DESIGN
*
SPONGE
at home

DESIGN

∗

SPONGE

at home

GRACE BONNEY

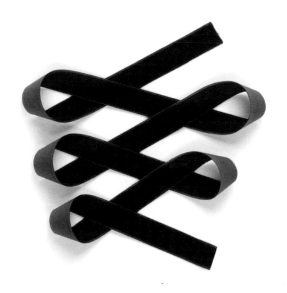

ARTISAN

TO ALL OF DESIGN*SPONGE'S READERS:
I hope this book will bring you the same joy,
inspiration, and excitement that you've shared
with the site over the years.

For photography credits, see page 390,
which constitutes an extension of this page.

Published by Artisan
A division of Workman Publishing Company, Inc.
225 Varick Street
New York, NY 10014-4381
www.artisanbooks.com

Published simultaneously in Canada by Thomas Allen & Son Limited

Library of Congress Cataloging-in-Publication Data

Bonney, Grace.
Design*Sponge at home / Grace Bonney.
p. cm.
ISBN 978-1-57965-431-3
1. Interior decoration—Amateurs' manuals. I. Title.
NK2115.B65 2011
747—dc22
2010039458

Design by ALSO Design
Illustrations by Julia Rothman

Printed in China

7 9 10 8 6

contents

FOREWORD BY JONATHAN ADLER vii

INTRODUCTION viii

SNEAK PEEKS 1

DIY PROJECTS 173

DIY BASICS 273

FLOWER WORKSHOP 293

BEFORE & AFTER 319

RESOURCE GUIDE 372

HOME & PROJECT CONTRIBUTORS 380

ACKNOWLEDGMENTS 384

INDEX 385

Jonathan Adler

Grace Bonney was a kid when she started her blog. She was too young to realize how preposterously daunting her endeavor was— to create a community of style warriors who through imagination and hard work transformed their spaces, their stuff, and their lives. She was also too young to imagine how influential and important her blog would become. Design*Sponge has become a daily (okay, hourly) must-read for me and the entire design world and has changed the rules of the game. It became the defining voice of design today, while remaining true to its optimistic, can-do ethos.

And now this tome that you're holding in your paws—four hundred pages of tips, inspiration, and general gorgeousness— perfectly captures the mood of the day. It reminds us that design is about inspiration, not snobbism. It's about empowerment, self-expression, and pluck.

I see Grace as a kindred spirit. When I quit my office job in 1993 (okay, full disclosure: I got fired from a string of jobs and was unemployable), I started making pottery and just hoped that if I stayed true to my creative vision of groovy and optimistic design, I would succeed. I had no idea what the hell I was doing, and it was really hard and isolating. In the eighteen years since (oy vay, long time), I've had some fab moments and some hard knocks. It's been fun, but it would have been a whole lot easier if I had had Design*Sponge to show me the way.

When Grace started Design*Sponge, she thought she was starting a design blog. But she wasn't just starting a blog, she was starting a revolution. And now the revolution has a bible.

Viva Grace Bonney, viva Design*Sponge, viva la revolución!

introduction

Sitting in front of my computer seven years ago, I had no idea how my life would change when I clicked a button on the screen that said PUBLISH. My blog Design*Sponge was born out of a desire to connect with people like myself—people who love design who want their homes to speak to who they really are.

I have always believed that great design doesn't have to come with a high price tag or require a professional degree. I certainly didn't have either of those things when I started my blog, happily chatting to myself about some of my favorite things: a classic red Eames chair, some gorgeous shelving from France, and a handmade wooden coffee table that I had stumbled upon at a student design show. Even though no one joined in the discussion at first, I was thrilled to have an outlet to express my love of design and decorating. It made me feel less like the crazy girl in the room who's always going on about cool wallpaper.

And yet, as it turns out, I wasn't alone. Within weeks, my blog was eliciting comments and e-mails and I felt like I was connecting with a community that I didn't even know *existed*. We started having online conversations about the kinds of things I previously thought interested only me: a particularly fabulous fabric on a couch in a movie, the eye-catching wrapper on my favorite kind of candy (and how great would that color combination look in a room?), the wide plank floors in old historic homes that I wished were mine. These conversations turned into larger discussions on the website, where we shared tips about furniture and paint, and created an online support system filled with new friendships, ideas, and endless amounts of inspiration.

Today, I wake up every morning and share news and inspiration from the design world with an audience that could fill Madison Square Garden. (How cool would it be if we could all meet up every day like that?) It is quite simply a dream job.

I grew up in Virginia Beach, Virginia, with parents who always encouraged me to try new things. For me, that meant getting out of Virginia Beach as quickly as possible and escaping to New York University to study journalism. As a freshman, I imagined an exciting future as a journalist. I'd write for newspapers while living a life inspired by *Sex and the City*'s Carrie Bradshaw (complete with the amazing shoe collection).

But those first few years didn't go quite as I'd hoped. I found myself quickly disillusioned with the world of newspaper journalism, which was more bureaucratic and competitive than I'd imagined. I moved back to Virginia, transferring to the College of William & Mary. Colonial Williamsburg wasn't the hotbed of activity that I had found in New York City, but it was this change of scenery that helped me to find myself.

After struggling to find a home in the college's English department, I drifted into the art studio, where I learned printmaking and studied the history of art. In between classes, I would head back to my dorm, plop down on the couch, and watch my favorite TV show, TLC's *Trading Spaces*. At first, it was just a way to decompress. But I quickly found myself inspired not only to redecorate my dorm room but also to reach out to my professors with questions about the history of interior and furniture design.

I was lucky to find a wonderful professor, Elizabeth Peak, who filled my arms with books about furniture design, decorating, and product design. She introduced me in particular to the work of several female designers like Ray Eames and Florence Knoll, whom I found infinitely inspiring. After graduation I moved back to New York and found a job at a small public relations firm that represented several companies in the furniture and design field.

One day, I was having brunch with my then boyfriend, Aaron (who is now my husband and partner at Design*Sponge). As I have been known to do, I was going on and on about the color palette in the room and how much I loved it. That's when Aaron had an idea: "Hey, have you ever thought about starting a blog about design? Maybe you could use it as a writing sample or a portfolio and use it to apply for a job at a magazine one day?" A few hours of excited conversation later, I was on Blogger.com setting up my very first blog. I decided on the name Design*Sponge because that's what I was—someone with an insatiable desire to absorb absolutely every tidbit about design that comes my way. Soon, I found myself writing my first blog post.

My first few months of design blogging were relatively solitary. There were only a handful of design blogs around, and the online design audience wasn't nearly as large as it is today. But I didn't care because I loved having an outlet where I could write about my passions. And the kind of design I was covering—accessible to all, regardless of budget—wasn't being written about in any design and shelter magazines that I could find.

The majority of my early posts were devoted to the design scene in my backyard of Brooklyn, New York. After work, I would throw my digital camera in my bag and go scout cool design shops and student shows, which I would then write about on the blog. The Brooklyn design scene was just starting to explode. And that incredibly creative scene—and the public's interest in it—brought Design*Sponge its first readers.

And to my surprise, they kept coming, hungry for design ideas that were relatable yet unexpected and that spoke to *their* needs. And what's more, they wanted to learn more about the people behind the design—the creators whose intriguing homes and products were becoming the backbone of the site. As Design*Sponge expanded, I realized I couldn't possibly do it all myself—at least not if I ever planned on sleeping. In 2007, three years after I started the blog, I redesigned the site and hired my first editors. I added do-it-yourself projects like monogrammed camp blankets and candleholders made from recycled wine bottles. Because I personally was becoming more interested in food and cooking, I also created a section featuring great recipes from my favorite designers. From there the site kept growing naturally. Additional editors came on board to address topics like interior design, design history, and floral and garden design. Because I feel that great design should be celebrated no matter where it is located, I added city guides to places as close to my home as Brooklyn, New York, and as far away as Auckland, New Zealand. When the economy took a nosedive in 2008 and everybody was cutting back, I decided to add an affordable shopping section with great products under $100. And then one day I realized that what began as my own personal blog had become the design magazine I had always wanted to read—and work for.

As much as I love the speed and immediacy of the web, there's something about having a tangible guide that you can dog-ear and bookmark to your heart's content that just can't be replicated online. Many readers of the blog have asked me to compile a collection of their favorite home tours to flip through or DIY projects to tackle on a rainy day. With this book I've tried to re-create the same sort of excitement, inspiration, and motivation that we strive for online, but now on the printed page. The first part of the book focuses on one of my favorite pastimes: sneaking a peek inside some of the most inspiring homes I've ever seen. Whether it's an apartment in London or a midcentury ranch house in Los Angeles, inspiration can come in many different shapes, sizes, and styles. Every home featured in this book is packed with ideas that anyone can copy in their own houses. In addition to practical tips on decorating and renovating, you'll also learn about the history behind design classics like Chesterfield sofas and Hudson's Bay blankets. By the time you're done reading, you'll definitely know your demijohns from your Dutch doors and your trompe-l'oeils from your Tolix chairs.

Inspiration and knowledge is only half the battle when it comes to designing the home of your dreams, so in the second part of the book we'll roll up our sleeves and get to work. This section features do-it-yourself projects that have been tested and created by both our team of editors and readers like you. (You'll even find an upholstered headboard that I made myself one weekday afternoon.) Then, inspired by one of the most popular sections on Design*Sponge, I'll show some of my favorite Before & After makeovers—with hints on how to turn a dowdy flea market dresser into a design delight, or on a larger scale, how to transform a dark hole of a kitchen into a chic modern space for cooking and entertaining.

This book would not have been possible without the hard work and contributions of both my blog's editors and our loyal readers. Design*Sponge readers are some of the most creative, inventive, and passionate people on the web and I hope that this book can provide them, and *all* design fans, with the tools to bring creativity and personality into their homes.

—**Grace Bonney,** founder of Design*Sponge

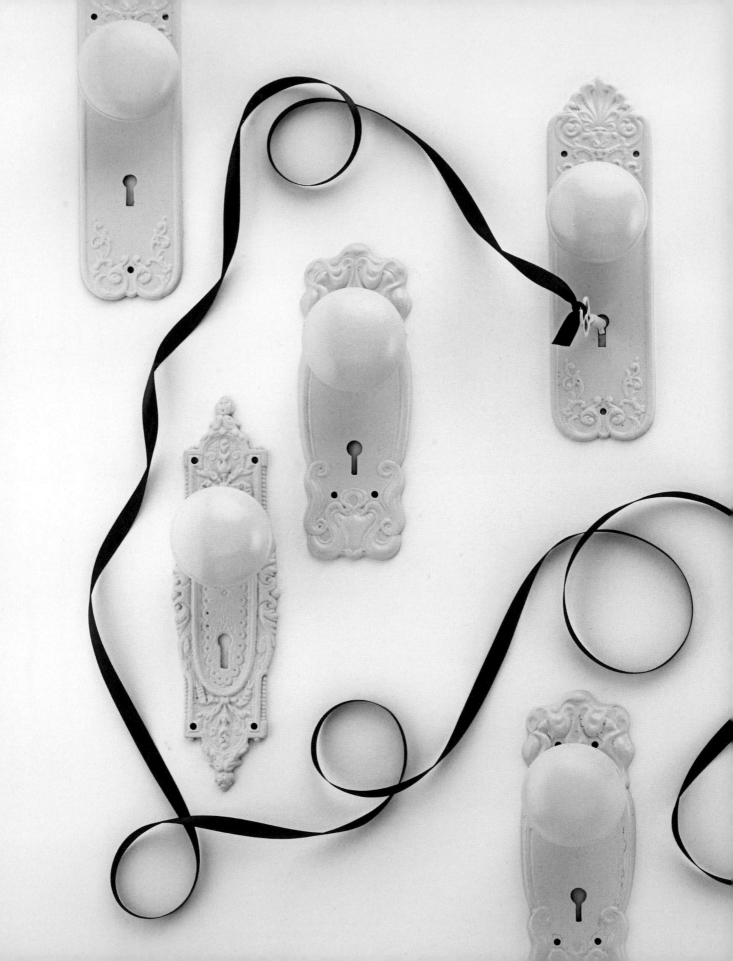

SNEAK PEEKS

*In the early days of the blog, I wrote about objects that inspired and amazed me—
a square vase by the designers (and brothers) Ronan and Erwan Bouroullec; a Tivoli*

radio that was simultaneously retro and modern. But before long, I was inviting readers to "sneak a peek" inside the Portland, Oregon, home of one of my favorite artists, Amy Ruppel. Though the post consisted of just a single image (a vignette on her hallway table), readers were thrilled and asked me to show more interiors on the site. Over the next few weeks I received hundreds of suggestions for homes to feature on Design*Sponge. Our first real column was born and the name "Sneak Peek" stuck.

I gravitate toward homes that grab me on some instinctual level, whether I'm attracted to an amazing wall color, a beautiful mixture of fabrics, or a furniture arrangement so artful that I'm tempted to move right in. When I select a home, along with Sneak Peek editors Amy Azzarito and Anne Ditmeyer, I'm looking for that intangible quality that will connect with readers and inspire them to make a change in their own homes. That quest for inspiration—which I believe comes in all shapes and sizes—has led us to amazing spaces

both small (less than 500 square feet) and large (well over 5,000). With each Sneak Peek, we hope to show how creative people have assembled spaces that reflect their personality— whether that means painting a rainbow wall mural in a bedroom or converting an old New England church into an amazing home and art studio.

Our hope is that these homes will speak to you, too, and inspire you to try something new or perhaps to view your own space in a new way. I've also used these homes as a jumping-off point for snippets of design history and interior design tricks and tips. And as an added bonus, Design*Sponge contributor Sarah Ryhanen at Saipua, a flower store in Brooklyn, has created flower arrangements inspired by some of my favorite rooms, together with simple instructions on how to re-create them. My goal for this section of the book, as with all Sneak Peeks we run on Design*Sponge, is to help you to turn your home, large or small, into a space that makes you happy and reflects who you are.

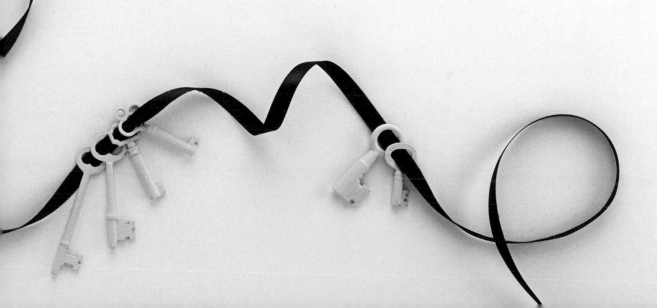

name

GENEVIEVE
GORDER

~~~~~~~~~~

location

NEW YORK,
NEW YORK

Red and white Astrid
chairs from Anthropologie
bring a bright splash of color
to the sunny living room.

A piano stool from
Genevieve's grandmother
acts as a side table
or extra seating during
get-togethers.

I've long been a fan of interior designer Genevieve Gorder. In fact, it was her dramatic moss wall, which she created as one of the original decorators on TLC's *Trading Spaces,* that inspired me to enter the world of interior and furniture design. Genevieve has gone on to host several television shows about houses and decorating, including *Dear Genevieve,* in which she solves design problems for people who write in to the show, and *Town Haul,* in which she helped give makeovers to small-town shops and businesses. Her home base is a beautiful townhouse, which she shares with her husband and daughter, in New York's Chelsea neighborhood. Originally from the Midwest, she sourced a number of her home's vintage design elements from old schools and houses in her home state of Minnesota.

Drawers salvaged from a bait and tackle shop in Maine are given a new life in the living room.

<<< Salvaged materials are a great way to add instant history and character to an empty space. Genevieve installed an old Minnesota public school door in the downstairs bathroom, along with fish scale–patterned bathroom tiles from Kaleidoscope Tile in Manhattan.

Outdoor space is limited in Manhattan, so Genevieve transformed her balcony into an urban oasis by installing a wooden daybed with a cotton canvas canopy.

Antique & Salvage Shops

Genevieve Gorder
loves these sources
for great vintage and
antique furnishings.

Architectural Antiques
Minneapolis, MN
www.archantiques.com

Material Culture
Philadelphia, PA
www.materialculture.com

Portland Architectural
Salvage
Portland, ME
www.portlandsalvage.com

Olde Good Things
New York, NY
www.oldegoodthings.com

Liz's Antique Hardware
Los Angeles, CA
www.lahardware.com

Paintings and pictures
aren't the only things
that can hang on walls.

Here, a piece of bitterroot,
which Genevieve discovered
in a local shop, hangs like
a natural sculpture in her
daughter's bedroom.

Staircase walls present a great opportunity to experiment with a diagonal art gallery.

A Tip for Creating Unity Within a Collection

Use frames with similar colors or stains to tie together disparate artwork. Or, if identical frames aren't your style, group artwork so that there's a color connection between pieces. For example, if you have a painting with a red background, place a small piece next to it that contains a red stripe, or some red element that will pull the two together and create a sense of flow.

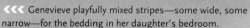

‹‹‹ Genevieve playfully mixed stripes—some wide, some narrow—for the bedding in her daughter's bedroom.

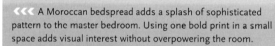

‹‹‹ A Moroccan bedspread adds a splash of sophisticated pattern to the master bedroom. Using one bold print in a small space adds visual interest without overpowering the room.

Unexpected details throughout Genevieve's home, like this salvaged Minnesota public school doorknob and iron gate, serve as conversation starters, inviting guests to engage and learn about places that were important in Genevieve's childhood.

This apartment illustrates how well industrial furniture can coexist with warm wooden pieces.

A teak table is paired with steel Marais chairs and antique metal cage lights to create a unique dining area for the family.

K in Ying Lee, head designer for the fashion brand Madewell, shares her sunny Brooklyn home with her husband, Dan Perna, and their children, Isabella and Marco. They live in a converted former guitar factory, where they have combined two apartments into one larger space with enough room for both their family and a home design studio. With views of the Manhattan skyline, their light-filled home has warm touches throughout that offset the building's industrial underpinnings.

An upstairs hallway, otherwise unused, was turned into a study area. The inexpensive shelving unit was made out of repurposed Ikea countertops. Instead of a larger rug, a group of hand-stitched Japanese indigo blankets were clustered together on the floor.

Affordable Shelving

Kin and Dan's study is a great example of using scale to make inexpensive materials seem more high end than they really are and add drama to your space. If your room can handle a full wall of shelving, consider using L brackets (available in most hardware stores) to hold pieces of found or salvaged wood cut to fit your walls. Try painting the L brackets and standards the same color as the walls to give the shelves a "floating" effect.

Kin and Dan's design studio is a great example of the couple's shared aesthetic. Both designers appreciate heritage details like embroidery and artisan-crafted hardware. They also collect utilitarian objects. Their upstairs studio is filled with vintage office supplies and furniture and denim jeans (a mainstay at Madewell).

Because children's tastes and needs can change quickly, you may not want to invest too much money in kids' play furniture. Why not make your own? Dan made this children's table out of used cardboard boxes. He even used the inside corrugated panels as decorative details. The room's chalkboard walls allow the children to decorate their space with their own artwork and writings.

The living room's charcoal-colored walls may seem like a risky choice, but darker-colored walls, when paired with the right pieces, can add richness to a room.

Kin's wooden credenza, an eBay score, brings out the warmer tones in the wall color. She turns even the humblest accessories into something special: A collapsible canvas camp chair holds a collection of plaid wool blankets, while a blown glass vase is filled with an arrangement of cotton branches from Kin's favorite florist, Sprout Home.

See page 102 for a glimpse of Sprout Home founder Tara Heibel's home.

name
ROSIE
O'NEILL
~~~~~~
location
LOS ANGELES,
CALIFORNIA

A heavy black dining room table adds a touch of masculinity and weight to Rosie O'Neill's pink dining room. A vintage Moroccan wedding blanket, found on eBay, was repurposed as a dining room rug, adding softness to the room.

Moroccan Wedding Blankets
~~~~~~

These shaggy, sequined blankets, known as *handira,* have important symbolic value to the Berbers, an indigenous people of North Africa, who create them as part of their wedding ceremonies. The bride-to-be and her family spend weeks weaving the sheep's wool blankets and hand-stitching thousands of flat sequin "mirrors" onto them. When finished, *handiras* are believed to have talismanic powers, bringing good luck to a marriage and offering protection.

Ever since Rosie O'Neill was a little girl, she dreamed of living in what she calls a "life-size Barbie Dream House." So it was appropriate that, as an adult, she landed the enviable job of director of Barbie marketing at Mattel in Los Angeles. The next step was to create her fantasy home. She knew she was on the right track when she discovered an art deco apartment with historic details and great light. She moved in and hired interior designer Kishani Perera, a graduate of UCLA's Interior Design and Architecture program, to update the ca. 1930s architecture with a romantic color scheme and with details that looked luxurious, even if they didn't cost an arm and a leg. They kept the budget in check by buying (and later reworking) furniture on Craigslist and eBay and at local flea markets. The resulting space is ultrafeminine but not overly sweet.

Rosie initially resisted the idea of adding a zebra rug to her living room's décor, fearing it would be too bold a gesture.

Kishani assured her the carpet would harmonize with the soft gray walls and the sofa's gray-blue velvet upholstery. The zebra rug is now Rosie's favorite feature of the room.

To update the bathroom's original green and black tile, Kishani accessorized the space with an inexpensive bead-print curtain and a candle sconce that she discovered at a Los Angeles flea market and glamorized by painting it black.

Knowing that Rosie loves purple, Kishani used two separate tones of her favorite shade (Pittsburgh Paint's Admiral on top and Ralph Lauren's Hotel Room on the bottom) to give the bedroom a girly but grown-up feel.

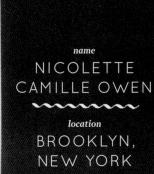

name
NICOLETTE CAMILLE OWEN
〜〜〜〜〜〜
location
BROOKLYN, NEW YORK

Caring for Houseplants
〜〜〜〜〜〜

Nicolette Camille Owen shares these tips for indoor greenery:

Focus on plants that work for the type of light you have in your home: Grow lights can help plants when light is scarce, but it's always best to be realistic about your light conditions as well as how much time you can devote to caring for your plants.

Create and stick to a consistent watering schedule: Try setting up a time each weekend when you clean, water, and feed your plants. Want to bring some green into your bathroom? Try ferns—they thrive on the humidity created by your morning shower.

Plant food is as important as water: Check directions for your particular plant. If you prefer to use a natural fertilizer, eggshell water is a great solution. Save your used eggshells until you have 20 of them. Boil the shells in a gallon of water for 5 minutes. Let steep for at least 8 hours and store in a jar under your sink (or in your garage). Work this liquid into your feeding schedule just like you would a premade fertilizer.

Soft blue walls in Benjamin Moore's Hydrangea create a sense of calm in Nicolette Camille Owen's urban bedroom. By keeping the bed and bedside tables (vintage crates) low, Nicolette was able to make the room look taller.

Floral designer Nicolette Camille Owen has brought her passion for the natural world inside her home. Because her work life in New York City can be hectic, she chose a palette of blues for her apartment as a tranquil antidote. As a result, the rooms flow together seamlessly, like a temperate blue sky shining on the casually lovely décor that Nicolette has assembled within.

Nicolette never buys new furniture. Instead, she scours flea markets and tag sales for finds, then mixes those pieces with family hand-me-downs. Not only is it a budget-friendly way to decorate, but because the pieces aren't expensive or precious, they can be repainted or restyled to suit Nicolette's changing tastes.

⌃ ⌃ Nicolette used a wall's panel molding as a frame for her collection of cloud photos.

⌄ ⌄ Open storage can give the appearance of clutter. Nicolette's clever solution was to create a striped curtain to cover the storage area under her sink.

The nature-inspired décor includes this set of antique Edward Lowe fern prints, shown here hanging above a daybed in the living room.

Turn to page 192 to learn how to make your own pressed botanical specimens.

Functional furniture doesn't have to be boring.

In the Brooklyn living room of P.J. Mehaffey and Dylan Hightower, vintage lockers were repurposed as media storage and a thrift store console was put into service as a television stand.

Prop stylist P.J. Mehaffey and his partner, Dylan Hightower, are both masters at finding new life in old things. In their apartment in the Prospect Heights section of Brooklyn, they have created a home that reflects them both individually and as a couple. P.J. describes their home as a "fun laboratory" where no specific design rules apply, but where everything manages to work because they follow a philosophy they can both agree on: Surround yourself with things that make you happy.

It can be difficult to blend a disparate collection of objects into a coherent display. P.J.'s solution was to use wall cubes from West Elm as minipedestals for his mismatched travel souvenirs. The result looks striking over the living room sofa, a throwaway that P.J. found on the street and reupholstered.

Any collection—however humble—can look wonderful if artfully displayed. The couple's vintage globe collection is placed on surfaces at different heights along one wall of the living room.

In the guest room, a vintage dental cabinet holds a television set and gives guests a place to store their things. A vintage hospital bed from a flea market is warmed up with a collection of colorful pillows from Hable Construction.

P.J. often finds treasure in other people's trash, like this vintage principal's desk he discovered outside the school across from his childhood home.

Above the desk, he hung an inspiration board that he made from a massive frame. Even an old gumball machine gets new life: P.J. transformed it into a fish tank.

13

If your passion for a particular theme is strong, carrying it through different rooms in your home can add a nice sense of cohesion. P.J.'s love of globes turns up in mobile form in the bedroom, which is decorated with a mix of affordable flea market finds and hand-me-downs. The walls above the picture rails were left white to give the ceiling an airy, cloudlike feeling.

P.J. and Dylan's kitchen is full of budget-friendly DIY projects. A microwave cart (found on Craigslist for $50) does double duty with its new butcher-block top: space for food prep above and storage below. As renters, they were not allowed to remove the kitchen's grungy tile floor. P.J.'s solution was to create a wall-to-wall floorcloth. The floor looks clean and brand new, and can be taken up when they move without damaging the existing tile.

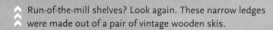

Run-of-the-mill shelves? Look again. These narrow ledges were made out of a pair of vintage wooden skis.

What do you do when your home doesn't come with enough closet space? If you're P.J., you repurpose a small room near your bedroom into a stylish and functional walk-in closet. Using autopoles and clamps (usually used as rigging for photo shoots and retail spaces), combined with metal rods and repurposed grocery store shelves, P.J. created a completely customized "closet." You can find autopoles at most photography/camera supply stores, or on Amazon.com.

A vintage card catalog found on eBay is put to work as a bedside table. The drawers keep lotions and eyeglasses organized.

Decorative Floor Coverings

An oil- or floorcloth is a cotton fabric that has been made waterproof with a coating of oil and pigment (or in P.J. and Dylan's case, with polyurethane). Floorcloths have a long history. They were first used as decorative floor coverings in eighteenth-century England, where wealthy homeowners used them in heavily trafficked areas of their homes. If you want to re-create this look, many companies still sell floorcloths online. You can even order a blank canvas and paint your own design (*www.canvasworksfloorcloths.com*).

name
CAROL NEILEY

~~~~~~~~~

location
LYON, FRANCE

An antique wooden door in Lyon, France, marks the entrance to the home of expat American entrepreneur Carol Neiley, her two daughters, and their dog, Daisy.

Carol Neiley is living every Francophile's dream. In addition to running a successful online store, Basic French, that sells all things French, from café au lait bowls to linen dish towels, she also calls two beautiful spaces in France home: a rustic country house and this chic city apartment in Lyon. Carol was drawn to the apartment's period architecture and to the neighborhood, which includes an abbey dating from the tenth century. The apartment serves as a base for her and her daughters, Halliday and Abigail. By using a restrained but ethereal color palette, Carol has created the perfect backdrop for her impressive—and eclectic—collection of antiques.

An everyday wooden bunk bed was transformed into a chic little nook for the girls with a coat of teal paint and a string of delicate flower lights from Habitat.

Grown-up details like a metallic silver pouf and an antique portrait add sophistication without detracting from the youthful feel of the room.

◄◄◄ The muted but lovely peach color scheme highlights the room's architecture, like this arched niche, and makes the space feel warm and feminine.

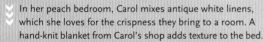

▼ In her peach bedroom, Carol mixes antique white linens, which she loves for the crispness they bring to a room. A hand-knit blanket from Carol's shop adds texture to the bed.

The peach palette in Carol's home inspired this fragrant arrangement.

Turn to page 311 to learn how to re-create this arrangement (and natural fragrance) in your home.

Carol is a master of artful display. Here in her office, she pairs a starfish sculpture with a coral print by Isabelle Grange.

Adam Silverman and Louise Bonnet are fearless experimenters when it comes to their home. Louise designed this hot pink and white wallpaper specially for their dining room. The chair rail and wainscoting were painted black to echo the black wooden Eames chairs around the dining table.

Create Your Own Wallpaper
~~~~~~~~~~

You, too, can create your own custom wallpaper like the design Louise made for the dining room. For design ideas, look to your own photographs or try drawing your own pattern. Here are some great online resources for creating your own custom wallpaper:

The Wallpaper Maker
www.thewallpapermaker.com

Design Your Wall
www.designyourwall.com

Atom Prints
www.atomprints.com/ wallpaper-mural.html

T rained as an architect, Adam Silverman worked in the field but then decided to instead pursue his love of pottery. He runs his own studio, Atwater Pottery, and is also a partner and studio director of the legendary Heath Ceramics. Together with his wife, artist Louise Bonnet, and their children, Beatrice, Charlotte, and Prudence, he lives in the Los Angeles neighborhood of Los Feliz, a hilly area north of Hollywood that is known for its midcentury houses and great nightlife. Adam describes their home as a "big, crumbling jalopy with enough room for all of us and a pool, right in the middle of the city." Crumbling or not, their home is a colorful space packed to the brim with inspiring artwork and furniture.

A long and narrow room can be a decorating challenge.

Adam and Louise divided their living room into two separate seating areas, each of which is anchored by an antique rug. To keep the separate seating spaces feeling different, they used furniture from different time periods in each grouping to create a harmonious arrangement.

‹‹‹ Some people would have painted over or removed the home's original knotty pine paneling, but Adam decided to keep it for his home office. The fire-engine red vintage desk, blue and red rug, and artfully arranged objects and artworks help lift the space so it doesn't feel drab.

‹‹‹ Borders don't have to be made of paper—and they don't have to be straight. Adam and Louise hand-painted this decorative border in the kitchen to echo the room's chair rail.

In the bedroom, chocolate brown walls get a jolt of bright color in the form of a pair of orange and red dressers from the legendary twentieth-century industrial designer Raymond Loewy. The orange bird pillow, created by the couple's friend Satbhajan Khalsa, is based on their wedding invitation. It sits on a vintage chair below a hand-drawn portrait of Adam and Louise's three daughters.

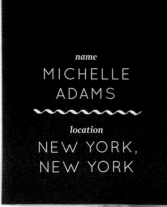
Small-space living never
looked so stylish.

Michelle utilizes double-
duty furniture whenever
possible to save space. Her
sleeper sofa from Room
and Board doubles as a
guest bed when friends
and family are in town.

Designer Michelle Adams is the founder of Rubie Green, an eco-friendly fabric
line, and the cofounder of online design magazine *Lonny*. With her great eye for
design, she has turned her 700-square-foot New York City apartment into a
stylish home that does it all, from entertaining to hosting her frequent houseguests. An
avid traveler, Michelle loves to collect treasures and uses them to add character to her
wallet-friendly décor.

Michelle made the bed the focal point of her tiny bedroom.

She ordered a custom headboard and had it covered in one of her own fabric designs. The yellow color palette is complemented by a black and white rug from Ikea, which adds a bit of visual width to the room with its horizontal stripes.

Turn to page 264 to learn how to make your own upholstered headboard!

⌃⌃ An inexpensive white Ikea bookshelf is filled with Michelle's favorite books and accessories, which she likes to arrange by color theme for decorative impact. A red bamboo chair covered in zebra fabric from Michelle's own line also adds a bright pop of color to the room without taking up too much space. Clear acrylic tables and chairs are affordable and great for small spaces, since they give plenty of surface space with very little visual weight.

⌄⌄ With space tight in the kitchen, a black Pottery Barn buffet table was employed as a stylish tabletop bar. While Michelle loves wallpaper, an entire room of it would be pricey. Instead, she invested in a small strip of sea grass from Phillip Jeffries, placing it behind the buffet to great effect.

One of Michelle's favorite space-saving tips is to cover side tables with a skirt.

This allows you to use the space underneath for storage without all of the visual clutter. Here, in her living room, she uses the room's panel molding to contain artwork, including Milton Glaser's iconic I ♥ NY print.

name
GRACE
BONNEY

location
BROOKLYN,
NEW YORK

In the bedroom, most people play around with colorful bedding and keep their headboard basic and neutral.

But there was a bold red fabric pattern that I was dying to try, so I decided to use the print on my headboard, which I upholstered myself. This bold stroke helps to highlight an accent wall in the room and gives me and my husband a soft place to rest our heads when we're reading in bed at night.

Turn to page 264 to learn how to make my headboard.

I share my apartment with my husband, Aaron, and our two cats, Turk and Ms. Jackson. I have fantasies of my dream home—or dream homes, actually: The city girl in me longs for a townhouse complete with a small backyard garden and fountain, while the country girl in me fantasizes about a farmhouse somewhere in rural Georgia. In the meantime, I make do with reality—our comfortable, sweet apartment in Brooklyn's Park Slope. We were living in a 500-square-foot studio when we first saw this space, which is about 900 square feet. I was swayed by the large bedroom and great location, which is a block or two away from some of the best restaurants, shops, and hot spots in the area. Perhaps that is why I managed to overlook some of the apartment's more *difficult* quirks, like a serious lack of natural light and a ten-degree slant throughout the rooms.

I have a penchant for red. But it wasn't until I brought home this vintage red horsehead lamp that all of the smaller red things I've collected over the years—from red highlights in the artwork above the couch to the floral stitching in the throw pillow from K Studio—really felt like a unified color theme in the space. It can be challenging to display small art prints such as the ones I love to collect on Etsy. On their own, they get lost on the wall; grouped together, they have a greater impact. I mount them in affordable frames from Ikea and hang them salon style.

<<< My closet was a mess of crumbling plaster and mismatched paint. Rather than repair and repaint, I hid the less-than-desirable details by covering the inside of the door and inside walls with an owl-print wallpaper from Trustworth Studios. I also attached caster wheels to a vintage wooden soda box to create a rolling shoe storage container.

One of my favorite design juxtapositions is the contrast between hard and soft textures. This Paul McCobb chair, which I bought at a store called Scout in Chicago, has a teak backrest and metal frame whose hard edges are softened by the seat's fuzzy plaid upholstery, which reminds me of a lumberjack's shirt.

Once again, red accents brighten the space—here in the form of the dining chairs and the lettering in our favorite print from the New York design studio Oddhero, which shows letters and numbers in a type font called Morgan Tower, designed in 2001 by the Portuguese designer Mario Feliciano.

23

Since space in our kitchen is extremely limited, I installed a Peg-Board rack but gave it a twist by painting it a bright red-orange (Benjamin Moore's Tomato Soup) to match the room's walls.

To learn how to make your own Peg-Board pot rack, turn to page 222.

The only wall in our kitchen not painted orange is the one that extends into the hallway and living room, which is white to match those other spaces. The orange flowers on a group of vintage plates act as a visual link to the other side of the room. I love terrariums and keep a small one filled with ivy and moss in my kitchen.

To learn to make your own terrarium, go to page 246.

⋘ To spruce up a generic dish drying rack, I swapped out the boring plastic mat it came with for a much more colorful plastic serving tray. I can change it out whenever I get bored with the pattern—and put it to work at parties.

I have a real weakness for chairs (Aaron and I joke that I own four chairs for every member of our household). I had this antique chair reupholstered by Chairloom in fabric from Rubie Green. I love the contrast between the fabric's modern zigzags and the more sinuous woodwork of the chair.

I don't like my kitchen to feel sterile. I prefer to treat it as an extension of the living room, with lots of personal decorative touches. Besides painting it orange, I added details like decorative cabinet handles and knobs. I also have a painting by the artist Zoe Pawlak above my stove. That last touch is unconventional, I know—especially since, to avoid damaging the painting, I have to remove it every time I cook (which at my rate works out to every other day). I think it's worth it to have something beautiful in the room.

A dark navy wall in the bedroom gets a jolt of brightness from a yellow sun sculpture and gold pillows and accessories.

The bedside lamps are similar in style and height—but look again: They are slightly different. "I love that they give the room symmetry, but throw it off a little, too," Corbett Marshall says.

Corbett Marshall and Jim Deskevich are the textile designers behind Variegated, which specializes in colorful bedding and accessories. When they opened a studio and showroom in the Hudson Valley town of Catskill, New York, they decided to move into the apartment above the store. Their new space consisted of small rooms—a big change from the loftlike spaces to which they were accustomed. For them, the tight spaces were an excuse to get creative with color and texture. Avid collectors of vintage furniture and artwork, they used paint and fabrics as a bridge to connect their décor with their apartment's old-fashioned spaces.

For a fun and functional touch in the kitchen, Corbett and Jim built shelves that run the length of the room.

With so much space, the couple lined up all of their favorite ceramics to create a colorful installation above an otherwise utilitarian area.

To draw attention away from the awkward paneling that wraps around the bottom section of the walls, Corbett and Jim painted it dark brown to make it recede, and used turquoise paint above. They made the console table by stapling an old cowhide to a piece of wood and attaching it to the top of a café table base.

Note the relationships between hues that extend from room to room. The living room's rich gold ties nicely to the golden brown shade they chose to paint the china cabinet in the adjoining dining room. Meanwhile, even the shelves within the cabinet get a special color touch in the form of coral paint, which in turn connects to the color of the decorative pig collection above the cabinet as well as to the pink runner on the antique dining table.

Using Fashion Textiles at Home

As textile designers, Jim and Corbett know all the tricks of the trade. One of their favorites is to decorate using fabrics not specifically designed for the home. They use fashion textiles—from shirting to velvets—to create everything from custom bedding to window treatments and pillows. Since clothing fabrics are available in endless materials and colors, there is no limit to the imagination. And since they are designed to be worn, they also have a very soft feel. To find interesting fashion and upholstery fabrics, check out stores like Purl Soho (*www.purlsoho .com*) and Jo-Ann Fabrics and Crafts (*www.joann.com*).

name
OLGA
NAIMAN

~~~~~~~~~

location
BROOKLYN,
NEW YORK

Olga Naiman created a platform bed by laying a piece of plywood on top of cinder blocks, which do double duty as storage for her shoe collection.

C reative director and prop stylist Olga Naiman had a very tight budget for decorating her railroad-style apartment in the Williamsburg section of Brooklyn. Except for one splurge—a Madeline Weinrib rug—she furnished the apartment with items found at flea markets or on eBay, or purchased inexpensively at Ikea. "My goal was to pull everything together and make it feel like a deliberate choice, not a collection of randomness," she says. Olga, who is of Russian descent, loves to incorporate touches of her heritage throughout her décor, from folkloric plates to black-and-white photographs of her grandparents taken in Russia in the 1940s. She loves her home's tall ceilings and exaggerates the effect by keeping her furniture low to the ground.

A kitchen ceiling provided an opportunity for some unexpected color and a chance for a visual trick. Painting your ceiling a soft sky color draws the eye upward and accentuates high ceilings.

Paint Magic

Olga Naiman has these tips for adding paint flourishes to your home:

Paint one wall in a room an unexpected color: Anything—even a basic white sofa or framed art—feels special when contrasted with a bold paint color.

Paint the floor molding a crisp color for a sharp and tailored effect.

If you don't have a headboard, paint one on! It should be the width of your bed, and you can go as simple or ornate as you like. Olga used gold paint to create the illusion of a tall headboard above her plywood-and-cinder-block bed.

Create a dramatic entrance: As you walk in the front door, how far do you see? Use paint to make that farthest wall sing.

Olga calls her home office, which is the biggest room in her home, her "inspiration room." She uses the room as a lab, experimenting with fabrics and different colors. Since the room faces the street, a bold pink curtain provides privacy and adds drama and brightness to the room. The center panel also conceals a large air-conditioning unit, which Olga uses only on the hottest days of summer.

Rather than rip out an old kitchen, Olga decided to instead add fanciful touches to the retro cabinetry and tile. A swath of lace hangs over the sink nook, while the cabinet front's 1950s design is enhanced with painted black outlines.

File cabinets can serve as inexpensive storage and can easily be repainted to match a room's color palette.

Olga found hers on Craigslist and spray-painted them apple green to go in her home office, which she also uses as an informal living room. A birdcage from Chinatown is paired with an Ikea vase by the Dutch designer Hella Jongerius—proof that interesting décor doesn't have to be expensive.

names
WAYNE PATE
& REBECCA
TAYLOR

location
BROOKLYN,
NEW YORK

Fashion designer Rebecca Taylor can't resist a lovely pattern like this sweet but sophisticated Nina Campbell wallpaper featuring birds.

It's a favorite of her girls, whose bedroom is also furnished with a coordinating floral rug from the fashion house Marni.

Wayne Pate, the illustrator behind Good Shape Design, lives in a wonderful Brooklyn townhouse with his wife, fashion designer Rebecca Taylor, and their three children, Charlie, Isabel, and Zoe. Working as they do in creative fields, both Wayne and Rebecca are surrounded by color and pattern on a daily basis. At home, they prefer to give their eyes a rest and keep things clean and simple, letting their standout pieces shine. Rebecca's love of feminine color and pattern is seen in the girls' cheerful bedroom, while Wayne's penchant for pared-down graphic pattern is showcased in the home's patterned tile floors.

The living room is painted pristine white to show off the antique architecture and the couple's collection of vintage furniture.

Rather than curtains, the windows have simple wooden roll-up blinds so as not to detract from the beauty of the original woodwork.

A classic white subway tile backsplash keeps the kitchen feeling clean, neat, and ready for cooking. Rather than the usual white grout, the couple opted for dark gray, to match the floor tiles. The extra-tall cabinets make great use of the ceiling's height, creating enough storage so the countertops remain clear.

A tiled floor in gray, black, and white adds a spectacular dash of pattern to the dining area, with its otherwise minimalist wooden table and metal Tolix chairs. A Fornasetti tray hangs over the dining table like artwork, echoing the floor's black and white theme.

The Tolix Chair

In France, this galvanized metal café chair is ubiquitous. It was born in the 1930s as Modèle A when designer Xavier Pauchard perfected the galvanizing process, in which a sheet of metal is bathed in a tub of molten zinc, which protects the finish from rusting. Light, easily stackable, and weather-resistant, the furniture was an immediate success and was used in cafés, brasseries, and even on the French ocean liner the SS *Normandie.* Tolix furniture is still manufactured in Pauchard's native town of Autun, France.

name
DAVE
ALHADEFF

location
BROOKLYN,
NEW YORK

A vintage industrial metal sliding door welcomes visitors to Dave's apartment. Antique barn and factory doors can be found on eBay or in salvage shops.

Dave Alhadeff has played an integral part in the independent design scene in Brooklyn, New York, for nearly a decade. Since it opened in 2003, his Williamsburg store, The Future Perfect, has been one of the best spots to discover up-and-coming designers (including local students) and view cutting-edge work. So it comes as no surprise that his home is filled with the same sort of innovative, exciting design. Through his deft use of color and imaginative décor, Dave has transformed this converted industrial loft into an inviting living space.

There is some question about whether the name Chesterfield refers to the English town in Derbyshire or to Philip Stanhope, the 4th Earl of Chesterfield, who is said to have commissioned the first leather sofa. Either way, this tufted couch is the epitome of English coziness and "a perfect fit for an eclectic aesthetic," Dave says. "It has a distinctly masculine feeling to it, but is super warm and cozy as well. And when complemented with other more modern furniture, the piece blends seamlessly while providing an interesting contrast element."

Nervous about mixing old things with new ones? Watch how a pro does it. Dave's living room is furnished with a vintage Chesterfield sofa, an Eames rocking chair, and a cutting-edge StopIt rubber stopper lounge chair from Redstr/Collective, one of the first designers Dave carried in his shop.

Another way Dave breaks the rules is to mix four different chairs around the table in the small dining area. Another Future Perfect designer, Jason Miller, created the ceramic antler chandelier that hangs over the table.

The bubblegum pink hue Dave chose for his bedroom instantly adds warmth to the space and ties together his collection of artwork, decorative objects, and a blanket on the bed. Though pink can be an unexpected choice for a man's bedroom, Dave says "it went up on the walls without hesitation" after he read physiological research studies involving this particular hue—known as Baker-Miller Pink—showing that the color reduces anxiety and increases melatonin production (which makes you feel happy and tranquil).

names
JACQUELINE & GEORGE SCHMIDT

location
BROOKLYN, NEW YORK

Jacqueline and George love to find ways to incorporate salvaged wood into their décor.

Their ten-foot-long dining room table was milled from a fallen cherry tree that they found near their cottage in Michigan.

Meanwhile, George recycled a piece of old particle board into hanging drawers, visible at left.

These talented designers are the duo behind Screech Owl Design, a studio that produces modern stationery and lifestyle products. They live in Greenpoint, Brooklyn, in an apartment with the woodsy feel of a summer cottage. The look, inspired by their Michigan country getaway, is achieved with hand-hewn touches helped along by George's carpentry skills. Their apartment, which they share with cats Mister and Pinky, is an oasis, helping them to escape from hectic city life. Just as they use recycled paper for their Screech Owl stationery, Jacqueline and George use recycled and salvaged materials at home whenever possible.

Wall-mounted lighting is a great way to add detail above a bed along with some much-needed functionality. The pillow is made from a Turkish kilim found at a Paris flea market.

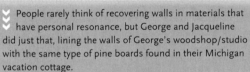

<<< The living room's décor exemplifies the couple's design ethos: Make the most of what you've got on hand, then add handmade things to the mix. Their interior design scheme includes hand-me-downs, like the room's cowhide rug, as well as such salvage finds as the floor lamp and file cabinet, and accessories made by local artists.

People rarely think of recovering walls in materials that have personal resonance, but George and Jacqueline did just that, lining the walls of George's woodshop/studio with the same type of pine boards found in their Michigan vacation cottage.

Store-bought kitchen islands can cost an arm and a leg. The couple's inexpensive alternative consists of a butcher block (purchased for a song at an Ohio flea market) mounted to a metal base from a restaurant supply store.

Reclaimed Wood

Salvaged wood adds tons of character to this home, from wall paneling to furniture. You can use a floor sander (which you can rent at most hardware or home improvement stores) to smooth down large planks of rough or aged wood before you build with them (be sure to wear safety goggles when sanding). Once you're done, clean the pieces with a damp towel and stain or coat to your desired finish. The wood is now ready to be used.

name
MARCUS HAY

location
NEW YORK,
NEW YORK

Stylist Marcus Hay prefers round tables in small rooms because they visually open up the space. He uses Eero Saarinen's classic Tulip Table for dining, entertaining, and working.

The pops of blue and hot pink in Marcus's kitchen inspired this floral arrangement.

Turn to page 317 to learn how to make it.

How do you live stylishly in an apartment with less than 500 square feet of space? As a professional stylist, Marcus Hay is a master at making any space look great. So when he fell in love with an apartment with panoramic views in New York's West Chelsea, he knew he could make it work despite the very limited square footage. "Because my apartment is high up, I feel like I am floating in the sky," Marcus says, which compensates for any lack of space. Meanwhile, by employing some great tricks of the trade, he has succeeded in making his apartment feel brighter and more spacious.

A pair of worn antique doors found at a flea market have been placed behind the desk as a backdrop, adding texture and atmosphere in an unexpected way.

Affordable Artwork

Strapped for cash and can't afford expensive artwork? Do what Marcus does. He gathers simple frames in varying sizes but all in similar tones, then groups them together in a gallery. You would be surprised how many things can look terrific this way: clippings, postcards, old photos you have lying around in drawers. Even new digital photo prints can look good. It helps to choose a theme for your gallery, such as black-and-white photographs or botanical prints. Marcus also likes to use thick frames—he puts the top edge into service as a ledge for small objects.

❮❮❮ Pale, butter yellow walls add airiness and are an interesting change from white. A Norman + Quaine sofa, shipped from Marcus's native Australia, is paired with a vintage coffee table from a local flea market. Marcus enjoys mixing flea market finds with high-end furniture because they make a room feel less perfectly composed.

For Marcus, even a bookshelf provides an opportunity for more display, with sculptures on the edges in front of the books.

Hanging a mirror over the bedside table makes the bedroom feel larger and adds light to the corner of the room.

Over the bed, the vintage metal fish sculpture reminds Marcus of his childhood spent near the sea in Australia.

An oak library ladder allows the couple to access every inch of their built-in storage—and adds an old-fashioned twist to the all-white space.

Designers Jill Robertson and Jason Schulte run a creative design, marketing, and advertising agency in San Francisco called Office. Though their aesthetic runs toward the modern, the couple also loves the kind of classic Victorian architecture for which San Francisco is so well known. After finding the perfect Victorian home, they modernized the décor so that it would be in sync with their design sensibilities, but without taking away from the good bones of the house. Their finished space reflects their love of clean, contemporary design while respecting the history and character of their home.

A soft green avocado wall color brings out the warmth in Jill and Jason's wooden bed.

Built-in bedside tables stretch the horizontal line of the bed farther, making the room feel wider than it is.

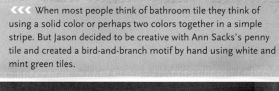

<<< When most people think of bathroom tile they think of using a solid color or perhaps two colors together in a simple stripe. But Jason decided to be creative with Ann Sacks's penny tile and created a bird-and-branch motif by hand using white and mint green tiles.

The rich gray walls in Jill and Jason's living room ground the couple's collection of artwork and furniture.

A classic Greek key rug brings pattern to the floor and picks up the black in the Eiffel chair and painting next to it.

The sunroom's pale gray walls are complemented by a slate gray Hella Jongerius sofa. Cool blue tones in the throw pillows and artwork act as accents.

As fans of book cover design, especially those by the artist Dick Bruna, the couple decided to showcase some of their favorites by hanging them on a wall. They used shadow boxes, which can highlight any three-dimensional collection. If there is too much space between a book and the frame glass, slip a piece of cardboard behind the book to hold it in place.

The couple's love of animals pops up in almost every room. These vintage butterfly plates, which add a graphic pop of color to the otherwise neutral kitchen, came from the Alameda flea market outside of San Francisco.

Panel molding, like this pattern of rectangles and squares in the living room, adds architectural interest to any room. Here, these details are highlighted by being painted white against the darker walls. The pirate-themed posters leaning against the wall were designed by Office for The Store at 856 Valencia, a shop cofounded by the writer Dave Eggers, which sells whimsical "pirate supplies" to fund a creative writing lab for children.

Adding Moldings

Many of today's new apartment buildings and homes are sadly lacking the detailing, such as wood or plaster moldings, found in older homes. But you can re-create the look by purchasing thin strips of molding (these usually cost just a few dollars at your local hardware store) and using them to lay out a pattern for your walls. Create panel molding, a faux chair rail—almost anything goes. Paint them white to pop against the painted background and attach them to the wall with finishing nails. Try painting the wall inside the panel molding a different shade to add even more interest to your room.

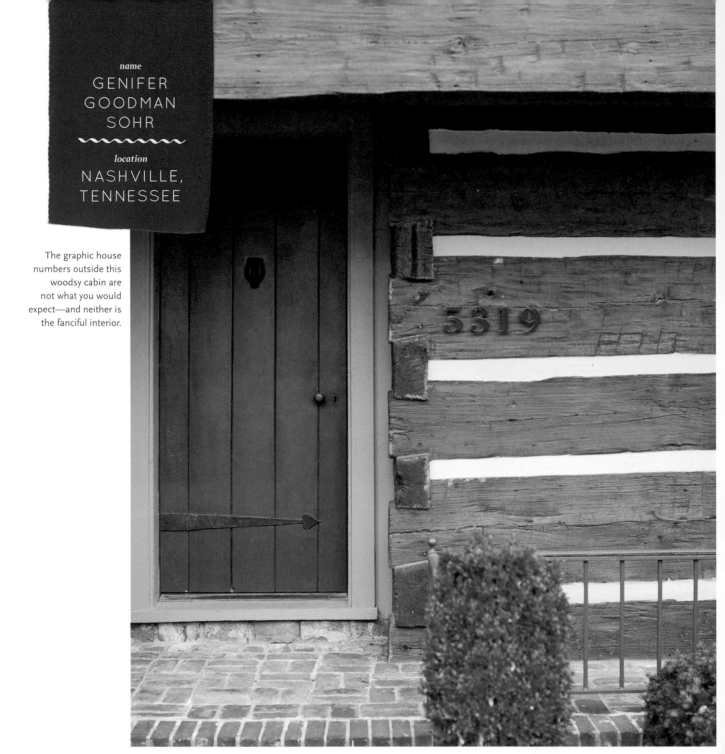

name
GENIFER
GOODMAN
SOHR

location
NASHVILLE,
TENNESSEE

The graphic house numbers outside this woodsy cabin are not what you would expect—and neither is the fanciful interior.

Interior designer Genifer Goodman Sohr and her husband, Benjamin, were drawn to the warmth of this log cabin in Nashville. They moved in with their children and updated the space with a modern spin. Splashes of red and pink brighten up the rich wooden walls and add a sense of playfulness that is perfect for this family of four.

Bright red accessories, including a dramatic chandelier, give the cavernous living room a hip, contemporary feel. Genifer played with the room's scale by choosing furniture that is low to the ground, making the already high wood-beam ceilings even more dramatic.

◄◄◄ Whimsical decorations, like this stuffed marlin over the sofa, are in the spirit of the house but feel modern when paired with clean-lined furniture and accent pillows that tie in the same blue hues.

The children's rooms have red accents to warm up the wooden walls—a continuation of the bold red accents elsewhere in the home.

This log cabin inspired this birch-wrapped arrangement.

Turn to page 308 to learn how to make both the vase and the arrangement.

If space is at a premium, consider building a custom wall desk like this one, which frees up floor space and blends effortlessly into the room's gray and white palette.

The white and gray sunroom has bright pops of color in the yellow dining room chair upholstery and the hot pink artwork, which is actually a framed kitchen towel.

Though the color palette in this room is different from that in the living room, the small accents of red and pink create a flow between spaces.

The master bedroom continues the sophisticated gray palette, with white sculptural decorations constrasting against the darker wall color.

Pops of pink and dark orange again recall the accent colors in other rooms of the home.

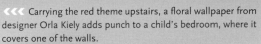
‹‹‹ Carrying the red theme upstairs, a floral wallpaper from designer Orla Kiely adds punch to a child's bedroom, where it covers one of the walls.

‹‹‹ Inexpensive paper shades hang above daughter Lucy's bed, bringing color to the ceiling and drawing the eye upward.

In the kitchen, the tightly edited gray and white palette encompasses even small details like the cabinet handles, which were painted to match, and the dishes. Genifer carries the home's playful accent colors to the room with the bright red tray. The neutral backdrop also allows for a quick change of theme: By adding colorful dish towels, plates, or a countertop runner, she can easily change the look and feel of the room whenever the mood strikes.

name

AMY
AZZARITO

~~~~~~

location

BROOKLYN,
NEW YORK

A cool gray and blue palette runs throughout the living room. Amy's collection of vintage seascape paintings, which remind her of her native California, are hung salon style above the gray velvet sofa.

Turn to page 369 to see her sofa before and after.

Design*Sponge editor Amy Azzarito shares her apartment in the Brooklyn neighborhood of Williamsburg with her two cats, Loki and Freya. Having recently completed a master's degree in decorative arts and design history at Parsons The New School for Design, Amy loves scouring flea markets and thrift shops for affordable antique furniture and objects.

> By repurposing a vintage machinist's cart into a rolling bar cart, Amy gave a flea market find a new life—and gave herself some additional storage space.

Amy and her friend documentary filmmaker Jessica Oreck created this incredible glass butterfly dome, which echoes the blue and gray color palette in the living room.

Turn to page 270 to learn how to make your own butterfly dome.

> Amy displays her many art and design books in the living room, where neat stacks double as decoration under the table (and invite guests to browse). She repurposed a vintage birdhouse found on eBay as a tabletop decoration.

Amy's butterfly dome looks beautiful from all angles. The backs of the butterflies are rich earth tones.

47

Amy's sunshine-filled bedroom gets a dose of pattern from butter-colored bedding from Dwell Studio.

A needlepoint horse pillow is a nod to her childhood love of horses.

The apartment was blessed with a dramatic porcelain pedestal tub.

To highlight the sculptural qualities of the tub, the adjacent wall was painted a dark blue-gray.

A vintage candle chandelier and upholstered seat make the space feel more like an elegant powder room than a city bathroom.

» A soft leather chair provides a comfortable reading spot in the bedroom. Suitcases from Amy's great-grandmother are stacked to serve as a side table.

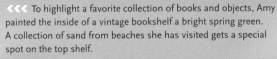

«« To highlight a favorite collection of books and objects, Amy painted the inside of a vintage bookshelf a bright spring green. A collection of sand from beaches she has visited gets a special spot on the top shelf.

Amy transformed her run-of-the-mill entryway by painting her front door a dramatic dark blue. She covered the nonfunctioning peephole with a tiny blue and gold mirror. Beside the door, an industrial metal rack now hangs as a landing pad for mail, keys, and accessories.

name
LYNDA
GARDENER

location
MELBOURNE,
AUSTRALIA

Vintage mirrors and an antique glass chandelier help reflect light in Lynda's sunny living room.

Lynda Gardener sells beautiful furniture and accessories in her Melbourne home furnishings shop, Empire Vintage. Lynda lives a dream life: She spends weekdays in her elegant home, complete with central courtyard, in town. Then on weekends, she retreats to her country house in the nearby village of Daylesford (see page 52). In Melbourne, her home has an open, airy feel, which acts as an antidote to the stress of her day-to-day city life. With features like an open central courtyard, wide plank flooring, and an abundance of natural light, it also serves as the perfect backdrop for her impressive collection of antique furniture.

Creamy white walls allow Lynda to mix a variety of patterns in this bedroom, like the peach floral upholstery on her chaise and the bed's blue upholstered headboard. She hung a trio of mirrors on the wall to reflect the natural light coming in from the courtyard, and used a collection of antique Christmas ornaments to add drama to a hanging crystal chandelier.

Taking advantage of the length of her living room, Lynda repurposed an old cutting table from a clothing manufacturer to use as her dining room table. After being cleaned, sanded, and repainted with a glossy white paint, the table now comfortably seats six on each side, making it perfect for parties and large get-togethers.

Lynda chose to make a statement in her bedroom by installing a functioning antique tub. Because the rest of the room is white and bright, a heavier piece like this tub is able to blend in, without adding too much visual weight. In addition to the bathtub, a collection of vintage upholstered chairs is arranged throughout the room to create different seating areas in the large, open space.

Lynda's collection of pottery inspired this tiny teacup arrangement.

Turn to page 314 to re-create this arrangement in your own home.

Lynda has spent years collecting cups, plates, and pitchers in a wide range of pastel hues. Together, they create a unified color palette and transform a storage area into an unexpected design detail. If your collection of china or pottery isn't cohesive, edit it down to colors or patterns that mesh well together. Display those in a collection and add to them whenever you visit a flea market or thrift store—they're great places to find inexpensive, matching dishware.

51

name
LYNDA GARDENER
〰〰〰〰

location
DAYLESFORD, AUSTRALIA

A dramatic claw-foot tub holds center stage in the bathroom.

By keeping the walls and accessories minimal, Lynda allows a few well-chosen antiques—an old scale and a glass chandelier, as well as the tub—to shine.

Traditional claw-foot furniture mixes with industrial accessories, including this floor lamp and a pair of metal buckets. The combination gives the room a modern feel and adds unexpected texture.

A small bedroom is transformed into a chic guest room with luxurious red-edged linens and sophisticated black and white toile wallpaper. A hanging light allows Lynda to use the room's limited surface space to display an antique trophy collection.

Lynda's vintage trophy collection inspired a floral arrangement in a trophy-turned-vase.

Turn to page 316 to find out how to re-create this arrangement in your home.

◀◀◀ Oversized vintage enamel pendant lamps hang above an old trestle table. A vintage cabinet acts as additional kitchen storage and picks up the green in the dining room table's finish.

The reading room plays a visual trick: Half of Lynda's library is real, while the other half is papered in faux-book wallpaper from Deborah Bowness.

name
BONNEE SHARP

〜〜〜

location
DALLAS, TEXAS

Painting the inside of a bookcase bright orange is a fun way to add a dramatic color to a room without a huge commitment.

Here, the hue picks up other orange accents in the room and highlights the owner's collection of white pottery.

Texas designer Bonnee Sharp is the creative mind behind Studio Bon, a collection of beautiful modern textiles that combine sophisticated neutral hues with playful patterns. Her Cape Cod–style home in Dallas shines with their vivid palette, which she uses to great effect throughout her home. Though her home's details are classic, the open floor plan feels contemporary, especially when furnished with Bonnee's modern-style furniture.

Rather than match the greens in her bedroom, Bonnee layered several shades of the color, from the grass green of her headboard to the moss of her walls. The combination of shades gives the room a springlike feel. With space tight, an Ikea desk serves as both a bedside table and a work center.

Bonnee's headboard inspired this spring bouquet.

Turn to page 309 to learn how to re-create this arrangement in your home.

⌃⌃ Bonnee matched her dining room's walls to her curtains, a nice detail that adds texture to the back wall without overwhelming the room. A vintage teak sideboard and dining table add warmth.

<<< In the hallway, framed seashells echo the colors in the window shade's scallop-patterned fabric.

With its beadboard wainscoting, the eat-in kitchen is a traditional space. But Bonnee gives it a modern twist by mixing and matching bold, op-art-like patterns. The trick is to create a cohesive theme—in this case, a circle motif.

name
MONIKA
BIEGLER
EYERS

~~~~~~~~

location
LONDON,
ENGLAND

Moroccan leather poufs rest on the floor as decoration until they're needed as informal seating during parties and get-togethers.

In 2007, Monika Biegler Eyers, a design editor, writer, and consultant, moved with her husband from a modern loft in Manhattan to a stately apartment in London's Holland Park neighborhood. The elegant space is packed with traditional details like panel molding, high ceilings, and huge windows that fill the house with light throughout the day. With an eye for high-end looks but a taste for budget-friendly prices, Monika used her editorial expertise to invest in key pieces that would stand the test of time. To counteract these more traditional pieces, she used less expensive, funkier details, like Moroccan leather poufs, to add a bit of fun and color to the home without breaking the bank.

A portrait of Monika, painted by one of her college classmates, hangs above her desk. Rather than creating a more traditional home office space, Monika chose to use rich fabrics to create a space that would blend in with the home's overall look and feel.

Instant Luxe

Monika's desk is a great example of how fabric can instantly make a room feel more high end. An old card table is instantly elevated to magazine chic with the addition of a colorful fabric and a glass top. Plus, you get the added bonus of hidden storage underneath!

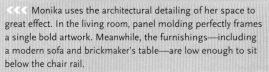

≪≪ Monika uses the architectural detailing of her space to great effect. In the living room, panel molding perfectly frames a single bold artwork. Meanwhile, the furnishings—including a modern sofa and brickmaker's table—are low enough to sit below the chair rail.

A common color palette can hold a mix of different patterns together.

Once again, Monika keeps the furniture and artwork low to the ground in order to showcase the room's impressive ceiling height.

≪≪ Monika fell in love with the existing deep teal of her kitchen so much that the space inspired her to take up cooking as a hobby. Her treasured collection of green and white chinoiserie china (in the drying rack) matches the room's palette so perfectly that she now uses it regularly and no longer saves it for special occasions.

This stunning bathtub was what sold Monika on her home. "I love the juxtaposition of unglazed stone against the sleek, cracked porcelain. It seems to channel the heyday of the Roman Empire, or something grand like that!" Monika says.

She chose to let the beauty of the tub stand alone in the room, with only an oversized shell as decoration and a holder for extra towels.

The matching gold
frames unify this set of
coral prints from Natural
Curiosities and tie in nicely
with the wall sconces.

name
AMY
MERRICK

location
BROOKLYN,
NEW YORK

The blues of Amy's collection of blue and white china coordinate effortlessly with the wall color and pick up the blue tones in her vintage quilt below.

esign*Sponge editor Amy Merrick's railroad apartment in Brooklyn is a favorite among the Design*Sponge team. Her love of antique furniture and handcrafted objects (many of which she made herself) instills each room with a sense of history. When she's not creating, Amy hunts for beautiful vintage clothing online and runs her own floral and styling business.

A big fan of wallpaper, but not the high price that often comes with it, Amy frequently scours eBay for affordable vintage patterns like this daisy print, which she used to paper the bathroom. Once a small, dark space, the room was transformed into a field of cheerful yellow and white flowers.

Amy's vintage bottle collection inspired this casual arrangement of Ranunculus.

Turn to page 307 to re-create this arrangement in your home.

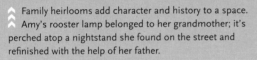

Family heirlooms add character and history to a space. Amy's rooster lamp belonged to her grandmother; it's perched atop a nightstand she found on the street and refinished with the help of her father.

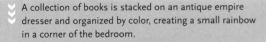

A collection of books is stacked on an antique empire dresser and organized by color, creating a small rainbow in a corner of the bedroom.

The spectacular garden-themed wallpaper in Amy's home office is a 1926 design by Charles F. A. Voysey, an English architect and textile designer, and a major figure in the arts and crafts movement. Amy chose the pattern, Apothecary's Garden, because it allowed her to bring a little bit of the outdoors inside—without all the maintenance. She bought the wallpaper from Trustworth Studios in Plymouth, Massachusetts. A vintage typewriter (still used for craft projects and correspondence) picks up on the greens in the wallpaper's pattern.

Turn to page 340 to see her office before and after from a different angle.

61

Amy loves DIY and renovated her sunny yellow kitchen herself.

Her favorite project was the painted floor in this room.

She tore up the damaged linoleum that came with the apartment, sanded the floors, and painted a black and white diamond pattern. Emboldened by the great results, she continued tearing up the linoleum in her home, room by room, and refinished the wood floors all by herself.

Though at first she didn't love the kitchen's mustard walls, Amy eventually embraced the hue and even painted her brown countertops yellow to match. Tiny hooks attached to the underside of a wall cabinet provide storage for teacups without taking up precious cabinet or counter space.

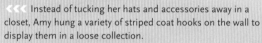

‹‹‹ Instead of tucking her hats and accessories away in a closet, Amy hung a variety of striped coat hooks on the wall to display them in a loose collection.

‹‹‹ Rather than fight the existing color of her kitchen's walls, Amy painted her refrigerator yellow to match. She keeps her houseplants above the fridge, where she knows she'll see them (and remember to water them on a regular basis).

Amy loves antique rugs, but didn't want to risk damaging this fragile find she purchased at a flea market. So she uses it as wall art, hanging it above a pew salvaged from a church in Brooklyn.

The fireman's pole running through the center of Alyn and Paul's living room says everything about their whimsical approach to life and design.

Alyn obtained this one from the Fire Station Museum in New Bedford, Massachusetts.

Artist Alyn Carlson and photographer Paul Clancy have lived inside a 110-year-old renovated church for the past twenty-eight years. The church was founded in 1900 by nondenominational factory workers, and its grounds include an outdoor swing, a chicken coop, and three acres of open meadow. With two artists in one home, this inspiring space has become a laboratory for design, color, painted surfaces, and all sorts of creative installations.

When they moved into their home, the couple painted their kitchen floor with a diamond pattern. It has worn over time, but they don't mind. In fact, they prefer its aged look.

<<< In another bold gesture, the couple hung a boat's timbers from the ceiling of their double-height living room. The space was originally the church's sanctuary and now houses a mix of vintage furniture and artwork created by the couple's children.

Avid book collectors, the couple created built-in bookshelves that run the entire length of the left and right sides of their expansive living room.

Alyn and Paul sleep in the closed converted choir of the church, with their bathroom in the steeple. The walls are painted to resemble the inside of shells, a nod to the area's nearby beaches. This decorative paint finish, as well as the floor, which was painted in a striped pattern, provided an inexpensive way to bring color and texture to the room without having to invest in new furniture or accessories.

Living Large

Whether you live in a church or a raw loft space, Alyn says, there are always ways to make your open space feel more cozy. In your mind, divide a large space into imaginary rooms—even if there are no wall separations. Pull furniture away from the walls, and create relationships between chairs and tables. Animate objects and spaces using floor or table task lamps, as opposed to more diffuse ceiling fixtures. Tactile materials—think velvet upholstery, thick textural rugs, and wooden surfaces—add warmth to a cavernous space.

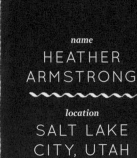

name
HEATHER ARMSTRONG

location
SALT LAKE CITY, UTAH

Heather and Jon's bedroom acts as a napping zone for the whole family, so they decided to furnish it with a king-size bed big enough to accommodate a family of four plus two pets.

The artwork's yellow and gray scheme is echoed in the bedding's palette.

Heather Armstrong, author of the hilarious blog Dooce, shares her Salt Lake City home with her husband, Jon, their young daughters, Leta and Marlo, and two lively dogs—a mutt named Chuck, and a miniature Australian shepherd called Coco. Perhaps best known for her writing on parenthood, Heather is also an active supporter of the independent design scene. Originally from Tennessee, she describes her personal style as "midcentury with a bit of a Southern born-and-raised twist."

Leather is a great option for family dining chairs, like the modern ones shown here; they are comfortable and easy to clean.

‹‹‹ Vintage signs and numbers introduce color into the blues and grays of the kitchen.

The alternating black and white matting of the photos echoes the graphic pop of the yellow and black chairs.

Julia Rothman created the Daydream wallpaper in Marlo's bedroom. The soft butter yellow coexists beautifully with the aged brass finish of the bed.

Brass Beds

The earliest brass beds were designed as "campaign beds" for military officers and could be quickly dismantled. In the mid-1800s, metal manufacturers developed hollow metal tubing, which was quickly adopted as a material for beds. In an era plagued by bedbugs, metal beds appealed to a broad public because, unlike wooden beds, the metal was pest-resistant.

Old-fashioned taxidermy looks modern and sculptural when paired with sleek gray walls and cool vintage furniture.

The living room sofa, originally in a bold floral print, was slipcovered to fit the room's sophisticated feel.

Rug designer Bev Hisey describes herself as a bit of a "junk hound." She can be found at least one day a week scrambling around Goodwill, hunting for a floor lamp or thick wool blankets. She displays these and other thrift store finds the way some people show off fine art or sculpture. Whether it's brand new or gently used, Bev always puts her own spin on her décor, creating a space that is uniquely hers.

Though her bedroom belies her love of color, it doesn't feel overdone. Bev makes it work by sticking to bright blocks of color rather than a mix of overwhelming prints.

The décor includes a rug of her own design, a blue gray love seat, and a side table (found at a yard sale) that she painted yellow.

Furniture from different styles and eras can easily be mixed as long as the colors blend well and have a neutral backdrop. Bev found one of her favorite possessions, the bull lithograph, at a Salvation Army store.

The Moderna Museet poster was a travel souvenir from a childhood trip to Stockholm. It inspired the wall color in her bedroom.

Rather than using a traditional headboard, Bev hung one of her own botanical die-cut fabrics behind her bed. The pattern pops against the wall's dark gray paint.

Bev's collection of West German pottery is displayed on top of the kitchen's storage lockers. Using closed storage like these lockers helps the kitchen stay clean, neat, and organized.

The dining room's gray walls are warmed up by Bev's collection of bent-ply Thonet chairs (for more on Thonet, see page 132).

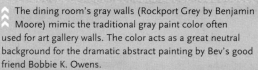

The dining room's gray walls (Rockport Grey by Benjamin Moore) mimic the traditional gray paint color often used for art gallery walls. The color acts as a great neutral background for the dramatic abstract painting by Bev's good friend Bobbie K. Owens.

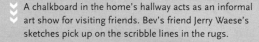

A chalkboard in the home's hallway acts as an informal art show for visiting friends. Bev's friend Jerry Waese's sketches pick up on the scribble lines in the rugs.

Bev artfully arranged a collection of wooden molds (originally used to make steel machine parts) on her dining room wall in a way that elevates them from industrial tools to colorful sculpture.

Industrial Parts

Industrial metal parts, wooden wheels, and other affordable flea market staples make for great displays when arranged in an interesting pattern. Other great sources include eBay's vintage section or your local Craigslist page. Looking for something really special? Try 1stdibs (*www.1stdibs.com*), which offers wonderfully unique options. Try using the search term "antique wheels" or "antique machine parts."

71

Alissa and Ryan have a ton of personal flair, which extends to their décor.

Their bedroom is furnished with a chunky crystal chandelier, modern artwork, and a playful self-portrait.

Design*Sponge editors Ryan Walker and Alissa Parker-Walker, who write our monthly bar column, are a talented young couple with impeccable taste. They maintain an online store, Horne, that is devoted to wonderful cutting-edge home accessories and décor. Meanwhile, their great sense of style is reflected throughout their Philadelphia home.

When original artwork isn't in the budget, framing a favorite poster or print is a great option. Not only does it make the piece feel more special, but it gives you a chance to choose a frame color that will tie the artwork into the room's décor. Above Alissa's desk, a framed Matisse poster holds court, picking up the blues in a vintage lampshade. The poster's metal frame coordinates with the vintage steel desk.

Investing in a great area rug can pull a room together.

And while it's unusual to put a vintage rug like this one in a kitchen, Ryan and Alissa consider it "art for the floor." The rich red colors make a nice counterpoint to their blue Formica table.

<<< A vintage clothing rack turns a favorite outfit into an eye-catching display.

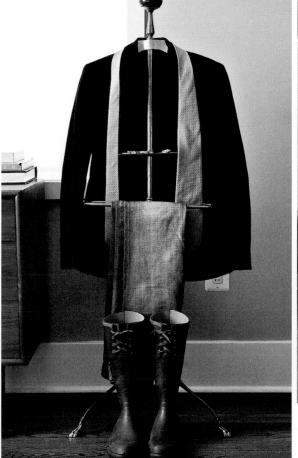

Ryan and Alissa need their living room to be multifunctional. They use it both as a place to relax and as a conference room where they can meet with designers whose work they are considering carrying in their shop.

A neutral palette balances such colorful furnishings as the patterned rug, orange floor lamp, and paintings by artists like America Martin.

A colorful suzani, a gift from Stephanie's mother-in-law, is draped over a daybed in the home's outdoor lounge area. A framed piece of Oaxacan fabric hangs on the wall above a set of cushions from Mokum's outdoor line. If you're afraid of using a bold print, try framing a small piece of it. It's a great way to test out the pattern in your room and also save a dollar or two. The flax mat on the floor, part of a wedding gift, is from Fiji and was handwoven in Stephanie's brother-in-law's village.

As the design director for Mokum, a vibrant line of contemporary textiles based in Australia, Stephanie Moffitt knows her way around pattern and color. So it was no surprise to find that her Sydney home, which she shares with her husband, was a mix of bold colors, prints, and sophisticated neutrals. By balancing her pattern choices with a calming palette of whites and grays, Stephanie created a home that feels fresh and modern no matter what patterns or textiles are changed and added. And after ten years of living in small apartments around Sydney, Stephanie was ready to create her own space in this larger home with a private garden.

A dramatic wall of glass doors opens onto the backyard from Stephanie's dining room and lounge.

A classic George Nelson bubble lamp hangs above the dining room table. Stephanie chose a dark gray color for the living room walls to create a cool, modern palette.

Rather than one large centerpiece, Stephanie likes to group collections of vintage bottles to create a relaxed focal point in the dining room.

Restored art deco sofas and chairs mix with retro furniture and lighting in the living room.

Stephanie loves combining soft patterns and textures to create a comfortable and relaxed space.

The pink rug is from Mokum's Tibetan line, which is handwoven in Nepal.

Stephanie used a mix of pink and gray accessories and bedding to give the bedroom a soft, ladylike feel.

Stephanie painted pale metallic gold panels on either side of the bedroom mantel to add a subtle bit of pattern to the room.

‹‹‹ Above the bedroom's fireplace mantel is a lei, handmade by Stephanie's friend Rochelle Cant. Small ceramic figures, passed down from Stephanie's grandparents, mix with candles on the mantel.

˅˅˅ A vintage café table and chair set is finished with a modern fabric to give the set new life. A grouping of succulents in planters acts as an easy-to-maintain centerpiece.

A patched kilim, purchased after a successful bargaining session in Istanbul's Grand Bazaar, echoes the living room's neutral color palette.

Kilims

Kilims have seen a resurgence in popularity over the past few years, but have a history that stretches back for centuries. Kilims are made throughout Asia and the Middle East and are produced using a flat tapestry-weaving technique. Often used as prayer rugs, kilims are now collected in museums across the globe, and can be found in more than fifteen different styles, ranging from designs with raised woven figures to thinner, striped rugs.

name
KATE BOLICK
〜〜〜

location
BROOKLYN, NEW YORK

Floor-to-ceiling bookshelves are great, but when they're so tall you can't reach everything, they lose their full functionality.

Kate picked up an inexpensive ladder from Ikea and painted it a pale lavender gray to match the wall so she could reach all her books.

Kate Bolick, a writer and former executive editor for *Domino* magazine, lives in a Brooklyn Heights high-rise apartment with a spectacular feature: a living room corner lined floor to ceiling with casement windows. The apartment is filled with vintage architectural details and blessed with high ceilings. A decorating buff, Kate considers her home to be a continual work in progress. She is forever redecorating, with a beautiful mix of vintage and contemporary items coming in and out of the house.

Fireplaces are beautiful, but when they no longer work it can be tough to decide how to use the space. Kate converted a simple garden urn (found on the street outside her apartment) into a dramatic sculpture by framing it in the fireplace.

Antique Urns

The urn in Kate's fireplace is reminiscent of eighteenth-century trophy urns, which were adapted from early Greek and Roman urns. If you'd like your own, check museum stores, which frequently sell replicas of the originals. Craft stores such as Plaster Craft (*www.plastercraft.com*) can be another source of inexpensive neoclassical-style urns. To search for an urn online, try these search terms: "Greek urn," "ancient vases," "garden urn," and "neoclassical urn."

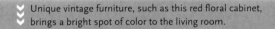

▲▲ Buying used furniture online can be scary—who knows what shape it will be in. But sometimes it can really pay off. Kate's antique green sofa bought sight unseen on Craigslist was a steal. As a safeguard, she asked the owner if she could test it out for a nap. It passed with flying colors and now lives in her sunny living room.

▼▼ Unique vintage furniture, such as this red floral cabinet, brings a bright spot of color to the living room.

While most people place sofas directly in front of a television, Kate put hers directly in front of her apartment's prize feature, the corner windows.

The placement not only looks dramatic, but when she wants to read a magazine or talk with friends she can take full advantage of the natural light.

SNEAK PEEKS

The bedroom's rich golden brown paint is a 1970s-inspired hue that contrasts nicely with the groovy vibe of Heather's vintage floral pillows.

Vintage Textiles

〜〜〜〜〜〜〜〜〜

Here are Heather's favorite online sources for vintage textiles:

Dots and Lines Are Just Fine: A blog that posts vintage textiles on a regular basis. *dotsandlinesarejustfine .blogspot.com*

True Up: This source guide links to loads of online sellers. *www.trueup.net*

Pindot: Fabulous online shop from Japan. *www.pindot.net/shopping.htm*

Retro Age: Australian online fabric resource. *www.vintagefabrics.com.au*

Purl Soho: A favorite for vintage-style fabrics. *www.purlsoho.com*

H eather Moore is the illustrator and designer behind Skinny Laminx, an Etsy shop filled with objects—from tea towels to aprons—made from the fabric she designs. Moore lives in Capetown in an apartment with a sweeping view of Table Mountain. Her home is filled with treasured items that she and her husband, artist Paul Edmunds, have spent years collecting. Never one to shy away from bold patterns, Heather is a master at using them throughout her home.

Yard sales are a great place to hunt for vintage fabrics.

Paul found this red floral at one such sale and Heather sewed it into cheerful bedroom curtains.

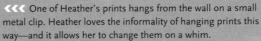

‹‹‹ One of Heather's prints hangs from the wall on a small metal clip. Heather loves the informality of hanging prints this way—and it allows her to change them on a whim.

‹‹‹ The kitchen came with a green paneled storage unit. Rather than tear it out, the couple transformed its appearance by adding wooden shelves and a coordinating wood island.

Even contrasting patterns look great when you mix and match.

Here, an assortment of pillows in vintage fabric finds a home on a vintage Ercol-style daybed.

81

Rugs serve as both floor and wall decoration in Jessica's home. The living room's neutral wall and curtain colors allow the rest of the room's bold patterns to breathe comfortably.

Photographer Jessica Antola's light-filled home in Carroll Gardens, Brooklyn, is full of treasures collected during her travels to such places as Turkey and Tunisia, as well as time she spent living abroad in Paris. Despite having traveled to so many exotic places, Jessica has enjoyed settling down in the heart of a bustling, creative area like Brooklyn, where she spends her time creating a comfortable home that combines her love of antique furniture with her flair for design and accessories.

To transform her small bedroom into a jewel box, Jessica painted the walls a vivid pink (Benjamin Moore's Peony) and added patterned pillows in coordinating colors.

In the dining room, Jessica made the most of a nonworking fireplace by decorating the mantel with favorite objects and using the space overhead to display artwork and a vintage mirror. The room's cream walls allow the contrasting pieces of art to fill the space with color and pattern.

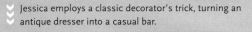
Jessica employs a classic decorator's trick, turning an antique dresser into a casual bar.

A pair of antique black chairs from Paris sits below a collection of Jessica's favorite pieces from around the world.

Caring for Older Rugs

If possible, keep antique rugs out of high-traffic areas.

To clean, shake rugs outdoors, then gently vacuum with the handheld attachment. Be careful not to touch the edges or fringe, as these delicate fibers are often ruined by vacuum cleaners.

Invest in a deep cleaning of your rugs by a trusted professional rug cleaner once a year. This will prolong their life and color.

Use rug pads or mats to prevent sliding and bunching, which can damage older rugs.

Tape down any frayed edges or loose strings with fabric tape (on the underside of the rug) to prevent the rugs from fraying any further.

Working with a consistent color theme in a small space can help create a sense of flow.

In the bedroom, green floral fabric at the head and foot of her bed is picked up in the edging around the pillowcases and curtains.

Rebecca Phillips, a photographer and yoga instructor, lives in a tiny Brooklyn apartment that is bursting with color and beautiful things. She loves design that is feminine but that also has an edge. With the help of her friend, decorator and Design*Sponge contributor Nick Olsen, Rebecca painted, sewed, and flea-marketed her way to a home that she describes as "a total expression of who I am."

Green is all over the tiny kitchen, too. Using varying shades of Benjamin Moore's Amazon Moss paint, Rebecca created a plaid backsplash. She even embellished her cabinet fronts with matching green grosgrain ribbon attached with a hot glue gun.

^^ In the bedroom section of her studio apartment, Rebecca painted chevrons onto an art deco dresser she found at the Chelsea flea market in New York.

Working with a Color Theme

"All greens go together," says Nick Olsen, who used to work for the interior designer Miles Redd. "Don't be afraid to pair different families of the same color," he adds. Rebecca painted her apartment mint green (a favorite color) when she moved in, but to Nick that shade looked too pastel. He added deep emerald accents, with enough white for grounding. "Decorating with one color doesn't have to look monochromatic if you consider value and contrast," Nick says.

An affordable couch from eBay gets a chic makeover with a white slipcover edged with kelly green piping.

Another inexpensive upholstery trick: This vintage chair was painted white and recovered in a Mexican blanket. To create her coffee table, Rebecca flipped an accent table from Urban Outfitters on its side and added a new Plexiglas top.

^^ Vintage artwork like this urban landscape can often be cleaned up and reframed for a fraction of the cost of new pieces. If you have a valuable piece of artwork on your hands, consider taking it to a professional cleaner, but if you're just looking to spruce up a five-dollar flea market find, gently rub the surface (and frame) of the painting with a damp cloth to remove dust and dirt.

Emerson and Ryan wanted to create a home that immediately puts guests at ease.

They've driven all over the Eastern seaboard picking up furniture and odds and ends, like this deep blue sofa in the library. The floors in the library were originally covered in a nonslip paint with sand bits in it, so Emerson and Ryan had the floors stripped to reveal a beautiful old heart pine.

Ryan and Emerson are the adorable couple behind the popular web shop Emersonmade. These designers create cheerful handmade paper and fabric flowers, housewares like cloth napkins, and clothing. After moving from New York City to New Hampshire, they bought a farmhouse that Ryan described as "in shambles." After renovating the home from top to bottom, leaving original details like exposed brick walls and pine floors, the couple have transformed their love of handmade design into a comfortable country home that celebrates vintage furniture and do-it-yourself décor.

Emerson and Ryan built a fireplace in their living room so they would always have a seat by the fire in the winter.

They salvaged the original (nonfunctional) fireplace's andirons so they could hold on to some of the details that it would have had more than 130 years ago. A nautical map on the mantel charts the ocean between New York and Maine, covering the area that the couple traveled in their move to New Hampshire.

‹‹‹ On the other side of the couple's library, a beaded chandelier hangs above a vintage round table stacked high with blue-covered books. When friends are over, this table can be cleared off to serve as an intimate spot for games or drinks.

‹‹‹ The kitchen pantry is designed to keep everything visible and easily accessible. Open shelving and storage can be a challenge to keep neat and clean, so basic ingredients are kept in clear glass jars to cut down on boxes and visual clutter.

The kitchen's country sink looks expensive, but was actually a bargain find from Craigslist. The butcher-block counter was built with prepping food in mind.

In the background, open storage highlights a collection of ironstone; Ryan first bought it for Emerson as an anniversary gift, and the collection has grown bit by bit over the years.

The couple loves to entertain so they brought a long wooden dining table home from a flea market excursion and set it up next to the fireplace in the living room. With space for eight to ten people to sit comfortably, it's the perfect place for warm winter meals. Emerson created the table runner herself and sells similar linens in her Emersonmade shop.

Homemade Table Runners

Custom burlap or raw linen runners are a great way to personalize your dining room or entryway tables without spending a lot of money. All you need is a piece of burlap or linen, or a fabric strip of your choice cut to size. Leaving the edges unfinished can add texture to the table, and you can easily customize the runner using stencils or iron-on decals in your family's initials.

Monogrammed pillowcases complement the striped sheets in the master bedroom.

Traditional details like brass sconces and an upholstered bed with nailhead trim give the room a sophistication that will last for years to come. To keep the room clean and simple, Emerson covered her books and sketchbooks (stacked under the beside table) in kraft paper.

In the guest room a pair of antique beds from Emerson's grandmother's childhood are painted a bright yellow to give them a modern feel.

A colorful, striped Hudson's Bay blanket (see page 91 for the history of Hudson's Bay blankets) picks up on the orange stripes in the duvet covers.

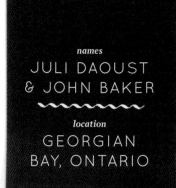

names
JULI DAOUST
& JOHN BAKER

~~~~~~

location
GEORGIAN
BAY, ONTARIO

While tearing down old drywall in the living room, the homeowners discovered the ceiling's wooden framework.

They loved the evidence of the craftsmanship that went into the home's construction so much that they decided to paint the framework white and leave a portion of the architectural detailing exposed.

Juli Daoust and John Baker—who own the Toronto home décor shop Mjölk, which specializes in Scandinavian design—inherited a family summer cottage in the Georgian Bay region of Ontario. Built in the 1970s, the cottage was in rough shape. Following a hands-on renovation, the couple furnished the cottage in the spirit of their favorite modern Scandinavian design—but with plenty of classic Canadian cottage touches, including de rigueur Hudson's Bay blankets.

The couple painted the interior of their home white in the spirit of the Scandinavian decorating style they favor.

In the living room, a rug by Swedish textile artist Judith Johansson ("Cliffs") lies at the foot of the home's original rustic fireplace. Rather than buy new lighting, they saved the home's old sconces, updating their look with a coat of matte black spray paint.

<<< The budget décor includes kitchen paneling improvised out of plywood sheets. The couple loves the look of unpainted plywood so much that they left it natural.

The contrast of different textures and materials keeps the living room interesting. A reindeer hide rug from the couple's shop, Mjölk, lies in front of a pair of telescopes, while an Isamu Noguchi paper lamp sits below a collection of vintage artwork.

The guest room is furnished simply with floor mattresses covered with striped Hudson's Bay blankets. Basic white clamp lights are attached to a plywood shelf.

Hudson's Bay Blankets

Incorporated in 1670 by a British Royal Charter, the Hudson's Bay Company is the oldest commercial corporation in North America. The company was initially focused on the fur trade, but their iconic wool point blanket became a regularly traded item in 1780. The "points" are the short black lines woven into the blanket just above the bottom set of stripes. The point system was invented by weavers in eighteenth-century France as a way to easily indicate the finished size of a blanket before it was felted. The higher the point value, the bigger and warmer the blanket. Though the blanket comes in solid colors, the classic version features green, red, yellow, and indigo stripes on a white background.

name
SCOTT ENGLER

∼∼∼∼

location
SAN FRANCISCO, CALIFORNIA

A casual display of Scott's favorite artwork, hats, and sculpture sits on a George Nelson slat bench in the hallway.

The deep chocolate brown walls match the floors and create a unified flow throughout the apartment.

W hile decorating his home in San Francisco's Castro neighborhood, Scott Engler's goal was to create a space that would feel like an escape from hectic city life. The owner of a busy online advertising agency, Scott wanted his home, which was built in 1900 and has airy, twelve-foot ceilings, to feel like a country retreat that is easily accessible to the city. By combining his love of classic design and "heirlooms in the making," Scott has created a space where he can be at home in his own "museum" of favorite things.

Scott retained his home's original vintage stove and found retro hanging lamps and a vintage sign to match. Open shelving from Ikea frees up counter space without adding a lot of bulk to the walls.

The deep chocolate color flows from the entry hall, seen here, to the second floor.

Rather than using white for all of the woodwork, Scott contrasts the brown walls with a soft tan bannister.

He is fearless when it comes to his wall art: Here, he displays a stuffed bat from the San Francisco gardening and natural sciences shop Paxton Gate.

The high-ceilinged living room sports a handblown glass chandelier created by New York designer Lindsey Adelman. The clear glass adds little to no visual weight in the room, like bubbles floating in the air.

Specimen Collecting

Collecting objects from nature, from butterflies to more unusual objects such as the bat in Scott's entry hall, has its roots in the great cabinets of curiosities of the Renaissance. As a sign of wealth, collectors acquired and carefully organized all types of objects—both man-made and natural. These carefully curated displays were early precursors to museum exhibits. Today's specimen collectors look for everything from insects to animal skulls and bones, taxidermy, and sea life.

The living room's décor mixes high-end contemporary furniture with flea market finds. The white lacquer and black walnut dresser is from the New York–based furniture maker BDDW.

A yellow and black theme runs through David's living room, using bold accent colors like red and lime green to keep the space bright.

Artist, designer, and event planner David Stark is known for the larger-than-life parties he plans, from charity fund-raisers to over-the-top bar mitzvahs—he famously created a "tornado" at a Robin Hood Foundation event by hanging shoes that were to be donated to children in need. So it was no surprise to find his Brooklyn home as full of whimsy and life as his incredible events. David describes his home as an "ever-changing collage." The wide array of colors, textures, and patterns gives his house a layered look that allows it to be both playful and beautiful.

Colors That Pop

David's home is a great example of living with bold colors. It's certainly not a look for everyone, but if you've been wanting to try some bright colors in your home, take a tip from David. In each of his rooms where there's an intense mix of colors, there is at least one wall that's painted a deep, neutral hue to give the eye a rest. The brown walls of the screened-in porch and the jet black wall in the living room ground the bright colors and keep things from going too far off the deep end.

Rich chocolate walls ground David's screened-in porch as a living space, while a multitude of potted plants and trees transform the room into a garden oasis. David's own twine flower designs (on the coffee table) for West Elm add texture and detail to the room without overshadowing the dominant color theme of green and brown.

In his bedroom, David uses a pale lavender wall color to ground graphic patterns like the black and white dots on the bedding and the striped window shade.

Bold geometric print curtains and a colorful striped rug work together in the dining area because they're grounded by the lime green color of the wall and chairs.

The bright orange lamp in the desk nook acts as a strong accent color, adding detail without distracting from the dominant palette.

name
ELISABETH
DUNKER

~~~~~~

location
GOTHENBURG,
SWEDEN

The collection of vintage floral paintings above the bed works well with the yellow and warm wood theme in the room.

Like many Swedish designers, Elisabeth has learned to mix disparate patterns expertly by focusing on similar color palettes and working with a range of pattern sizes.

Designer, illustrator, and stylist Elisabeth Dunker's home is full of pieces with special meaning. Whether she designed them herself or collected them from friends, she has created a home that is full of stories. Along with her husband, Dennis, and their children, Tovalisa and Otto, Elisabeth has grown to love her home for its lived-in feeling. Her flair for mixing vintage floral patterns and working with a warm color palette of olives and yellows harkens back to styles that were popular in the 1970s.

Create a Plate Wall

A display of dishes is colorful and graphic, and a great way to show off plates that are too special or fragile to use on an everyday basis. To create your own, pick up a set of plate hangers (available at most hardware stores and any housewares shop) and try one of these layouts to create a custom display in your home.

Symmetrical layout: Nothing's easier than working with a balanced layout. Try a simple design—three rows of two plates, or a square arrangementof four plates.

Small to large or large to small: This arrangement works particularly well if you have a very long or very tall wall to work with. Choosing a selection of plates in different sizes, hang them on the wall in a pattern that starts with your smallest or largest plate and work toward the opposite end of the scale.

Focal point: If you have a favorite plate, try hanging that plate first and adding plates to the wall as you go. Don't be afraid to adjust plates midstream; tiny nail holes can easily be filled.

︿︿ Repurpose vintage baskets for laundry or storage. These baskets (originally used for picking blueberries) store hats, scarves, and gloves in the entry hall.

︿︿ A small collection of plates, which were designed by Elisabeth and her children, hangs on the dining room wall, complementing the pale blue walls.

︿︿ A bold print from legendary Swedish graphic designer Olle Eksell hangs above a collection of patterned pillows on the living room sofa. A mix of textures in the room (the white wall covering, needlepoint pillows, aged paper prints) adds detail to the space without overwhelming the room.

︿︿ A vintage flat storage cabinet gets a new life in Elisabeth's living room, serving as both storage and a place to display favorite items. Cabinets like this are perfect for storing linens or other treasured objects that need to be kept flat.

name
ABIGAIL
AHERN
~~~~~~~
location
LONDON,
ENGLAND

Abigail installed a dramatic wire chandelier above her claw-foot tub. This luxurious touch inspires her to slow down and relax with a nice, candlelit bath.

London-based Abigail Ahern is an interior designer and stylist whose shop, Atelier, sells housewares that showcase her impeccable taste and eye for modern design. But her stylish home isn't restricted to the contemporary. She loves such cutting-edge combinations as a solid concrete chair (one of her favorite pieces) and vintage finds (like her worn-in dining room table). She uses bold color around her home to bring a happiness to her space that counteracts London's frequently gloomy weather.

In the Dark

Don't be afraid of decorating with a dark palette. "Dark colors are my idea of heaven, and it's a big misconception that you need to live in sunny climates or have huge rooms to pull it off," Abigail says. "Dark, smoky colors make rooms look and feel sophisticated and grown-up by enveloping the walls and floors with their intense, strong notes (making them a statement in their own right). The trick is to use an abundance of intense accent colors (think hot pink, acid yellow, burnt orange). Couple these intense pops of color with plenty of lighting and you will have a beautiful space that has been transformed from a shy flower of a room to a head-turner."

⌃⌃ Play around with scale; ignore traditional rules about keeping everything in proportion. This dramatic porcelain chandelier is Abigail's favorite piece in her home—even though it was so big she had to hire the company that installs chandeliers in Buckingham Palace to deliver and hang it.

⌃⌃ Abigail embraced a bold theme in her kitchen and dining room, playing with both the shade and scale of the objects. In the corner an oversized, blue-velvet-wrapped Anglepoise lamp (which can be placed in a number of positions without the need for clamps) adds a touch of humor to a sophisticated space.

<<< A piece of pop art from Abigail's shop adds a bright dose of color to the walls of the living room.

The back wall of the home was replaced with a wall of glass to bring in more light. The dramatic, dark walls are offset by brightly colored furnishings, including a pink lamp and mohair chair that is a favorite cozy space for reading. The faux-book wallpaper is the same as that used in Lynda Gardener's country home (see page 53), but where there it worked as trompe l'oeil, here it is used as an accent!

names
LINDA
& JOHN
MEYERS

~~~~~~

location
PORTLAND,
MAINE

Consider fabric as a wall covering if you want to add some additional texture to a room.

Linda covered her dining room's walls in a patterned fabric she found at a flea market in France. Fabric can be used just like wallpaper —simply iron your fabric, clean your walls with soap and water, allow them to dry, and then apply thin coats of liquid starch and hang the fabric on the wall. Use a plastic straightedge to smooth out any bumps in the fabric, just like you would with wallpaper.

Linda and John Meyers are the talented husband-and-wife team behind the design studio Wary Meyers. Perhaps best known for their amazing projects repurposed from found materials (documented in their book, *Tossed & Found: Unconventional Design from Cast-offs*), they have filled their home with an eclectic collection of thrift store finds and lovingly worn-in vintage pieces. Whether they're repainting an old canoe with a classic Blue Willow pattern or covering their walls with vintage fabric, John and Linda are always creating unique decorations for their home.

The couple set out to create a guest bedroom with the décor of what they call a "groovy reading nook." They layered multiple patterns in the form of cushions, wallpaper, and bedding, and lined the walls with vintage artwork and books.

A vintage shag rug and restored Eames loungers create a 1970s feeling in the living room.

The look is modern and retro with a funky twist, epitomizing the Wary Meyers style. The living room's walls are made of exposed lathing, and was discovered when the plaster coating was removed. The look reminds the couple of the exposed beams in Alvar Aalto's home in Helsinki.

The natural, 1970s-style accents in Linda and John's home inspired this colorful driftwood arrangement.

Turn to page 310 to learn how to re-create this arrangement in your home.

Using a favorite color object for inspiration can lead to a beautiful new room. Linda walked into Home Depot with a box from the jeweler Tiffany & Co. and asked them to match the color. The store came up with Behr's Sweet Rhapsody, which now covers the living room walls.

The home office is decorated with a bold pink and black mural, harking back to the 1970s but looking very now.

Candy-colored accessories and furniture—including the purple swivel office chairs—add fun to the white space.

name
TARA HEIBEL
〜〜〜〜〜〜
location
CHICAGO,
ILLINOIS

Tara combined vintage furniture with colorful, modern accessories to create a sophisticated but fun living room in what was once a neighborhood bodega.

The building's original brick walls were left exposed, and a dramatic open staircase was added to access the upstairs living room and master bedroom.

ara Heibel is the owner of Sprout Home, a popular nursery, flower, and modern design shop with locations in Chicago, Illinois, and Brooklyn, New York. To look at her modern, airy home in Chicago's West Town neighborhood, it's hard to believe it was once a corner bodega that had shut down due to fire damage. "The solid, simple exterior drew me," she says. "I loved the industrial feel of the building. The fact that it was on a corner lot was a huge plus as well, as it allowed for more windows for plants and light." Seeing the potential it held, Tara personally oversaw a renovation to transform the derelict building into the airy space she now calls home.

Tara's large combined kitchen and dining room is grounded by a bright yellow accent wall. A collection of potted plants, terrariums, and cut flowers keeps the minimalist modern space feeling green and fresh.

We were inspired by Tara's collection of succulents to create this modern arrangement.

Turn to page 313 to learn how to re-create this arrangement in your home.

<<< In a sunny lounge on the upper floor, shelf lengths are staggered to create visual interest.

For entertaining, Tara installed a walnut bar and vintage swivel bar stools in the living room (opposite the sofa).

To keep the fun rolling, vintage pachinko machines (a cross between a slot machine and pinball) were hung on the wall.

<<< Medical posters have become a popular wall decoration and can easily be found on eBay and Etsy, as well as in thrift shops around the world. Tara's vintage medical poster is from the Edgewater Antique Mall in Chicago. The blue echoes the color of the walls in the upstairs lounge a few steps away.

names
CARL &
CHRISTY
NEWMAN

location
WOODSTOCK,
NEW YORK

The dog portraits on the walls of the screened-in porch were discovered in the house, where they were laminated to the backside of the home's original backsplash. Christy had them framed and relocated them.

When Christy Newman and her husband, musician Carl Newman (lead singer for the band The New Pornographers), bought their midcentury cabin in New York's Catskills region, they spent an entire summer renovating and pulling out old carpet. Their goal was to create a "groovy ski lodge" motif that combined the home's original style and purpose (a country getaway) with their own modern tastes. When the hard work was finished and they were ready to move in, Carl and Christy loved their new home so much they decided to rent out their apartment in Brooklyn and move to Woodstock full-time.

The "groovy ski lodge" motif in Carl and Christy's home was inspired by the massive stone fireplace at the center of their living room.

A sectional sofa allows the couple to face both the television and the fireplace.

A solid beech coffee table from artist Michael Arras, that Christy found on Etsy, echoes the pile of cut logs stacked by the fireplace.

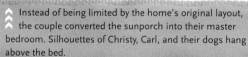

Instead of being limited by the home's original layout, the couple converted the sunporch into their master bedroom. Silhouettes of Christy, Carl, and their dogs hang above the bed.

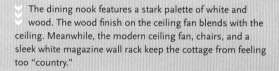

The dining nook features a stark palette of white and wood. The wood finish on the ceiling fan blends with the ceiling. Meanwhile, the modern ceiling fan, chairs, and a sleek white magazine wall rack keep the cottage from feeling too "country."

Christy loves the home's original Dutch door with leaded glass. She added a vintage key knocker to the front to replace a traditional doorbell.

Dutch Doors

As its name suggests, the Dutch door originates from the Netherlands and was typical of pre-Revolutionary homes in areas of Dutch settlement such as New York and New Jersey. Divided in half with independently opening top and bottom portions, the Dutch door was designed to allow air and light in, while keeping livestock and pests out. This style of door regained popularity in the 1950s and is still a favorite today.

Few things can beat the sense of history that aged plank floors give a room. Christine and Paul restored the kitchen's 1931 Glenwood stove to working condition, and it now serves as the focal point of the room.

Christine Foley and Paul Sperduto are the owners of the home goods shop Moon River Chattel in Williamsburg, Brooklyn (specializing in vintage-style tableware and accessories as well as antique furniture and lighting), and like old-fashioned shopkeepers they live above the store. Known for their excellent taste in vintage furniture and accessories, it was no surprise to find that their sunny apartment, which they share with sons Jack and Silas, was decorated with the same rustic but elegant style as their store. Christine and Paul did the majority of the work on their home by themselves over a period of twelve years. The couple sees themselves as caretakers of their home, rather than owners. "Our blood, sweat, and tears are in everything we see and touch each day," Paul says, "making our guardianship of our home, for our time, very personal."

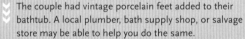

The kitchen renovation combines a vintage farmhouse sink with new countertops made from reclaimed Southern yellow pine.

In the minimal parlor, the vintage sofa came out of the Brooklyn office of the Waterfront Commission of New York Harbor, originally formed in 1953 to fight corruption among longshoremen (a situation which later inspired the Marlon Brando movie *On the Waterfront*).

The couple had vintage porcelain feet added to their bathtub. A local plumber, bath supply shop, or salvage store may be able to help you do the same.

Old Doors

Looking to add character to your home but don't know where to start? Try adding antique doors and hardware. Salvage yards, eBay, and Craigslist often list doors. Make sure if you buy one that it fits your door frame. Don't be afraid to experiment with doors that would have originally belonged in schools or other types of buildings (for more ideas, see Genevieve Gorder's apartment on page 2).

Paul and Christie seek out salvaged furniture for its sense of history.

In their office, bookshelves from Columbia University Teacher's College were hauled down four flights of stairs and trucked to their home in Brooklyn. The couple always keep their ears to the ground for word about sales or spring cleaning taking place at local shops, schools, or historic buildings. You can often get word of these events through local antique stores, listings online via sites like Craigslist, or local newspapers that specialize in neighborhood news.

names
MICHAEL &
SARA PENNEY

location
TORONTO,
ONTARIO

Michael and Sara combined contrasting red and green hues in their bedroom. Their four-poster bed, an inexpensive model from Ikea, was painted white to keep the room feeling crisp and clean.

Style editor, decorator, and stylist Michael Penney and his wife, Sara, live in a beautiful downtown Toronto apartment. They were drawn to the home's high ceilings and historic details like crown molding and a quaint brick fireplace. Both Michael and Sara love to live with their collections on display, and are happy that they were able to come up with a look that was both functional and beautiful. Their décor may be traditional, but thanks to artful styling it still feels young and fresh. "The little quirks here and there loosen it up and the colors allow us to have fun and express any mood we feel," Michael says.

Broken furniture is often just one repair shop visit away from being as good as new.

The living room's standing lamp had a faulty switch and had been abandoned in the basement of a shop where Michael used to work. The basement's humidity had tarnished the brass and given it a gritty patina that Michael loved, so he scooped it up, had the switch fixed at a local lighting shop (many will do this at low cost), and added a new drum shade.

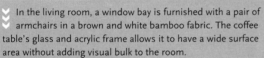

❮❮❮ In the bedroom, a dresser top is layered with objects, including a piece of dried coral and a vintage mirror, which bring a sense of depth to the room.

≫ In the living room, a window bay is furnished with a pair of armchairs in a brown and white bamboo fabric. The coffee table's glass and acrylic frame allows it to have a wide surface area without adding visual bulk to the room.

Cane chairs, vintage green bottles, and an antique silver vase add character to the dining room and signal the traditional side of Michael and Sara's style.

Michael painted the back wall of the china cabinet (which was original to the house) brown to highlight a collection of brown transferware plates.

In the kitchen, decorative touches like blue and white Thibaut wallpaper and a retro hanging light (a thrift store find) make an often overlooked space feel more like an extension of the couple's living area. The wicker storage baskets above the cabinets also add warmth to the room.

A Nonworking Fireplace

Even if your fireplace has been sealed, there are still plenty of ways to decorate and disguise this visual dead zone.

Decorative screens: Fireplace screens, which come in a variety of materials—from fabric to wood or metal— are a great and easy way to cover a fireplace while bringing a little bit of color and/or pattern to your room. Try covering a piece of plywood with wallpaper to create your own "screen" to place in front of the fireplace. If wallpaper isn't in your budget, beautiful patterned wrapping paper can work just as well.

Mirrors: Mirrored tiles or a cut-to-size piece of mirror mounted on plywood are a great way to turn your dark fireplace hearth into a space that reflects light and makes your room feel larger. Mirrored tiles can be applied with Velcro, adhesive tape from 3M, or putty for easy removal down the road. If you're using a mirror on plywood, place it in the hearth, propping it against the back of the fireplace. You could also have a small stand built so the mirror can stand freely at the front of the hearth.

Chalkboard paint: If you're up for something a little more "out there," try painting your fireplace hearth or the screen in front of it with chalkboard paint. You can write your favorite poems or quotations on the chalkboard or draw yourself a toasty two-dimensional fire.

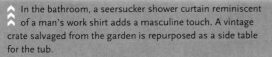

˄ In the bathroom, a seersucker shower curtain reminiscent of a man's work shirt adds a masculine touch. A vintage crate salvaged from the garden is repurposed as a side table for the tub.

˅ To turn this nonfunctional fireplace into a clean, modern display area, Michael and his wife painted the brick white. Antique andirons with birch logs were added to keep the fireplace feel without all the smoke and soot.

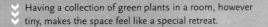

˅ Having a collection of green plants in a room, however tiny, makes the space feel like a special retreat.

˅ A painted Peg-Board adds functional and stylish storage space to the kitchen.

Turn to page 222 to learn how to make your own kitchen Peg-Board.

names
HALLIGAN
NORRIS &
ADAM SMITH
〜〜〜
location
PHILADELPHIA,
PENNSYLVANIA

Adam and Halligan's living room is where they spend most of their time, so they wanted it to be as comfortable as possible.

For a young couple, expensive furniture isn't a high priority, so inexpensive pieces like a green Ikea couch are coupled with flea market finds like a small shelving unit (currently acting as a plant stand) and wire chair.

Design*Sponge contributor and jewelry designer Halligan Norris met her husband, designer and bike mechanic Adam Smith, while they were both studying at the Savannah College of Art and Design. After their 2009 wedding in Georgia, Adam and Halligan moved north to make their home in the Fishtown area of Philadelphia. Both of them are champions of do-it-yourself design, so they've filled their home with furniture and decorations that they or friends and family have made.

The living room's wire chair was a Philadelphia yard sale score that Halligan says "cost next to nothing." It's coupled with another quirky flea market find, a deer hoof footstool. The Fraktur on the wall was painted by Adam's grandmother to commemorate Adam and Halligan's wedding day.

Fraktur Artwork

Fraktur, like the piece painted by Adam's grandmother, is a style of calligraphy and artwork created by the Pennsylvania Dutch. Dating back to the late eighteenth and early nineteenth centuries, Fraktur works were primarily based on Germanic folk art, focusing on images of birds and flowers.

A hand-me-down mirror from Halligan's grandmother hangs above the mantel. Hiding under an antique bell jar is Halligan and Adam's wedding cake topper, designed by Jennifer Murphy.

A colorful collection of books and globes is displayed on these shelves, which mimic the stairway leading up to the bedroom.

Halligan and Adam love to travel, so vintage maps and globes are used frequently as decoration throughout their home.

Adam and Halligan used a vintage frame and corkboard to tie together a disparate collection of Halligan's handmade vintage doll clothes and Adam's collection of quirky old tools.

Adam's father, furniture maker Bradford Smith, made this bed as a wedding gift for the couple.

The bars that make up the headboard are vintage farm tool handles.

The "parentheses" around the name above the bed are actually a set of chair arms Adam and Halligan found while Dumpster diving.

<<< In their small upstairs bathroom, Adam and Halligan decided to indulge in their shared love for "creepy critters" by hanging artwork depicting mice, snakes, and lizards.

A vintage armoire makes a dramatic statement in the bedroom.

Investing in classic pieces like this and mixing in less expensive pieces from flea markets and shops like Ikea allows you to create a home that will grow with you.

115

Brick walls: love them or hate them? Maya is on the fence and was anxious to have the one in her bedroom blend into her breezy white home. She whitewashed the brick to make it visually recede while retaining the texture it gives to the room. The worn-white finish coordinates well with soft, butter yellow bedding from Dwell Studio. The reproduction fan above her bed was such a hit with her visitors that she now stocks it in her store.

Maya Marzolf is the owner of a popular antique store in Brooklyn called Le Grenier, so I was excited to see what sort of beautiful antique treasures her home would hold. In addition to a wide selection of gorgeous furniture, Maya's duplex houses an impressive collection of artwork and accessories collected on trips and during shoots while working as a fashion photography producer. She decided to leave the walls of her 1870 brownstone white, to make the space feel brighter and to let her eclectic mix of furniture shine. Few changes had been made to the home since it was built in the 1870s, so Maya spent more than seven years transforming the space to fit her needs. Along the way she repaired the entire structure of the building—the floors, lighting, the backyard garden, and the roof.

To accent the antique feel of her tin-ceilinged kitchen, Maya installed a trio of hanging light fixtures from one of her favorite antique shops in upstate New York.

The decorative ceramic hands on top of her reclaimed wood counters were originally used in factories as glove molds.

Maya has been collecting skeletons since she was a little girl. She displays a few of them inside a nonworking fireplace whose mantel she found in an antique shop in upstate New York. Her coffee table is made out of an old sand mold from a metal foundry in St. Paul, Minnesota. Maya had a piece of glass cut to fit the top of the mold.

Without small children in her home, Maya felt safe to leave the stairway open. A crystal chandelier, purchased during a trip to Holland, hangs at the foot of the stairs.

An alligator bench, purchased in Bali, is another reminder of Maya's world travels.

The duplex didn't have an extra room for an office, so Maya created a small alcove under a loft bed. She had it built by local carpenter Sebastian Trienens using wood scraps salvaged from her store, which he also renovated.

Trouble Lights
~~~~~~~~~~
Originally used by workmen as they moved around job sites, trouble lights are a single bulb encased in a metal cage. They have hooks, which allows them to be easily hung from any surface. Here, Maya hangs hers from a metal arm found at an antique shop. You can find trouble lights on eBay or 1stdibs, and often through stores like Anthropologie, where reproduction lights are sold.

DESIGN✳SPONGE
AT HOME

Maya's cat Grendel peers from an old fire escape ladder that connects the guest loft on the top floor of her duplex to the rooftop terrace above.

<<< Architects' drafting tables can work well at home for almost any purpose because they are easily adjustable to different heights. In Maya's dining room, a drafting table is surrounded by a mix of flea market stools.

<<< The "roof" of the office nook doubles as a cozy guest bed for visitors. Simple canvas curtains were installed along the ceiling beams for privacy.

To create a seaside feel in her bathroom, Maya hired local artist Weston Woolley to paint a mural featuring some of her favorite beach imagery like horseshoe crabs, coral, shells, and starfish.

Silhouettes

The art of creating a portrait that is a black outline of the subject goes back to ancient times, when the Greeks and Etruscans used them to decorate pottery. In the era before photography, silhouette artists worked quickly and cheaply to capture a likeness. Augustin Édouart (1789–1861), one of the most highly regarded silhouette artists, is credited with cutting more than 100,000 portraits in England and the United States. The silhouette's connection to ancient Greece made it extremely popular from 1750 to 1850, the era of neoclassicism.

In the bedroom, an antiqued paint finish is the perfect backdrop for a collection of vintage and contemporary silhouette artwork.

Along with her dog, Pablo, and cats, Georgia and Alro, self-taught painter Trish Grantham has called this cozy Oregon bungalow home for more than twelve years. Trish is known for her work depicting fantasy characters "playing out classic themes of good versus evil and romantic love," often painted directly on wood panels. It is this same sense of fantasy and playfulness that Trish has infused in her home's décor, which includes small treasures she has collected from all over. She makes an effort to spend as little as possible on the pieces she brings home, and where she saves on shopping costs, she splurges on the amount of time she invests in making her home feel welcoming and full of love.

Trish found her living room sofa on the side of the road and had it re-covered in exchange for one of her paintings.

The Swiss army blanket provides a soft spot for the cats to nap while protecting the upholstery from wear and tear. Deep gray walls (Iron Mountain by Benjamin Moore) act as a rich backdrop for Trish's collection of artwork, including this piece by Portland artist Dan Ness.

⌃⌃ The entryway is livened up by this collection of Trish's favorite artwork and objects, which covers almost an entire wall above a Danish credenza. A vintage wooden cuckoo clock, wooden whale sculpture, and ship's wheel clock are mixed in among the artwork.

Trish attached an inexpensive piece of wood to dramatically curved legs to create the table in her kitchen nook.

You can re-create this look in your own home by searching for legs at thrift shops, flea markets, and salvage yards, and on eBay and 1stdibs, and then having a local carpenter attach a sturdy wooden, metal, or marble top.

Artwork doesn't need to be perfectly centered. The paintings around Alyson's cabinet are erratically placed and give the room a sense of movement.

Austin-based artist and designer Alyson Fox and her husband, Derek Dollahite, owner of the interactive design agency Coloring Book Studio, have lived in their 1940s-era house for more than five years. After a large-scale (but low-budget) do-it-yourself kitchen renovation that involved the help of both family and friends, the couple feel that their home is finally finished. A "perfect canvas" of bright, open space, it's the ideal balance between feminine and masculine styles.

> Alyson's office is filled with the primary hues she loves: She pairs a red thrift store desk with a bright yellow chair. The mix of old and new reflects her artwork, which draws on the look of vintage illustrations while giving them a contemporary twist.

> Working on a tight budget, this crafty couple renovated their entire combined cooking and dining space mostly themselves. They found affordable countertops, cabinets, and a sink from Ikea. Open wooden shelving keeps the space feeling airy and echoes all the wood accents elsewhere in the home.

> The couple's pet, Stache, sits atop a bed custom-made by Alyson's brother-in-law, Blake Dollahite. The walls are painted a soft blue gray hue (Balsams, by Ralph Lauren).

> In the living room, a green classroom chalkboard serves as both a message center and an ever-changing backdrop for a rotating selection of paintings.

Renovating on a Budget

Alyson shares these tips.

Before you start: Always remember to measure twice and cut once, get help from friends to keep costs down, and take advantage of inexpensive building materials that can be customized to create a luxe look.

Do your research: Look at a wide range of stores and options before settling on a product. A little research can add up to big savings. We really wanted a farm sink in our kitchen, but most were in the $600 range. Then we looked at Ikea and found one for $225!

Go construction-grade: Don't just rely on high-end furniture stores. Builders' materials can look great, hold up well, and save you money. The open shelves above the kitchen sink were made from a laminated veneer lumber called Microlam, which is similar to plywood but much stronger.

List your priorities: Start with the things you absolutely want and go from there. Sometimes second best really won't do, and that is okay. Just be sure to budget around the pieces you can't live without.

Think long-term: In two years, will you still like the color you painted the cabinets? If you love to cook, will the countertops hold up? In the end, function will outlive design trends, so invest in pieces you won't have to replace in a few years.

Ask your friends: Get sources and ideas through word of mouth from people whose home renovations you admire. They will often lead you to affordable resources.

names
KELLY &
ALEXIS

location
PORTLAND,
OREGON

In the stairway, the brown color palette, together with fresh greenery, emphasizes the home's theme of bringing the outside in.

Portland, Oregon—based interior designer Jessica Helgerson is known for her eco-friendly design projects. With degrees in both interior and environmental design, she has been recognized for her impressive (and stylish) green projects, which earned her a place on *House Beautiful*'s list of America's top young designers. Jessica oversaw a complete renovation of Portland homeowners Kelly and Alexis's split-level ranch. After remodeling the kitchen and the master bath and refinishing the floors, Jessica focused on using a wide range of earthy colors to bring the feel of nature inside. In keeping with her green philosophy, she made sure all of the furnishings were vintage finds that could be reupholstered and refinished. The only exception was a beautiful maple coffee table made by her husband, architect Yianni Doulis.

Demijohns

These highly collectible antique bottles are characterized by their large size and short, narrow necks. Sometimes called carboys, they were popular in the nineteenth century, when they were used to transport and store bulk liquids such as alcohol and wine. Color can often help identify age, as newer bottles tend to be greener. Demijohns of European origin, such as the example in this home, have a globe shape, while their American counterparts tend to be more cylindrical. You can find the most common colors, green and clear, on eBay and 1stdibs, and at flea markets across the country. Try turning demijohns into lamps with the aid of a conversion kit, which can be found at most lighting or hardware stores.

Rather than replace the living room's original flooring, Jessica had the wooden floors patched and ebonized. The Yianni Doulis coffee table was made from a slab of locally salvaged Eastern hard rock maple. Portuguese eel traps hang above the mantel, while vintage demijohn bottles filled with branches create the feeling of a live tree.

<<< Small bathrooms are often the best places to experiment with bold patterns. When space is limited, you only need to use a small amount of wallpaper. The result—as with Cavern Home's Blackbird used here—can look bold but not overwhelming. To keep things simple, Jessica painted both the ceiling and the walls black to allow the wallpaper to shine. Bright accessories from Jonathan Adler carry the home's green theme into the room.

Kirei Board, a low-VOC-emission material made from reclaimed sorghum stalks, was used to create the cabinets in the master bathroom. A long wall of brown curtains behind the bed not only gives the room privacy from the windows behind it, but also acts as a wall of color against which the wooden bed pops.

names
MATT CARR &
JOYCE LO

~~~~~~

location
TORONTO,
ONTARIO

Ceilings are often neglected when decorating a room. But when Matt and Joyce saw the classic William Morris wallpaper that their home's previous owners had used on the ceiling, they jumped at the chance to use one of the pattern's central shapes as a frame for the chandelier.

Ceiling Style
~~~~~~

Don't forget to look up! Sometimes the best place to use a bold pattern is in an unexpected place. This home's wallpapered ceiling is a great example of turning a traditionally overlooked space into a room's focal point. A stamped print, wallpaper, or just a coat of bright paint can add visual interest to a room without making the space feel too busy. It's also a great way to draw the eye upward and make a room feel taller!

M att Carr, design director of the housewares company Umbra, shares his Toronto home with his girlfriend, artist Joyce Lo. She is the director of the Drake General Store, a fun shop attached to the city's groovy Drake Hotel. When the couple first saw their prospective home during an open house, they were charmed by the arts and crafts–style floral wallpaper that seemed to cover every surface. They enthusiastically took on the considerable work that needed to be done to make the house their own, from refinishing floors to hauling heavy furniture up several flights of stairs. In the end, they created a home that combines their love of eclectic modern design with their taste for more traditional furnishings.

Inspired by coffee table legs, Matt designed these Biblioteca shelves for U+ (Umbra's more experimental studio line of home accessories and furniture) and now uses them in his living room next to two outdoor sconces that he spray-painted black. Parisian café chairs contrast nicely with the couple's rough wooden table and a colorful rug from Canadian designer Bev Hisey.

Turn to page 68 to see Bev Hisey's home.

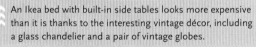

An Ikea bed with built-in side tables looks more expensive than it is thanks to the interesting vintage décor, including a glass chandelier and a pair of vintage globes.

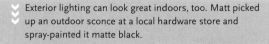

Exterior lighting can look great indoors, too. Matt picked up an outdoor sconce at a local hardware store and spray-painted it matte black.

A wooden fox figure, a Parisian flea market find, welcomes guests to Matt and Joyce's home. The vintage map and marble console table were both purchased at Machine Age Modern, a favorite shop of the couple's in Leslieville.

Turn to page 188 to learn how to make storage boxes from vintage maps.

names
JOY & TYLER THIGPEN

location
WINDER, GEORGIA

Joy's living room is a celebration of color and pattern, kept in check by simple white walls. Her bold floral drapes were sale finds from Marimekko, while both the rug and chair were purchased at Anthropologie. Because the room's primary furnishings are so bold, a Lucite table gives the other pieces room to breathe.

P hotographer and wedding stylist Joy Thigpen shares a colorful home with her husband, Tyler, and their children, River and Oswin. Joy describes their house as a happy retreat where her kids can run, squeal, and play, but also a place where she and her husband can relax. To create a home that is hospitable to both children and adults, the couple used a fairly adventurous color scheme in the living room and children's bedrooms, but chose a more neutral palette for the master bedroom.

River's rainbow room inspired this colorful bouquet.

Turn to page 315 to learn how to re-create this arrangement in your home.

A rainbow fade of paint colors is a great way to give a child's room a sense of energy and movement. Joy used seven Sherwin Williams paint samples to create the rainbow effect. The colors, from top to bottom, are: Lively Yellow, Optimistic Yellow, Oleander, Charisma, Begonia, Dynamo, and Aquaduct. To get the graduated effect between stripes Joy swept a clean brush through the wet bottom layer of one color over the stripe above it, blending the paints together.

When the rest of your home is full of bold color and pattern, a space that uses a calm, neutral palette can be refreshing. Joy and Tyler's serene bedroom acts as a peaceful retreat from the energetic color in the rest of their home.

Oswin's playful bedroom features a mural that combines his favorite color, blue, with a whimsical indoor palm tree. To create more play space, Joy removed the door to Oswin's closet and placed his dresser inside. Small rooms often benefit from taking the doors off of closets. The closets can remain open and reveal a colorful wallpapered interior, or can be simply covered with a fabric curtain that takes up less space than a door and covers up laundry or hanging clothes.

names
SUSAN &
WILLIAM
BRINSON

location
NEW YORK,
NEW YORK

Susan and William's style is all about contrast: black and white, light and dark, masculine and feminine, old and new, rustic and modern.

But their bedroom is a bit more feminine and softer than the rest of the loft. Much of their furniture is vintage and handed down from family, including their headboard, which originally belonged to William's grandparents.

Art director Susan Brinson and her husband, commercial photographer William Brinson, are high school sweethearts. After meeting at William's sixteenth birthday party, the two quickly became an item and attended the Savannah College of Art and Design together. Shortly after graduation they moved to New York City, which has been their home for the past ten years. After moving into their new loft in the NoMad area of Manhattan ("north of Madison Square Park") in 2009, Susan and William spent a few months converting its 2,000 square feet into a work space for Susan's stationery line, Studio Brinson, and William's photography studio. The couple loves when their home is filled with visitors, and most days you can find both friends and clients gathered around the loft's huge dining table.

Another Savannah score, a vintage three-drawer dresser, holds a teacup collection to which Susan's grandmother, mom, aunts, and friends have contributed.

<<< A tall armoire purchased in Savannah holds Susan and William's clothes. A collection of antlers and vintage finds like a birdcage and metal fan not only serve as decoration, but are also great props for William's photo shoots.

Susan made sure their bedroom was large enough for a sitting area where she can relax in privacy if William is shooting in the other part of the loft.

A vintage metal scrap piece (left over from the industrial process of knife creation) hangs on the wall at the other end of the Brinsons' kitchen.

Bright white walls and tall windows allow William, who shoots mainly with natural light, to turn almost any space in their home into a backdrop for photos.

The lighting fixture in Susan and William's dining room is a DIY project the couple tackled together. It has 100 bulbs, but they chose to wire only ten, which highlights the inactive bulbs. The couple, who use this long table both for client meetings and dinner parties with friends, love how the glass bulbs reflect light. A collection of classic Thonet bentwood chairs acts as everyday seating at the table.

The Thonet Chair

~~~~~~~~

The classic bentwood chair, called Model #14, was designed by Michael Thonet in 1859 as a response to the overcomplicated production methods for wooden chairs in the mid–nineteenth century. Using only six pieces of wood, Thonet created this masterfully simple chair, which became an instant classic in both high- and low-end markets.

Susan and William created a large, open kitchen space because William often photographs food and needs a bright, open space to shoot.

They combined inexpensive countertops, cabinets, and a sink from Ikea with vintage lighting and a kitchen table found on thrifting trips throughout the United States and Canada. To make their kitchen feel aged and worn-in, Susan and William covered the walls with embossed wallpaper then painted over it with a dark, high-gloss outdoor paint.

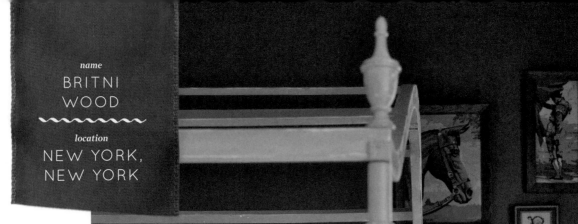
Britni painted a vintage four-poster bed bright coral, which pops against the ash gray walls in her bedroom. A collection of paint-by-number paintings hangs over her nightstand.

Go for Kitsch
~~~~~~~~~~

Do you collect velvet paintings? Love garden gnomes? Don't be afraid to embrace your love of kitsch. Take a cue from Britni and her paint-by-number paintings and group your oddball collectibles together to make a statement. For small objects, try shadow boxes (see page 174) or small wall shelves to display a collection. Homeowner P.J. Mehaffey did the latter.

Turn to page 13 to see how great it looks.

As a style expert for *Martha Stewart Weddings* magazine, Britni Wood is always on the go. So at home in her apartment in New York's Chelsea neighborhood, she has created a haven for herself where she is surrounded by all of her favorite things. Her jewel box of a home is filled with memories of travel, hand-me-downs from loved ones, and whimsical collections.

Britni filled her living room with personal treasures like the artwork by Bjørn Wiinblad and mineral specimens from her grandmother's collection. Upholstering a sofa in two-toned fabric can be a great way to jazz up an older piece, as Britni did with her prized Billy Baldwin sofa. The folding side tables are from Ikea; Britni expands them to create a dining table when guests are over.

An antique desk from Florence, Italy, sits in front of the living room window, which has a *Mary Poppins* view of neighboring chimneys.

<<< The old-fashioned look of silhouettes in fanciful gilded frames contrasts with the classical blue-and-white stripes in the hallway.

Britni created her own cabinet of curiosities (see page 93) by prominently displaying her favorite books, pottery, and milk glass in a vintage bamboo armoire.

A pink-and-white striped rug in the living room makes the room feel wider than it actually is.

The skull hanging on the wall was collected by an old friend traveling around the desert.

Interior designer Jennifer Barratt lives in a colorful 1950s bungalow. Based in Indianapolis, Jennifer runs a design business, The Arranger, inspired by her love of eclectic items and finding ways to make them work together. Because Jennifer is an expert arranger, it's no surprise that her collection of art, objects, and furniture is masterfully mixed and displayed in her 1,700-square-foot house. She loves to entertain, and her home is often the setting for small gatherings of family and friends.

The living room, with its pink and red palette, has a mix of vintage furniture and lighting, and retro-looking accessories like a lampshade from Anthropologie.

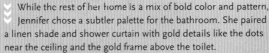

〈〈〈 A pair of vintage gold stools adds pizzazz to the kitchen bar. The leopard-print cushions make the seats more comfortable for guests.

∨ Jennifer's pink bedroom is home to some of her favorite vintage finds, like a collection of religious icons over the bed. Despite the wide range of patterns, the room flows easily into the next because of the common color palette.

∨ While the rest of her home is a mix of bold color and pattern, Jennifer chose a subtler palette for the bathroom. She paired a linen shade and shower curtain with gold details like the dots near the ceiling and the gold frame above the toilet.

DIY Window Treatments

Dealing with small or nontraditionally sized windows? Sometimes a custom, do-it-yourself window treatment is the most affordable option. Try cutting your own piece of fabric, sewing the edges closed, and hanging it from a simple tension rod to create a quick and easy curtain. Take it up a notch by gluing a colorful ribbon border or adding fringe or a decorative pattern around the bottom. If you have a standard-sized window, you can customize inexpensive drapes from a store like Ikea by stenciling on a pattern or adding iron-on decals.

The Signature pattern wallpaper, from Interiors Europe, emphasizes the high ceilings in Kathy's entryway.

A vintage dog needlepoint from a French flea market adds to the hallway's playful feel.

Kathy Dalwood is an English sculptor and designer whose work includes concrete figurines, plaster friezes, and concrete urn sculptures. Along with her husband, artist Justin Mortimer, Kathy has spent years collecting found objects, art, and vintage textiles to decorate her eclectic nineteenth-century home in the Queen's Park section of London. Their décor is pared-back simplicity with white walls and painted gray floors, which allows both the original architecture and their serendipitous finds to shine.

In the bedroom, the wall is covered floor to ceiling with art collected over the years from flea markets, junk shops, and thrift stores.

The colorful floral bedding picks up on all the different colors in the artwork and frames.

‹‹‹ Kathy found this beautiful nineteenth-century Victorian folding screen at a salvage yard in the English countryside. Sometimes beautiful vintage options are left in salvage shops because they require a little love and extra work. Kathy saw potential in this piece and had the frame and artwork professionally cleaned before bringing it home.

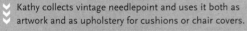

Kathy collects vintage needlepoint and uses it both as artwork and as upholstery for cushions or chair covers.

Colorful pillows are piled high atop a comfy gray sofa. A vintage brass music stand is used to display and highlight a thrift store painting of flowers.

Needlepoint

The art of embroidery is thousands of years old. Embroidery on canvas is called *needlepoint* and was originally intended to re-create the look of expensive woven tapestries. This craft was particularly popular in colonial America, where it was used for creating pictures, upholstery fabric, and fashion accessories. To demonstrate their mastery of needlepoint stitches, young colonial girls often created samplers. Samplers have since become popular collectibles, with pieces often selling on eBay, 1stdibs, and Craigslist. Estate sales are great places to find samplers and often provide pieces that are in good condition because they've remained protected in someone's home.

name
LESLIE
OSCHMANN
~~~~~~
location
AMSTERDAM,
THE
NETHERLANDS

Leslie clusters a section of a wall in her living room with some of the painted portraits she collects. She finds them at flea markets all over Europe.

American designer Leslie Oschmann's love of rehabilitating and updating old furniture started early in life. At age five she learned to help her father, who was born and raised in Holland, with his carpentry business, and she used those skills working for brands like Conran's-Habitat and later when she became the visual director for Anthropologie. After leaving her work in retail, Leslie moved to Europe to start her own business, Swarm. With her dog in tow, she set up a home and studio in Amsterdam, where she now collects and refurbishes old furniture from flea markets (and sometimes the street). Surrounded by some of her own furniture rescues, Leslie has created a home that reflects her love of Dutch design and handcrafted objects.

Leslie's dog, McDuff, lounges next to an original Thonet chair Leslie found sitting in a trash can. She loved the layers of paint on it so much she decided to leave it as is. She used a vintage metal stand originally meant for a science lab as an unconventional living room table.

The bedroom is deliberately left as simple as possible, relying on different textures to give the space visual interest. "It's a place to rest my eyes and not have so much sensory overload." The lamp on the bedside table was wrapped in a neutral fabric so that the form and shape would blend in more with the colors of the room.

Three of Leslie's designs mingle in a sunny corner of her home. The cabinet is a German oak sideboard she refinished using a splatter paint technique. The chair is covered with vintage embroidery, and the piece of wall décor above it is made from old velvet curtains that have aged beautifully from the sun.

A wooden strip and a series of clamps create a casual gallery for Leslie's paintings; it allows her to change out the art easily.

Displaying Artwork

Artwork doesn't always need to be framed and hung on the wall. If you have a collection of objects that you don't mind having out in the open, consider some of these ideas for displaying your favorite pieces on a budget.

Foam core and frame ledges: Try mounting your prints with spray adhesive on foam core, wood, or cardboard and then lining them up on a frame ledge. They're easily moved but still have the support of a firm board behind them so they don't bend.

Wire and clips: Because small artwork and objects often get moved around the house, try using a fishing line or metal wire and hanging clips to display your collection.

Bulldog clips and nails: Try collecting metal clips from flea markets or antique shops for a unique look. Simply tap a few finishing nails into the wall, hang your clips from them, and use them to hold your favorite prints or papers.

Clipboards: You can buy oversized clipboards and artist sketch boards that are up to 19 inches wide that will allow you to clip larger artwork and papers to a board that can be hung on or leaned against the wall.

names
**LYNDSAY
CALEO &
FITZHUGH
KAROL**

~~~~~~~~~

location
**BROOKLYN,
NEW YORK**

Taking advantage of the home's high ceilings, Lyndsay and Fitzhugh created a guest room loft that can be accessed via the living room's sliding library ladder. The room's structural beams were exposed during demolition and were left as architectural details during the remodeling process.

Jewelry designer Lyndsay Caleo and woodworker and sculptor Fitzhugh Karol first met when they were graduate students at the Rhode Island School of Design. After completing their studies, they moved to New York to start their design cooperative, The Brooklyn Home Company, which specializes in real estate development, design, and architectural consulting. Lyndsay and Fitzhugh were thrilled to find a classic brownstone in Park Slope. The home had great bones, but needed more light and space for guests and storage, so the couple set about renovating from the ground up, opting for a clean, open layout that would make the most of the 55' x 20' brownstone (while leaving three of the four floors available for renters). Lyndsay explained, "We approached the project like a puzzle, and it was just a matter of how it would all fit together." The final product is a sun-filled modern home that makes the most of every space available.

Open shelving stacked from the countertops to the ceiling makes the most of the room's high ceilings and allows for as much cooking and prep space as possible.

A custom wooden counter on the kitchen island has built-in slots for knives and can double as a casual table for in-kitchen dining.

The open floor plan creates a clear flow from the kitchen to the living and dining areas.

Keeping the walls white and the accent details in warm wood tones makes the space feels unified. An area rug clearly defines the seating area, separating it from the rest of the room. Fitzhugh built the white wood sculpture above the fireplace. Lyndsay found the Indian daybed at a salvage yard for next to nothing.

Lyndsay searched eBay for weeks to find the perfect barn door to lead into the bathroom, and ended up finding one in the sheep run behind Fitzhugh's family's farm in New Hampshire. Lyndsay loves the worn patina and the warmth it brings to the room.

A wall of windows in the ground-floor sitting room provides a peek into the brownstone's backyard. Lyndsay and Fitzhugh made the couch platforms from reclaimed brownstone beams and used twin mattresses for the cushions so they can double as guest beds. Oliver, the couple's dog, lounges next to a pair of wooden sculptures made by Fitzhugh.

Wainscoting

Wainscoting is decorative wooden paneling often applied to the lower half of walls in a room. Originally used in sixteenth-century England to protect walls from dampness, wainscoting is now used to add character and detail to a room, whether on walls, ceilings, or floors, or to add detail behind open shelving or on the fronts of furniture.

Lyndsay was inspired by a ship's cabin when creating this cozy guest room. Fitzhugh created the underbed storage. To save money on lighting, floor models were purchased at a discount and installed above the bed. White wainscoting was used on the walls and ceiling.

name
GRAHAM
ATKINS-
HUGHES

~~~~~~~

location
LONDON,
ENGLAND

A rattan wicker lamp, by Michael Sodeau, and a crocheted throw bring warmth to a corner of the living room.

Adding in natural textures like wicker and leather brings a sense of depth to a room and adds visual interest.

Photographer Graham Atkins-Hughes shares his lovely London townhome with his wife, Jo, and their sons, Digby and Kit. The family endured a top-to-bottom renovation, including a winter without heating and lots of take-out meals while the kitchen was being finished. "When I start to think about our house, I am reminded of all the hard work we put in—and are still putting in," Graham says. "But I am also reminded how the house has given back all that energy in double and triplicate amounts."

A wall of blue closet doors masks much-needed storage and acts as a wall of bright color in the bedroom.

Inspired by a classic Verner Panton light, Jo and Graham decided to make their own chandelier by hand-stringing capiz shells.

Kitchen Renos

Graham has this advice for anyone embarking on a kitchen renovation.

Consider function: Take into account how you really use your kitchen, and design for things like extra sinks, lower counters, or built-in knife holders.

Be honest with yourself: For example, if you don't keep your dishware clean and organized all the time, don't choose open shelving just because you like the look. It's always best to design with real life in mind.

Consider the floor plan: If you like to cook and entertain at the same time, consider an open floor plan that lets you move, cook, and talk with guests all at once.

Look for inspiration: Most people only look at kitchen or home magazines for design ideas, but if you keep your eyes open you might find color, design, or decoration ideas in unlikely places—airports, restaurants, museums, train stations—which can be great sources of inspiration for anything from tilework to floor plans.

‹‹‹ Enamored of the home's marble fireplace, Graham and Jo decided to leave the wall above it empty, save for a grouping of vases, so it would stand out as sculpture. The living room's vintage chrome lamp, to the left of the mantel, was purchased on a trip to Italy.

˅ A vintage glass chandelier (a lucky find from Camden market) hangs in the stairwell. The chandelier's small pops of color stand out against the home's gray color palette and add just enough brightness.

˅˅ Working with complementary colors, Graham and Jo chose olive green walls to accent the red cabinets in the remodeled kitchen.

An oversized vintage bee print makes a long wall feel more proportional to the living room.

Vintage Educational Charts

Originally intended for classroom use, vintage educational charts (like Molly's bee print) are now collected as stylish wall decorations. To find your own, search online auction sites using terms like "scientific German educational charts," "botanical charts," "vintage educational charts," and "vintage educational posters." If you come up empty-handed when searching for the vintage version, try a reproduction—stores like Evolution Nature Store (*www .theevolutionstore.com*) sell great reproductions of original German educational charts.

Actress and model Molly Sims travels constantly for work. When she sat down to decorate her SoHo apartment with Los Angeles—based interior designer Kishani Perera (who also decorated Molly's L.A. home, and the homes on pages 8 and 154), she knew she wanted to create a home around the vintage and antique pieces she has collected from across the globe. Kishani helped her to supplement her own treasures with new finds from Parisian flea markets. Together, they created a décor that combines Molly's love of luxurious antiques with her modern lifestyle.

Working with a classic butter yellow and gray color palette, Kishani was able to mix a range of patterns together in Molly's bedroom, like damask fabric (on the headboard) from Christopher Hyland and Romo Lasari's Opal wallpaper.

<<< Molly's kitchen is filled with Parisian flea market finds, including an antique French chandelier, botanical prints, and stools, which she had covered in a polka-dot fabric from Scalamandré.

<<< The elegant gray palette continues in Molly's sitting room, which is lit by an ornate antique chandelier. The gray built-ins allow the objects on its shelves to stand out like works of art.

Kishani combined a range of gray colors and textures in Molly's living area. Velvet upholstery assures the colors will feel warm and luxurious, rather than cold and flat.

name
EMMA CASSI
~~~~~~~~~~

location
LONDON,
ENGLAND

Emma's office is a mix of new and old items.

She repurposed a plastic lace bicycle basket into file storage and turned an antique chest of drawers into office supply storage. A sheer string curtain allows for a feeling of privacy without blocking out light.

I n 2005, designer Emma Cassi was house-hunting in the Richmond Park area of London, along with her husband, Bertrand, and son, Anton. When she saw the apartment that would become her home, she immediately knew it felt right. "I loved how bright and large the living room was," she says. "I knew it would be perfect for working in while my son is away at nursery school." By focusing on a mix of pastel colors, Emma was able to add the sorts of patterns and textures she loves to her home, while still creating a calm space where her family can relax.

When a headboard feels too heavy, creating a faux headboard can be a great alternative.

Emma used wallpaper from Cath Kidston to create this clever one that echoes the pink ceramic cups and sculptures on the mantel and shelves. For another example of a faux headboard, see page 69.

In the kitchen, a cozy nook has Laura Ashley curtains and a vintage wooden table. A wall of family photos becomes a mural when spread across the wall at an even height.

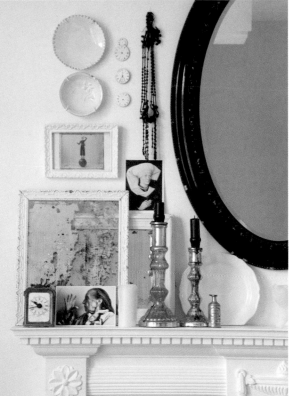

A selection of vintage finds and mercury glass candlesticks graces Emma's living room mantel. By mixing together a range of weathered patinas, the collection feels cohesive and blends with the home's existing décor.

Mercury Glass

The name of this beautifully reflective material is actually a misnomer. Although elemental mercury was used for mirrors, it was too expensive and toxic to be used for tableware. Mercury glass is silvered glass. Silvering is a nineteenth-century technique in which clear glass is blown double-walled and then filled with a liquid silvering solution.

name

SARA H
RYHANEN

〜〜〜〜

location

BROOKLYN,
NEW YORK

Sarah's living/dressing room glows in the afternoon sun. While some may be scared to experiment with paint, Sarah picked her living room's color—Desert Rose, by Valspar—on a whim. She loves the final result.

Design*Sponge contributor Sarah Ryhanen is one of my favorite Brooklyn florists, and created a monthly garden and floral column for the site called "Weeder's Digest." In addition to her work with the site, Sarah spends her time creating beautiful arrangements for weddings and events, and running her Red Hook soap and flower shop, Saipua. Her home, which is right around the corner from Saipua, is decorated with a mix of Sarah's favorite vintage furniture and plants brought home from the shop.

The bedroom closet was abandoned because of its shallow shelves. Now it's a gallery for a vintage painting and a few odds and ends and serves as a bedside table.

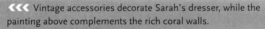

‹‹‹ Vintage accessories decorate Sarah's dresser, while the painting above complements the rich coral walls.

‹‹‹ If closet space is limited, invest in a stunning piece of furniture to hold your everyday wardrobe. An antique wooden dressing table and mirror serves as part of Sarah's open closet and adds warmth to the room.

Sarah's kitchen is her favorite spot to entertain friends. Jars of homemade kombucha tea rest on the counter, casting a beautiful amber light onto the butcher block.

name
DAVY
NEWKIRK
〜〜〜〜
location
LOS ANGELES,
CALIFORNIA

The mirrored lamp in the bedroom helps brighten up the dark space.

Davy Newkirk loves how modernist homes, in their heyday, were furnished with unusual things that their occupants brought back from their travels to exotic places. Inspired to create the same feeling in his home, Davy started collecting treasures from his trips abroad. Working with interior designer Kishani Perera, Davy indulged in his love of British and French antiques while mixing in small odds and ends that he collected from local street markets in his spare time. The result is a home that is full of memories and stories.

By incorporating natural elements like a raw wood mantel and cane chair, the living room gets an added dose of warmth and texture.

Curating Collections

Designer Kishani Perera shares her tips for working with a disparate collection of memorabilia or souvenirs. "I often create groupings of varied objects that are seemingly unrelated in order to create an eclectic, globally inspired vibe. To keep the collections from appearing random, I only incorporate one object from each style and ensure that there is a common thread, however small, tying the pieces together. Color is usually the simplest theme to keep in mind, but a specific detail could also unify a varied collection. For example, you could combine a vintage vase from Paris with an antique picture from India and a curio box from Syria if they all have some element of the color cream, or perhaps a brass detail, throughout."

The green in Davy's master bedroom is carried through to the guest room, contrasting here with colorful orange throw pillows.

Benjamin Moore's Hale Navy paint gives the guest bathroom a luxe feel without a high price tag. A custom-made ikat fabric shower curtain adds another decorative touch.

155

name

LUCY ALLEN GILLIS

〜〜〜〜

location

ATHENS, GEORGIA

The butter yellow walls bring out the warmth in the blue-painted tiles and keep the nonworking fireplace from feeling too empty and cold.

Lucy Allen Gillis, her husband, Jim, and their dogs, June and Milo, spent three years fixing up their Athens, Georgia, home. Working on a strict budget, they decorated with hand-me-downs, thrift store finds, and antiques inherited from family. The goal was to create a home that would be equal parts quirky, warm, meaningful, adaptable, and most of all, happy.

The living room features a number of vintage finds gathered during family vacations in Maine, including vintage portraits and a colorful rug.

Rather than frame the portraits, Lucy chose to leave them unframed to highlight the beautifully curved edges of the paper.

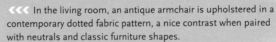

<<< In the living room, an antique armchair is upholstered in a contemporary dotted fabric pattern, a nice contrast when paired with neutrals and classic furniture shapes.

A pair of antique wooden beds (on loan from Lucy's mom) fill the guest room, which is painted pale blue. Framed pictures of birds in flight add a sense of lightness to the room and tie in to the room's soft color.

K2LD Design worked with Aun and Su-Lyn to create an airy living room that would let in as much natural light as possible.

A striking red Double Octopus chandelier from Autoban hangs next to the floor-to-ceiling bookshelves in this double-height space.

Singapore-based bloggers Aun and Su-Lyn write a popular food blog, Chubby Hubby, that chronicles their love of food and design, as well as their marriage. The couple, who also run a lifestyle consultancy specializing in restaurant development, work out of a stunning home in Singapore. From their bright red door to their state-of-the-art kitchen, Aun and Su-Lyn's space is a study in great design.

A vivid red door welcomes guests and enhances the warm brick exterior of the house. A black cast-iron lion's head doorbell traveled all the way from Venice, Italy.

The rich color of Su-Lyn and Aun's door inspired this arrangement of red tones.

Turn to page 312 to learn how to re-create this arrangement.

<<< By mixing chairs, lighting, and a dining room table in different styles, Aun and Su-Lyn were able to create an eclectic but modern feel in their dining room.

<<< When planning their kitchen, Aun and Su-Lyn thought about how they actually used the space. Because they both enjoy cooking and contributing to meals, the kitchen was designed so that Aun and Su-Lyn could cook comfortably side by side or across from each other.

An antique French chair, a gift from Su-Lyn's brother-in-law, sits next to a tray table in the couple's bedroom.

name
SAMANTHA
REITMAYER
〜〜〜〜〜
location
DALLAS,
TEXAS

Mirrored furniture reflects light in a room and gives a luxe look.

Samantha's mirrored desk is actually an affordable version from Target. Behind it are a pair of antique doors, a favorite find of Samantha's from Four Hands Furniture in Austin.

Designer Samantha Reitmayer of style/SWOON, an interior design studio and blog, lives in a stylish home in the center of Dallas. She loves its mix of glamorous and rustic details because it always provides something interesting to see. Samantha's love of antiques has resulted in a home that is chock-full of special pieces that remind her of her adventures traveling throughout Texas.

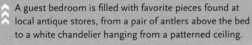
A guest bedroom is filled with favorite pieces found at local antique stores, from a pair of antlers above the bed to a white chandelier hanging from a patterned ceiling.

To create more storage space in the bedroom, Samantha designed this chaise with hidden shelves for magazines and books.

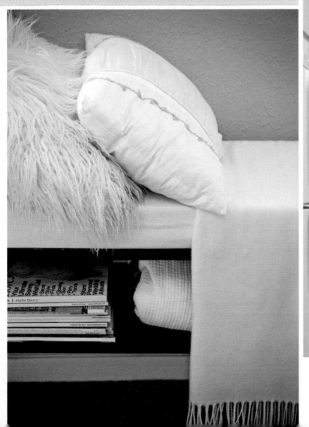

A pair of Indian mermaid goddess brass handles from an antique store in McKinney, Texas, dresses up the bedroom closet and makes an everyday storage space feel special.

In the kitchen, the ceiling was covered with lumber that had been left to age for six months in the backyard. Samantha loves the weathered patina. A chalkboard wall at the back of the room is great for grocery lists.

161

name
MORGAN
SATTERFIELD

location
HEMET,
CALIFORNIA

The entry hall is furnished with a shelving unit that Morgan built by herself using black pipes. A bold kilim adds rich color to the space.

F irst-time homeowner and author of the blog The Brick House, Morgan Satterfield spent two years renovating her home on a budget. With help from her boyfriend, Jeremy, she decorated it almost exclusively with thrift store, bartered, or flea market goods. Armed with an eye for great finds and a little do-it-yourself power, Morgan has created a beautiful modern environment that fits her style—and budget.

Morgan painted her living room fireplace black to create a neutral backdrop for a collection of modern art. An inexpensive butterfly chair found at a local thrift store looks more luxe in a leather seat cover.

Butterfly Chairs

Now a college dorm staple, the butterfly chair was designed by Jorge Ferrari Hardoy in 1938. In 1947, Knoll purchased the U.S. production rights to the chair, which was such an instant success that knockoffs began to flood the market. When Knoll lost its claim of copyright infringement, the company dropped the chair from production and it became part of the public domain. More than five million butterfly chairs were produced in the 1950s alone.

A low bed with built-in storage tables enhances the width of the bedroom. A mix of thrift store artwork, a vintage quilt, and Ikea bedding adds color to the room.

‹‹‹ Morgan did a trade for her den's shelving unit at the Long Beach Flea Market and found the glass pears and stools for less than $10 each at a thrift store. Accents of green in the room bring a fresh feeling to the space.

The dining room, like the rest of Morgan's home, is an example of her incredible eBay and thrifting skills.

The table and chairs were vintage finds and the hutch was a Long Beach Flea Market trade.

name
MEG MATEO ILASCO
∼∼∼∼∼
location
PINOLE, CALIFORNIA

A bold orange wall (Outrageous Orange, by Benjamin Moore) highlights a vintage Po Cadovius wall system in the living room.

Philippine rattan chairs, a gift from Meg's parents, echo the wooden details throughout the rest of the home.

Designer and writer Meg Mateo Ilasco is a busy woman. She is the author of several popular craft-based books, runs a series of design-based Internet sample sales called Modern Economy, and produces the Mateo Ilasco line of stationery and gifts. She and her husband, Marvin, are parents to two young children, Lauryn and Miles. Meg, who is of Filipino descent, describes their California home as a mix of vintage, modern, and ethnic décor—with a nod to the 1970s. "We love it because it's expressive of our personalities, interests, and culture."

Meg is the author of *Crafting a Meaningful Home*, a book on how to incorporate elements of your own culture or family into your home. She shared these tips.

Don't be afraid to mix and match contemporary pieces with cultural/ethnic pieces. For example, in her bedroom, Meg paired pottery by artist Sara Paloma with a Philippine tribal pot. The ensemble is unexpected, but it works well together.

You can bring your culture into your home in subtle ways by using materials or techniques that evoke your culture. It doesn't need to be completely obvious to your guests. As long as an object has cultural meaning for you, that's all that really matters.

You don't have to preserve cultural items in their original form. As long as it's not a family heirloom, consider spray-painting it if it doesn't fit in with your home décor. Or cast folk art in another material.

›› Meg used ribbed wallpaper from Ferm Living to create an accent wall in the bedroom. Meg's own pillow design picks up on the red tones in the wooden dresser.

›› Meg uses complementary hues like orange and blue in the dining room to create a bright but harmonious scheme.

‹‹‹ Soft gray wallpaper is warmed up by a wooden sink base and mirror. Unhappy with the premade sink options on the market, Meg and Marvin made their own sink by combining a sink top they found on Craigslist with a salvaged cabinet and hairpin legs (from hairpinlegs.com).

A warm golden brown wall ties together colorful wall hangings and floor mats from Urban Outfitters in the children's playroom.

names
TRACI & BILL FLEMING

~~~~~~~~

location
LOS ANGELES, CALIFORNIA

The Flemings' front porch got a modern face-lift with the help of lead gray paint accented by a bright yellow door.

The gray and yellow color theme is carried from the exterior of the house to interior.

As parents of two young children, Traci (who is the founder and president of Nursery Works) and her husband, attorney Bill Fleming, had some very specific goals for their newly purchased one-hundred-year-old craftsman bungalow. So they turned to Los Angeles—based designer Tamara Kaye-Honey of House of Honey to lighten up the space and create a furniture and color plan that would be both modern and livable for a young family. Looking to keep their budget low, Traci and Bill worked with Tamara to refinish and retain existing furniture and art and find a mix of vintage and new furniture that wouldn't break the bank.

Striking vintage peacocks found at the Rose Bowl flea market hang outside the office on a classic Dutch door (for more about Dutch doors, see page 105).

The porch's yellow and gray color theme is echoed in Traci's pale blue and yellow office. Painted vintage screens from a flea market were repurposed into a clip board for fabric samples.

For their daughter's room, Tamara chose a pink and coral color scheme that would grow with her as she matured. Vintage Murano glass lighting from the 1960s hangs on either side of the bed, and with vintage bedside tables, gives the room balance.

Children's Rooms

Great design and kids' rooms can coexist without compromising on style. Children's spaces should be both practical (lots of closed storage) and fun (great art) yet sophisticated enough to allow the child to grow with the room. To me, kids' rooms make the most sense as an extension of the overall design of the home. Start with a special piece and build a room around it that is unexpected and exciting for both adults and little ones. Allowing children to collect art and special pieces creates respect for their space and appreciation for their surroundings. It's also a wonderful way to begin learning how interiors can inspire us all.

name
MICHELE VARIAN

location
NEW YORK, NEW YORK

To add color in the kitchen's reading nook, Michele repurposed vintage sari fabric to create custom curtains.

Along with her husband, musician Brad Roberts of the Crash Test Dummies, New York designer and shopkeeper Michele Varian lives in a spacious SoHo loft. After numerous changes and upgrades, the couple now feels totally at home in their space at the center of the city. For Michele, the best part is the fact that each piece tells a story. She explains, "When I come home at the end of the day I feel transported to another time and place." Thanks to her deft styling skills, Michelle has created numerous displays of artwork and collectibles that bridge the gap between past and present. Her ability to combine antique and contemporary pieces in the same space give the apartment a uniquely modern feel.

Michele used her collection of vintage glass flytraps to create a sheer hanging "wall" between the den and kitchen.

Glass Flytraps

These glass bottles were once the standard tool for catching flies. Sugar water placed inside the bottle attracted the insects, which were able to get in, but not out. Early examples of the bottles were handblown, making the once utilitarian object a beautiful collectible.

‹‹‹ An old pedal sewing machine base was transformed into a dining room table with the addition of a Herman Miller desktop. Neisha Crosland wallpaper, reproduction Woodard wire chairs, and stuffed ducks give the dining area a dark but sophisticated feel.

‹‹‹ The living room's shelves were made from pieces of Douglas fir that Michele sanded and stained. Near the top of the shelves sits an armadillo Michele brought all the way home from a Detroit junk shop on her lap.

An aged yellow dresser, found on the street in Park Slope, Brooklyn, sits next to the bedroom door.

To let light into the bedroom, Michele and Brad used inexpensive heating grates to create a decorative panel near the ceiling.

names
SHAY-ASHLEY
OMETZ & JEFF
BARFOOT

location
DALLAS,
TEXAS

Shay's graphic designer husband prefers posters and screen prints, while she likes fine art and odds and ends. They managed to compromise for this hallway wall, which features some of Shay's favorite objets d'art and Jeff's prints.

S enior art director at Fossil, Shay-Ashley Ometz has lived in her midcentury home since 2006. Along with her husband, artist Jeff Barfoot, and their children, Calder and Milo, Shay focused on keeping the original features of her home while creating a space that would provide surprises around each corner. Whether it's colorful tray tables or a whimsical collection of toys and ephemera, Shay and Jeff have created a home that is both welcoming and playful.

Custom Tray Tables

Tray tables are a practical necessity for those of us who like to eat and watch our favorite shows at the same time. Sadly the TV tray design market is somewhat lacking, so rather than abandoning your favorite trays, try giving them a modern spin. Simply cut a piece of your favorite wallpaper or gift wrap to size and attach it to the top of your tray with spray adhesive for a quick and easy new look. Then cover it with a layer of Mod Podge craft glue to protect your new tray from spills.

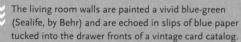

Brightly colored doors with octopus illustrations welcome guests into the couple's home screen-printing studio.

The stripes of color in Shay and Jeff's Flor carpeting are repeated in the tray table tops, found on eBay.

The living room walls are painted a vivid blue-green (Sealife, by Behr) and are echoed in slips of blue paper tucked into the drawer fronts of a vintage card catalog.

Jack Summerford's *Eggs* print hangs over the home's built-in kitchen grill and playfully references the room's primary use.

DIY PROJECTS

Making things by hand hasn't always been second nature to me. I grew up surrounded by stacks of magazines and catalogs, tearing things out that I hoped to buy one day,

never imagining that I could possibly create something similar on my own. But over the past ten years, there has been a rebirth of the do-it-yourself (DIY) movement that has inspired me to finally put down the catalogs and pick up a staple gun.

With the introduction of independent craft shows like the Renegade Craft Fair and e-commerce websites like Etsy (www .etsy.com) that allow artists to easily sell their handmade work to a worldwide audience, the air is practically buzzing with DIY fever. From the most novice crafters (that would be me) to the most experienced artists, the design community has wholeheartedly embraced the idea of creating both home products and home decorations by hand.

Design*Sponge has embraced the handmade movement since the beginning, choosing to feature both handmade work and do-it-yourself projects from a team of talented editors. In this section of the book, I've chosen twenty-five of my favorite posts from the Design*Sponge DIY archives,

along with twenty-five new projects from our readers and contributors. Each project is broken down by time, cost, and difficulty, so you can easily choose a project (or flag one for later) depending on your skill level, budget, and available free time. Some of the projects require templates, which are available for download at www.designsponge.com/templates.

This section of the book—and DIY in general—is about providing actual examples of how you can create the home of your dreams. Not only do these projects show you how to build something with your own two hands, but they'll offer additional suggestions for further personalizing each piece so you have a truly special object when you're done. I hope these projects will inspire you to create something meaningful for your own home, whether it's quick and easy like a yarn vase, or more detailed, like the upholstered headboard I made for my own bedroom. A more personal space that truly reflects who you are is only a snip, clip, or hammer away.

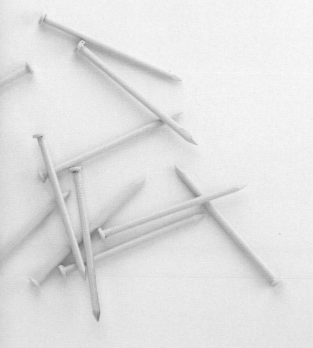

No matter what size our home is, most of us are always in need of more storage space. Rather than covering up more precious counterspace, Design*Sponge contributors Derek Fagerstrom and Lauren Smith decided to add wall shelves made from recycled wine crates they found at their local wine shop. To add more detail, Lauren and Derek lined the back of the shelves with colorful, inexpensive gift wrap to act as a backdrop for their favorite books and tiny treasures.

DESIGNERS
Derek Fagerstrom and Lauren Smith

COST
$10

TIME
1 hour

DIFFICULTY
★ ★ ★ ★

MATERIALS

Tape measure

Wine crates

Gift wrap or other fancy paper

Pencil

Straightedge

X-Acto knife

Bone folder

Spray adhesive

Sawtooth hangers (1 per crate)

Hammer

Small nails (2 per sawtooth hanger)

Rubber bumpers (2 per crate)

Hanging hardware (1 per crate)

INSTRUCTIONS

1   Use a tape measure to measure the interior of each crate to make sure you have enough fancy paper to line all of them.

2   Next, draw out the measurements in pencil on the back of the paper. In order to avoid any potential gaps along the interior edges, add a 1-inch allowance as follows:

Long sides	Add 1 inch to each of the three edges that border the interior of the box.
Short sides	Add 1 inch to the edge that borders the back of the box.
Back piece	No allowance necessary

3   Using a straightedge and an X-Acto knife, carefully cut out each piece of lining paper (five per box). Create fold lines by scoring along the 1-inch allowance with a bone folder. Finally, miter each of the interior corners at the allowance by cutting a 45-degree angle from the outside edge in.

4   In a well-ventilated area, apply spray adhesive to the back of each of your long pieces. Place them carefully inside the box, lining up the folded edges with the inside edges of the box, and smoothing out any air bubbles that may appear in the paper. Next, spray and apply the short pieces. At this point, all four sides of the box will be lined, and the back will have a 1-inch border all the way around it. The last step is to spray and apply the back piece to the box. Smooth away any air bubbles and let dry completely before proceeding to the next step.

5   Decide on the orientation of your boxes, and attach a sawtooth hanger along the top edge of the back of each box using a hammer and small nails. Apply peel-and-stick rubber bumpers at the bottom corners on the back of each box, to ensure that they hang flat against the wall.

6   Mark the position of each box on the wall with a pencil and attach the boxes using the appropriate hanging hardware.

SAFETY NOTE: Spray adhesive is pretty toxic, so you'll want to wear a mask and open your windows while you spray. Spray in short spurts and let your room fully air out before proceeding.

U sing mismatched plates and a variety of candlesticks and vases, Kate created a decorative set of cake stands out of otherwise unused items. Whether you're celebrating a birthday, showcasing holiday treats, or just looking to creatively display everyday snacks, these stands are a great way to decorate your table without spending a lot of money.

DESIGNER
Kate Pruitt

COST
$10

TIME
**1 hour
(plus drying
time)**

DIFFICULTY
★ ★ ★ ★

―――――― INSTRUCTIONS ――――――

1   Test the pieces you want to put together: The plate should be able to balance on the base without any adhesive.

2   Clean all plates and vases/candlesticks thoroughly. Dry completely.

3   Measure the back of each plate and mark the center with a dot.

4   Prepare some epoxy, following the package directions. When ready, apply the epoxy to the top edge of the base and gently place it upside down onto the back of the plate, using the center dot as a guide.

5   Let the epoxy set up, following package directions, then gently press the plate down on the base to hold it in place while wiping away any excess epoxy with the Popsicle stick. Apply masking tape on four sides to anchor the cake stand, and let it dry overnight.

MATERIALS

Old plates (any size) and candlesticks or vases (look for anything that is wider at the bottom, with a sturdy base and a flat top)—larger plates (like dinner plates) will require a larger base

Ruler

Marker

Epoxy
(from a hardware store)

Paper plate or
scrap cardboard
(something to mix the epoxy
on that you can throw out)

Popsicle stick or
cotton swabs with the
cotton removed
(something to apply
the epoxy with)

Masking tape

Rags and cleaning solution

Tip

While these are sturdier than you would expect, they are not dishwasher-safe. Instead gently clean by hand.

REBECCA SOLNIT

RIVER OF SHADOWS

EADWEARD MUYBRIDGE AND THE TECHNOLOGICAL WILD WEST

PUSHKIN'S BUTTON

Serena Vitale

FARRAR STRAUS GIROUX

AMY VANDERBILT'S ETIQUETTE

The Guide to Gracious Living

Doubleday

Merriam Webster

Collegiate Dictionary

TENTH EDITION

delicious new york

red lashes

U sing bricks as bookends has been a popular college dorm room trick for decades. While Kate appreciated the affordability and ease of the idea, she wanted to jazz it up a bit to suit her style. Using inexpensive sheets of gift wrap to cover the bricks, Kate was able to modify this classic idea to not only suit her personal style but also fit her budget.

DESIGNER
Kate Pruitt

COST
$5

TIME
1 hour

DIFFICULTY
★ ★ ★ ★

MATERIALS
—————

2 sheets of decorative paper
or wrapping paper

2 sheets of thicker
weight paper
(drawing paper will work)

Dust mask

Spray adhesive

2 paver stones or bricks
(found in the garden/
outdoor section of
hardware stores)

Scissors

Hot glue gun

Decorative embellishments

~~~~~~~~~~~~~~~~~~~~~~~~~~~~~~~~~~ INSTRUCTIONS ~~~~~~~~~~~~~~~~~~~~~~~~~~~~~~~~~~

1   Lay out the decorative paper facedown on a clean work surface.

2   Lay out the drawing paper and cover it with an even coat of spray adhesive. Flip it so that the adhesive side is down, lay it on the backside of the decorative paper, and smooth out any wrinkles.

3   Place the brick or paver stone on the backside of your paper. Cut out enough paper to wrap it like a present.

4   Begin to wrap the brick like a present, folding the paper over to the back and overlapping it to create a snug fit around the brick. To secure, add hot glue to the right side of the brick's back surface and refold the right side of the paper over the glue and smooth down. Then add hot glue to the left side of the brick's back surface and the edge of the first fold of paper. Fold the second flap over the first. Smooth down.

5   Cut slits up each of the corners of the paper at the bottom until you reach the edge of the brick. You now have the brick wrapped like a present, but there are four flaps of paper at the bottom of the brick. Fold the side flaps in first and glue them down to the brick. Then fold the flap from the back to the front and glue down. Lastly, fold the flap from the front to the back and glue down. During this process you may need to cut away excess paper to create a clean fold. Always try the fold first to see what it will look like, then unfold, make any necessary cuts, and try again. Make sure you have neat, clean folds before gluing. Repeat with the top of the brick.

6   Repeat the wrapping and gluing process with the second brick. When both bricks are complete, add decorative images, decals, or embellishments, if desired.

SAFETY NOTE: Spray adhesive is pretty toxic, so you'll want to wear a mask and open your windows while you spray. Spray in short spurts and let your room fully air out before proceeding.

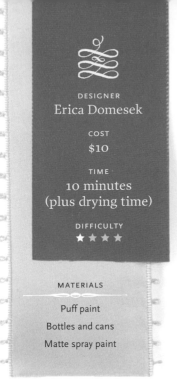

DESIGNER
Erica Domesek

COST
$10

TIME
**10 minutes
(plus drying time)**

DIFFICULTY
★ ★ ★ ★

MATERIALS

Puff paint
Bottles and cans
Matte spray paint

project
FAUX PORCELAIN VASES

I t's hard to turn a page in a home magazine without seeing a collection of beautiful porcelain vases in someone's home. But the price tag that comes with some designer vases can be a little hard to stomach. So do-it-yourself queen Erica Domesek of P.S.-I Made This came up with an ingenious way to turn everyday bottles and cans into elegant faux porcelain. All you need is a little puff paint and some white spray paint.

〜〜〜〜〜〜〜〜〜〜 INSTRUCTIONS 〜〜〜〜〜〜〜〜〜〜

1   Paint your desired pattern onto the can or bottle with puff paint. You can create shapes or stick with a simple line-and-dot pattern.

2   Once the puff paint has dried, spray paint over the entire can or bottle and let it dry. Repeat if necessary until the can or bottle has a smooth, solid coat. Let that dry, and you'll be ready to fill your new "vases" with flowers or just display them around your home.

DESIGNERS
**Derek Fagerstrom
and Lauren Smith**

COST
$2

TIME
10 minutes

DIFFICULTY
★ ★ ★ ★

MATERIALS

Glass vase or bottle
(ours is rectangular, but any
shape would work)
Double-stick tape
Yarn

Craft projects involving yarn always remind me of Girl Scout camp, but Derek and Lauren found a way to use yarn that feels fresh and modern. By wrapping a simple glass vase with brown and teal yarn, they created a modern design that feels right at home with the rest of their décor. If you're looking for something more dramatic, try using a range of colored yarns to create Paul Smith—style stripes.

INSTRUCTIONS

1   Apply a few strips of double-stick tape to your vase, down the length vertically and around the top and bottom.

2   Starting at the bottom, begin wrapping the yarn, making sure to stack the layers (don't overlap) and tuck the loose end under the first couple of rounds. When you're ready to switch colors, cut the yarn and secure the trimmed end to a piece of the double-stick tape.

3   Continue wrapping until you reach the top of the vase. Tuck in the tail end at the back of the vase under the top couple of rounds.

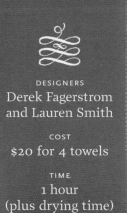

Resist-dyeing, like batik or tie-dye, is a lot of fun, but can be a mess—especially for those of us completing projects at home. Design*Sponge editors Derek and Lauren discovered that bleaching a pattern onto predyed fabric using a gel bleach pen is a much easier, cleaner way to achieve a similar effect on a limited budget. So the next time you pick up a bleach pen to work on your bathroom tiles, consider trying your hand at faux batik dyeing using inexpensive, colorful fabric.

DESIGNERS
Derek Fagerstrom
and Lauren Smith

COST
$20 for 4 towels

TIME
1 hour
(plus drying time)

DIFFICULTY
★ ★ ★ ★

INSTRUCTIONS

1   Wash and dry the fabric and cut it into quarters. Fold the long sides in ¼ inch and press with a hot iron. Fold in another ¼ inch and stitch. Repeat on the short sides, and with the rest of the fabric pieces.

2   Protect your work surface with a plastic drop cloth or sheets of aluminum foil. Wear work clothes in case the pen brushes against you, and open your windows for ventilation. Lay the towels down on the work surface and draw patterns on the fabric with the bleach pen. We like the look of free-hand, slightly wavy lines, but you can also draw your desired pattern onto the fabric beforehand using tailor's chalk and trace over it with the bleach pen. Let the finished towels sit for 30 minutes.

3   Wearing rubber gloves to protect your hands from the bleach, rinse the towels in cold water. It is very important to rinse off all the bleach in order to avoid smearing.

4   Let the towels dry, and give them a final wash before use.

NOTE: One yard of 54-inch-wide fabric will yield four tea towels that measure 26 × 17 inches.

MATERIALS

1 yard of dark-colored linen

Scissors

Iron

Sewing machine

Matching thread

Plastic drop cloth
or aluminum foil

Clorox Bleach Pen
(2 pens should be enough
for 4 towels)

Tailor's chalk (optional)

Rubber gloves

DESIGNER
Grace Bonney

COST
$40

TIME
1 hour

DIFFICULTY
★ ★ ★ ★

O ne of my favorite pastimes in life is attending flea markets. The endless possibilities, the hidden treasures, the chance of finding something amazing for less than $10—it all makes me weak in the knees. The Brimfield Antique Show in Massachusetts is one of my favorite flea markets to visit, and during my last trip I picked up this vintage mercury bottle for a song. Originally I assumed it would work as a vase, but the neck was so narrow I decided to use a lamp conversion kit to create my own custom desk lamp. All I needed was an inexpensive shade and it was good to go!

MATERIALS

Bottle
(try eBay and flea markets
for affordable versions)

Cork lamp kit
(this version is from
National Artcraft and is
available at Amazon.com)

Lamp shade
(be sure to buy the kind that
clips directly onto the bulb)

Fabric (optional)

Scissors

Marker

Hot glue gun and glue sticks
(optional)

Decorative details like ribbon
or studs (optional)

INSTRUCTIONS

1   Clean out the bottle to ensure there isn't any mold or organic matter that could be left to rot when sealed with the cork.

2   Assemble the lamp kit and gently slide the cork lamp unit into the neck of the bottle. If the bottle feels top-heavy, remove the cork unit and fill the bottle with sand or small pebbles as ballast. If your cork is too big, you can carefully shave the sides to ensure a snug fit.

3   If you want to decorate your lampshade like I did, cut the fabric so it is 1 inch longer in height than the lampshade, and ½ inch longer in length than the circumference of the lampshade. (Just wrap it around the shade to measure. If you have a shade that doesn't have straight sides, you'll need to cut your fabric at a bit of an angle. Just lay it on top and mark with a marker where you need to cut.)

4   Using a hot glue gun, run a line of glue around the bottom inside lip of the lamp shade. Wait 10–15 seconds for the glue to cool down a bit and then lay your fabric flat against the outside of the shade. Do not try to pull it taut, but rather let it lay gently on the shade and fold the bottom ends up and press them into the glue until they stick. Your fingers will get a bit messy but they won't get burned if you've allowed the glue to cool.

5   Repeat step 4 with the inner top lip of the shade, until your fabric is completely attached. (If you have any excess fabric on the inside, cut it with a small pair of sewing scissors—any extra fabric will show up when the light is on.) Run a line of hot glue along the edge of one side of the fabric and press the other side on top. This seam will be visible, so position your shade so the seam side is at the back of the lamp. Let the shade dry before clipping it to the lamp.

Inspired by elegant, moss-covered statues from her local garden tour, Design*Sponge reader Shannon Crawford decided to create architectural elements for her own garden using common hardware store materials. With simple glass lighting covers and a bag of quick-setting concrete, Shannon designed beautiful (and affordable) concrete spheres that will age gracefully tucked inside her backyard garden.

DESIGNER
Shannon Crawford

COST
less than $20

TIME
30 minutes
(plus setting time)

DIFFICULTY
★ ★ ★ ★

INSTRUCTIONS

1   Spray the inside of the lighting covers with nonstick cooking spray—it helps in separating the glass from the ball at the end! Then set the lighting covers in a pile of dirt or sand so they won't roll away while you're filling them or while they are setting.

2   Mix quick-setting concrete in the bucket (Shannon used about half a bag of fine-gravel quick-setting concrete), adding water until it reaches the consistency of peanut butter . . . or maybe a little bit runnier. You don't want it too runny, but not too hard, either. Play around with it!

3   Use a small garden shovel to fill the balls. After every scoop, give the ball a shake or twist to help it settle and break up any air bubbles. Fill the ball to the top and try to make it as level as possible. Then let the balls sit for at least twenty-four hours to set up.

4   When the concrete has lightened, it's ready to be freed. Put on safety goggles and gloves, and use a hammer to lightly tap the glass to break it away from the concrete ball.

NOTE: When buying lighting covers, make sure there are no cracks in them or they will break when you fill them with concrete.

MATERIALS

Glass lighting covers
(try a thrift store or hardware store for cheap options)

Nonstick cooking spray

Quick-setting concrete

Bucket

Small garden shovel

Safety goggles and gloves
(for when you break away the glass)

Hammer

D esigner and stylist Bettina Pedersen loved the idea of being surrounded by maps so much that she decided to incorporate them into her home décor. This simple box project uses a variety of different maps, from countrywide themes to detailed city street layouts, and can be adapted to work with any type of map you like. If you enjoy the look, you could easily expand your collection to create an entire themed desktop with pencil holders and file folders.

DESIGNER
Bettina Pedersen

COST
Free

TIME
15 minutes per box

DIFFICULTY
★ ★ ★ ★

MATERIALS
—
Rectangular or round
cardboard boxes

Maps
(Bettina's included maps of
Denmark and Europe from
an outdated school atlas,
a Miami street map, and a
tourist map from Africa)

Scissors

Pencil

Brush

Mod Podge

~~~~~~~~~~~ INSTRUCTIONS FOR RECTANGULAR BOXES ~~~~~~~~~~~

1   Measure the perimeter of the box bottom and the box height (without lid). Add ½ inch to the perimeter and 1¼ inches to the height. Cut a piece of map with these dimensions.

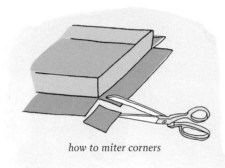

how to miter corners

2   Brush an even layer of Mod Podge on the back of the map and wrap it around the box sides so there is ⅝ inch extra at top and bottom.

3   Miter the corners and fold the ⅝ inch of extra paper over the top edge and onto the bottom and glue to secure.

4   Measure the height of the box lid. Place the box lid over the image chosen for the top and trace around it with a pencil. On each side of the resulting rectangle, add the height of the box lid, plus ½ inch. Cut out the piece of map.

5   Brush an even layer of Mod Podge on the rectangle you drew on the map and attach it to the top of the box. Add glue to the edges of the map and wrap the box top like a present. Miter the corners and fold the ½ inch of extra paper over the top edge of the lid.

~~~~~~~~~~~ INSTRUCTIONS FOR ROUNDED BOXES ~~~~~~~~~~~

1   Measure the circumference of the box bottom and the box height (without lid). Add ½ inch to the circumference and 1¼ inches to the height. Cut a piece of map with these dimensions.

2   Brush an even layer of Mod Podge on the back of the map and wrap it around the box so there is ⅝ inch extra at top and bottom.

3   Cut slits ½ inch apart all the way around both top and bottom. Fold these pieces over the top edge and onto the bottom and glue them to secure.

4   Place the lid over the image chosen for the top and trace around it with a pencil. Cut out the circle just inside the traced outline.

5   Cut a piece for the edge of the lid in the same way as for the box bottom. Cut slits, fold, and glue in the same way. Finish by gluing the round motif on top.

project

PRESSED BOTANICAL SPECIMENS

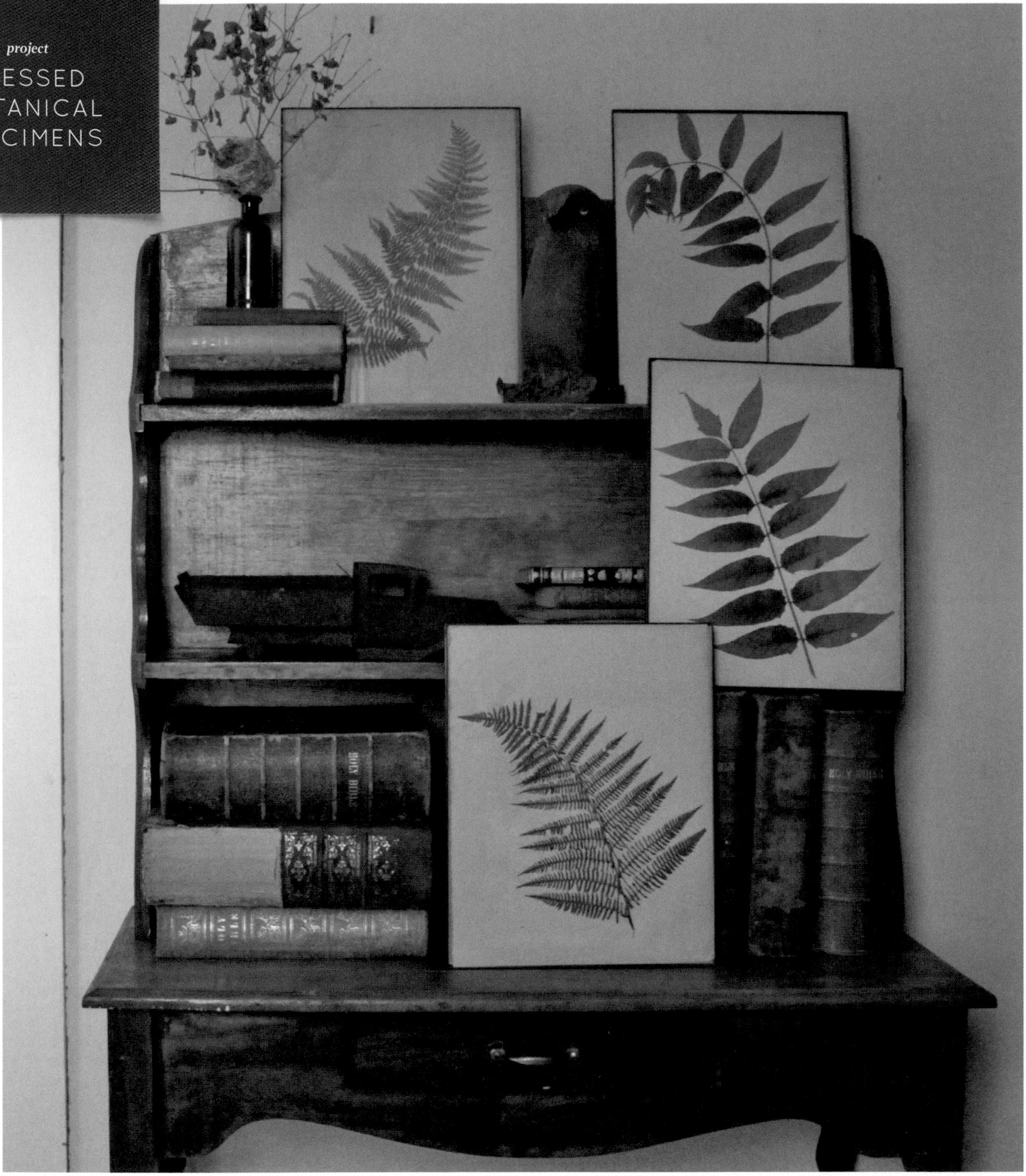

For those of us with limited access to nature, finding ways to bring the outdoors in can be crucial. Amy Merrick decided to press and frame some simple vines and ferns, found in an abandoned lot in her neighborhood, to create the look and feel of fancy botanical prints. Using heavy books to press the specimens flat, Amy used found frames and kraft paper to create an antique look that cost less than $25.

DESIGNER
Amy Merrick

COST
$20

TIME
1 week

DIFFICULTY
★ ★ ★ ★

MATERIALS

Several fronds from ferns or other flat-leafed plants

Frame

Scissors or knife

A large pile of heavy books, including a phonebook

Rubber cement

Kraft or decorative paper

INSTRUCTIONS

1 Locate and clip a few different varieties of fern fronds or other flat-leafed plants and bring them home. These can be from your garden or something found growing in between sidewalk cracks!

2 Hold each frond or stem against the background of its frame and trim the specimen, stripping some of the leaves to fit, if necessary. Decide on the basic layout of your specimens. Should they curl to the right or left?

3 Place each frond vertically or diagonally between the pages of a heavy phone book. Warning: Now is not the time to get out your lovely art book collection, as this process will leave the pages bumpy. It's best to use a book you don't mind getting a little messy! Once your specimens are in place, lay several heavy books on top of the phone book and leave alone for a week.

4 When dry, add a few small dabs of rubber cement to the back of each stem or frond, attach them to the decorative paper, and place the specimens in the frames.

DESIGNER
Amy Merrick

COST
$20

TIME
2 hours

DIFFICULTY
★ ★ ★ ★

F̲ew memories of mine are as vivid as when I would stick clover between book pages as a child. I loved finding it months, even years, later—flattened and perfectly preserved in time. Design*Sponge editor Amy Merrick created this do-it-yourself flower press as a way to preserve the art of pressed flowers without leaving stains on your favorite book pages. Whether you're saving a flower from your wedding or a buttercup that reminds you of summer picnics, this easy press will make framed botanicals a quick and simple process.

MATERIALS

2 rectangular wooden boards, about 6 × 12 inches

Measuring tape or ruler

Power drill and ⅛-inch drill bit

Several cardboard boxes

Watercolor paper (to absorb moisture during pressing)

4 bolts and 4 nuts

∽∽∽∽∽∽∽∽∽∽∽∽∽∽∽∽∽∽∽∽ INSTRUCTIONS ∽∽∽∽∽∽∽∽∽∽∽∽∽∽∽∽∽∽∽∽

1   Measure a 1-inch square at each corner of each board and drill a hole at the interior corner of each square. Corresponding holes need to line up exactly when the boards are placed on top of each other.

2   Make a template for the sandwiched layers that will separate your flowers, ½ inch smaller on all sides than the measurements of the wooden boards. Cut the corners of the template at a 45-degree angle to accommodate the bolt holes. Cut out 5 sheets of cardboard and 4 sheets of watercolor paper in this shape.

3   Alternate cardboard and watercolor paper in a pile and sandwich the stack between the two wooden boards. Line up the holes and insert the bolts into each corner. Screw on the nuts to tighten.

4   Decorate the cover, if desired. Now let's all get out and collect some flowers to press!

NOTE: To press your flowers, place them in between the watercolor paper (which has cardboard above and below it) and screw the press tightly into place. Set aside for at least two days, then unscrew to reveal your pressed flowers.

Every summer a new battle wages between backyard parties and the seasonal mosquito invasion. Kate decided to take matters into her own hands by creating citronella candles at home. Using inexpensive tin cans as decorative holders, Kate used citronella from her local health food store and a mix of old wax candles and crayons to create a custom candle that will keep the bugs at bay when the weather gets warmer.

DESIGNER
Kate Pruitt

COST
$25

TIME
1–2 hours

DIFFICULTY
★ ★ ★ ★

~~~~~~~~~~~~~ INSTRUCTIONS ~~~~~~~~~~~~~

1   Clean out your jars and tin cans. Dry completely.

2   Place a pot with 2 inches of water in it on the stove over low heat, and place the wax-melting container in the water.

3   While the water is heating, attach the wick bases to the bottom center of the jars and tins with a dab of hot glue.

4   When the water is 140 degrees, add the wax and crayons to the melting container. Stir every once in a while as it starts to melt. When all the wax is melted to an even liquid (it will be the consistency of olive oil), add a few drops of citronella oil and stir (2 or 3 drops of oil for every 8 ounces of wax). Then remove the melting container from the water and pour the wax into your containers, leaving about ½ inch of wick exposed. Let cool.

MATERIALS

Old pickle or jam jars
or tin cans

Container for melting wax
(a saucepan with another
heat-safe container inside
will be fine, or you can
purchase wax containers at
a craft store)

Wicks
(available at craft stores)

Hot glue gun and glue sticks

Thermometer

Old wax candles, or any type
of safely meltable wax

Crayons
(optional, for color)

Stir stick or spoon

Citronella oil
(available at health food
stores, online, and at some
specialty hardware stores)

Tip

If you want to give the jar
candles as a gift, cover the
lid of the jar with some
pretty fabric and screw it
back onto the jar. Wrap the
tin can candles with a little
kitchen twine and finish
with a bow.

Some people may be "turned off" by the industrial look of a bare lightbulb, but Kate embraced the look with this clever outdoor lamp design. By attaching two inexpensive wire planter baskets with some fine-gauge wire, and threading a pendant socket and lightbulb through the top, Kate designed a striking lamp that's perfect for any outdoor occasion.

DESIGNER
Kate Pruitt

COST
$20

TIME
**1–2 hours
(plus drying time)**

DIFFICULTY
★ ★ ★ ★

INSTRUCTIONS

1 Place the wire planters outside on a tarp or newspaper and spray paint them with a white primer, allowing one side to dry and then turning to spray from all angles to ensure an even coat. Let dry.

2 If you want to paint them a color, use the same method to spray them with an even coat of color.

3 Screw the lightbulb into the socket and place it between the two planters. Thread the cord through the top of one planter and wire the two planter bases together with the fine-gauge wire. Make sure you like how the vertical seams line up (or don't line up).

4 Use wire snippers to trim wires at the connection spots to ¼ inch.

5 Use the garden twine to hang the planter lamp in your desired location. Plug in.

MATERIALS

Two matching wire
planter baskets

Tarp or newspaper

Spray primer

Spray paint
(optional)

Lightbulb

Pendant socket set
for lightbulb
(available at Ikea)

Fine-gauge wire

Wire snippers

Garden twine
(for hanging the lamp)

Tip

The fine-gauge wire is quite pliable, so it's easy to separate and reconnect the planters at the connection spots if you need to change the bulb.

I f you're like me, you want to have privacy in your home, but without sacrificing bright, natural light. Design*Sponge editor Kate Pruitt solved this problem by using inexpensive window film to create decorative decals for her French doors. Because the window film peels off easily, you can swap out the designs when you're ready for a new look or want to rearrange the design.

DESIGNER
Kate Pruitt

COST
$25

TIME
3—4 hours

DIFFICULTY
★ ★ ★ ★

MATERIALS

Ruler

Window film, clear
(found at hardware or home
organization stores)

Scissors or X-Acto knife

Tape

Paint pen

~~~~~~~~~~~~~~~~~~~~~~~~~~~~ INSTRUCTIONS ~~~~~~~~~~~~~~~~~~~~~~~~~~~~

1   Measure the windowpanes and transfer the dimensions to the back of the window film. Cut out the rectangles. I recommend using a ruler and an X-Acto knife, but if you draw a clean line and can cut neatly with scissors, that will work just as well.

2   Tape down the edges of your window film cutout with the paper side down. This ensures you will be painting on the nonsticky side of the window film. Using the paint pen, draw out your design on the window film. Let the paint dry at least ten minutes.

3   Carefully peel the paper backing away from the film and place it on the windowpane. Slowly pull the paper down and smooth down the window film with a piece of paper or a book with a rounded spine.

DESIGNER
Christine Chitnis

COST
$10—$40

TIME
1 hour

DIFFICULTY
★ ★ ★ ★

MATERIALS

Lace doilies

Pins

Needle and thread
or sewing machine

project
**LACE DOILY
TABLE
RUNNER**

W riter and crafter Christine Chitnis decided to update her collection of doilies by turning them into a custom table runner. Simple hand-stitching was all Christine needed to create a loose design that was perfect for a romantic dinner at home. Even the most inexperienced sewers can tackle this project on a rainy day and have something beautiful to dine on by dinnertime.

INSTRUCTIONS

1   Arrange the doilies across a tabletop to create a long runner, overlapping the edges of each adjoining doily. Once the runner is laid out, carefully pin the doilies together.

2   Using either a needle and thread or a sewing machine, stitch the doilies together.

DESIGNER
Kate Pruitt

COST
$18

TIME
2 hours

DIFFICULTY
★ ★ ★ ★

MATERIALS

Wooden log
(you can also use premade
wooden coasters)

Saw
(chop saw or a regular
tooth saw and miter box)

Pencil

Stemless wineglass, drinking
glass, or a clean glass jar.

Wood-burning tool with a
medium, rounded tip

Design*Sponge editor Kate Pruitt has fond memories of growing up sitting around a crackling fire in Maine, watching her dad chop firewood outside. While she no longer has access to firewood, she wanted to find a way to bring those memories of wooden logs back into her California home. Using found logs from a neighbor's tree cutting, Kate created wooden display jars to house her most treasured objects.

INSTRUCTIONS

1   Cut the log slice. It can be anywhere from 1 to 3 inches thick, but make sure both sides are flat so it sits level.

2   Flip the glass over, center it on the log slice, and trace around the rim with a pencil.

3   Working very slowly and carefully, use the wood-burning tool to burn the ring into the wood so it is indented by ⅛ to ¼ inch. When tracing the ring with the wood-burning tool, work along the inside of the line you traced to be sure the glass will fit snugly. Stop every few minutes to place the glass in the ring to see if your shape is right. I recommend not trying to burn the entire ring at once, but instead burning tiny dots, one right next to the other, and then running over them again and again to connect them into a continuous shape.

Many of us long to have a lush backyard filled with trees and room to garden but are faced with the reality of limited space, fire escapes, and cement patios. Looking to create an "urban greenscape" for the backdrop of her wedding ceremony, Lily Huynh of Nincomsoup decided to turn to bricks to create the structure she would need for her wall of greenery. By planting tiny succulents into the holes in each brick, Lily was able to get the lush, green feel she wanted without having an actual garden out back. She loved her finished succulent wall so much she decided to move it from the background of her wedding ceremony to the front, where it served as a makeshift altar. Whether you're planning for a wedding decoration or just want to create a small wall of greenery on your deck, this is a fun and affordable way to build a small greenspace without a backyard.

DESIGNER
Lily Huynh

COST
$80–$90

TIME
2–3 hours

DIFFICULTY
★ ★ ★ ★

MATERIALS

Potting soil

Cactus soil

Large plastic bucket
(a 4 gallon works well)

Succulents
(look for mature succulents
that have anywhere from a
2-inch blossom diameter to
a 3-inch blossom diameter)

9 × 12-inch baking pan

Engineering bricks
(these come in a variety of
types, most commonly with 3
large holes, although you can
find some that have 10 or 16
small holes)

1 long, skinny spoon

~~~~~~~~~~~ INSTRUCTIONS ~~~~~~~~~~~

1 Mix the potting soil and cactus soil in a 1:1 ratio, filling a bucket, and set aside.

2 Separate the succulents into individual florets that will fit the various sizes of the brick holes, and trim the roots to about 1 inch in length.

3 Fill the baking pan with about ½ inch of water.

4 Place a brick into the baking pan with the holes facing up. Spoon the soil mixture into each hole, until the holes are loosely full. Then, using the back side of the spoon, pack the soil into the holes a bit (not too tightly).

5 Arrange the different sizes of florets into each of the brick holes. Pack the florets with additional soil mixture, making sure that each is held firmly in place. Remove the brick from the baking pan and set it aside. Repeat the process, replenishing the water in the baking pan as needed, until you have created enough bricks.

6 Let the succulent-filled bricks sit upright for a few days to acclimate, then stack the bricks on their sides to build the wall of succulents. If the succulents begin to look dry, spray them with a spray bottle.

NOTE: The number of bricks and succulents and the amount of soil needed depend on how large a wall you plan to build.

Premade block-printed duvet covers can be pretty expensive, so Design*Sponge editor Kate Pruitt decided to try her hand at a do-it-yourself version. Using scrap cardboard she had around the house, she made a simple pinecone template, which yielded a rough, slightly uneven print that Kate really loved at a fraction of the cost of a store-bought design.

To Make the Cardboard Printing "Block"

1   Draw your pattern on the Kraft paper, including the parts you plan to cut out. When planning your design, try to keep it simple, with big shapes. Don't try anything too intricate or dainty; the cuts can't be too narrow or the cardboard will break down. Try to keep all printing surfaces of the cardboard at least ½-inch wide. Cut out the pattern pieces that need to be removed using an X-Acto knife. What is left will be exactly what your painted surface will look like.

2   When you are satisfied with the final design, trace it onto the cardboard with the permanent marker, including all the cutout parts, and carefully cut it out of the cardboard, making sure all cuts are clean. Replace the knife blade often to keep the cuts sharp.

To Print the Design

3   Prep the fabric according to the directions on the fabric paint and iron out wrinkles. Lay the duvet cover on the work surface and consider how to print your design. If you want exactness, you will need to measure and make small marks with a pencil or tape on the duvet cover to show where you want to place the block each time. Otherwise, you can start at the top of the duvet cover and work downward, eyeballing the design as you go.

4   Mix the fabric paints, preparing a large amount in the plastic cup. The paint should have the consistency of house paint from a can. If you have thicker fabric paint, you may need to dilute it with water.

5   Pour some of the paint in the paint tray and cover the foam roller evenly and heavily with paint. Roll the paint onto the cardboard and cover evenly, then place the cardboard paint side down onto a piece of scrap fabric. Cover it with a piece of clean scrap paper or newsprint and use one hand to hold the cardboard in place while using the other hand to press down and rub over the entire image. Press firmly over every inch of the surface of the cardboard, just as if you were gluing the cardboard down. Then remove the paper and—using one hand to hold the fabric down—carefully peel the cardboard off. Repeat the practice printing a couple of times. This will give the cardboard time to absorb paint so it will release more paint onto the fabric. It will also allow you to see how much paint you need to use and how firmly you need to rub on the design.

6   Once you have practiced the printing process and are confident, begin printing on the duvet cover one print at a time. The cardboard pattern should hold up for the whole process. If you are doing both sides of the duvet cover, you will need to make two cardboard shapes and use a fresh one for the flip side. The first one will start to break down after thirty uses or so.

7   Continue printing the pattern, using fresh sheets of paper to cover and press down on the template. Take care not to drip or smear paint on the fabric. When complete, leave the duvet cover to dry flat. You may need a hand to help you transport or hang it somewhere.

8   Follow the directions on the fabric paint to set the pattern, which will allow you to wash the fabric again and again without losing the pattern.

NOTE: If you are willing to spend the money, a large linoleum block will provide you with a sharp, clean printed image. This project shows you that you can get a pretty nice image with a cheap material like cardboard, but it does create a rough, imperfect look, which may not suit your style. If you want to make your design smaller (fist-sized for example), I would recommend using a linoleum block. The method described here is best for bigger prints.

DESIGNER
Kate Pruitt

COST
$25

TIME
**4 hours
(plus drying time)**

DIFFICULTY
★ ★ ★ ★

MATERIALS
―――――――――

Kraft paper

Newsprint or scrap paper
(at least ten sheets of this)

Pencil

X-Acto knife and extra blades

Scrap cardboard
(you need one or two large
flat pieces with no bends or
tears that can fit your stencil)

Permanent marker

Large working surface

Duvet cover
(or fabric to make duvet,
or a cotton sheet, etc.)

Iron

Fabric paints
(enough paint to fill a
regular-sized plastic
drinking cup)

Plastic cup

Paint tray (or paper plate)

Small foam roller

W reaths aren't everyone's cup of tea, mainly because they can require a lot of maintenance. But artist and crafter Kirsten Schueler found a way to create a wreath that wouldn't require any upkeep, and would allow her to recycle some leftover materials. Working with an old wool sweater and a foam wreath form, Kirsten cut pieces of the sweater and hot-glued them to the form to create a unique sweater wreath that can be used throughout the year.

DESIGNER
Kirsten D. Schueler

COST
$13

TIME
3—4 hours

DIFFICULTY
★ ★ ★ ★

MATERIALS

Wool sweater
(needs to be at least 90
percent wool), women's
size L or men's M

Scissors

Steam iron

Low-temp hot glue gun
and glue sticks

Fabric to wrap wreath form
(a 16-inch wreath
will use ¼ yard)

Styrofoam wreath form

〜〜〜〜〜〜〜〜〜〜〜〜〜〜〜 INSTRUCTIONS 〜〜〜〜〜〜〜〜〜〜〜〜〜〜〜〜

1   Wash the sweater in the washer with some old towels, using the maximum amount of soap and the hot wash/cold rinse cycle. You want to really rough up—felt—your sweater, so don't be shy: Use the machine's maximum settings. Dry it on the maximum settings also.

2   Once the sweater has dried, turn it inside out and cut it up along seam lines using a sharp pair of scissors. Cut away any decorative details, ribbing, and thick seams. Then, using a medium-hot steam iron, press the sweater pieces on both sides, until they are flat and smooth.

3   Cut leaf shapes out of the sweater pieces, with as little waste as possible. Don't worry about all the leaves being identical in shape and size—once they are on the wreath no one will notice and it adds visual interest when they are all a bit different.

4   Let your low-temp hot glue gun heat up while you prepare the wreath. Cut or tear 1-inch strips of fabric. When the glue gun is ready, wrap the fabric strips around the wreath form, tacking the fabric into place with dots of glue as you go. Wrap neatly and tightly, trying to avoid wrinkles.

5   Attach the leaves to the fabric-covered wreath, layering them like shingles all in one direction. Attach each leaf with a dot of hot glue. Sometimes I like to layer the leaves close together and sometimes I give them a bit more space. Either way, layer them so you can't see your fabric-covered wreath form. Cover only the front part of the wreath, leaving about an inch uncovered on the back to help it lie flat against a wall or door.

DESIGNERS
**Derek Fagerstrom
and Lauren Smith**

COST
$25

TIME
2 hours

DIFFICULTY
★ ★ ★ ★

Sometimes, affordable, everyday materials can create a beautiful high-end look. Design*Sponge editors Derek and Lauren scoured their favorite local hardware store and found budget-friendly strips of wood veneer, which they used to create a curved wall sconce. Inspired by the bent plywood designs of Charles and Ray Eames, Derek and Lauren loved the way a humble material could be used to create such a dramatic, sophisticated design.

 INSTRUCTIONS

1   Use a chop saw (or ask your local lumberyard) to cut your 1-inch × 4-inch plank to the following lengths:

> One piece at 12 inches
> Two pieces at 10 inches
> One piece at 8 inches

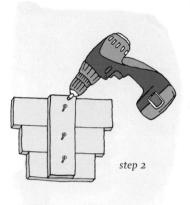

step 2

2   On a flat work surface, line up the 12-inch piece, one of the 10-inch pieces, and the 8-inch piece of wood from large to small, making sure the centers are aligned. Apply a bead of wood glue down the length of the remaining 10-inch piece and place, glue side down, on top of the other three pieces. Then secure the 10-inch crossbar by drilling through both layers of wood with three 1½-inch screws, one for each of the three lengths of wood.

3   Drill a ¼-inch hole through the fixture, about one-third of the way up from the bottom of the cross bar, to allow the socket's wires to pass through to the back, then attach the light socket to the front with the last 1½-inch screw. Pull the wires through the ¼-inch hole to the back.

4   Attach the sawtooth hanger to the crossbar, near the center top.

5   Using scissors, cut the wood veneer into three 4-inch-wide strips that measure 18 inches, 16 inches, and 14 inches in length. Starting with the shortest piece, attach the wood veneer to the shortest board of the base along the sides, flush with the top edge of the 1 × 4. At first, use a bead of wood glue to tack the veneer in place, then attach with the finishing nails, three per side. Since 1 × 4s aren't technically 4 inches wide, the veneer strips will overlap just a little.

6   Continue with the middle and longest pieces of veneer, attaching them in the same way (first with glue, then with 6 finishing nails).

7   Sand down any rough edges, apply a stain or wood oil of your choice, and let dry.

8   Secure the wires of the fixture to those coming out of the wall with electrical tape (black to black, white to white). Gently push the wires into the wall (or, if you don't have wall sconces, run the wire down to the floor beneath a strip of wire molding). Screw a lightbulb into the fixture to test.

9   Insert a drywall screw into the wall and mount the fixture using the sawtooth hanger.

MATERIALS

Chop saw

One plank of 1-inch × 4-inch wood (at least 4 feet long), cut to the measurements listed in step 1

Wood glue

Drill with screwdriver bit, or a screwdriver

Four 1½-inch screws

Light socket with tab for attaching vertically to fixture

Sawtooth hanger

Scissors

Wood veneer that measures at least 18 inches × 12 inches

18 finishing nails

Hammer

Sandpaper

Wood stain or oil

Stain brush or clean rag

Electrical tape

Electrical wires

Lightbulb

Drywall screw (and wall anchor, if necessary)

Many of my fellow editors at Design*Sponge have seen my vintage box obsession in action and can attest to the fact that I rarely leave a flea market or thrift store without lugging a few wooden boxes home. I love the character of old wood, the faded stamps from factories across the country, and imagining who might have lugged these same boxes around decades and decades before me.

At the Brimfield Antique Show in Massachusetts I got a great deal on an oversized vintage box that previously held parts for the Boston Rubber Shoe Company. Looking to store our rather embarrassingly large collection of video game equipment, I decided to attach some casters to the bottom of the box, create a quick upholstered top, and turn my flea market find into a rolling storage bench. Our cat, Ms. Jackson, immediately claimed it as her favorite sleeping spot.

DESIGNER
Grace Bonney

COST
$40

TIME
2 hours

DIFFICULTY
★ ★ ★ ★

MATERIALS

Old box (try thrift stores, Craigslist, flea markets, and eBay for similar versions)

Casters and mounting screws

Screwdriver

Measuring tape or ruler

Sturdy, midweight plywood (for your lid)

Saw
(if you choose to cut your own lid)

Sandpaper

Foam
(use 2-inch foam at least, to create a comfortable seat)

Box cutter or electric knife

Batting

Scissors

Fabric

Staple gun and staples

Hinges (optional)

INSTRUCTIONS

1 Flip your box upside down and attach the casters to the four corners. Be sure to use screws that are short enough that they don't come through to the interior of the box. If they do, you can place an extra piece of foam in the bottom to protect your stored items.

2 Flip the box upright and measure from edge to edge for your box top. Cut your plywood box top to fit, and sand the edges. (Most Home Depot and Lowe's stores will cut plywood you buy in their stores for you.)

3 Lay your foam on the floor and place the box lid on top. Trace around the edges of the plywood lid and cut the foam to size with a utility knife or electric knife.

4 Repeat step 3 with the batting, leaving a 3-inch border of batting on all sides so you can pull it over the foam and staple it to the back of the plywood lid. Repeat the process with your fabric.

5 With the fabric facedown on the floor, center the batting and then the foam on top. Place the wooden lid on top of these three layers and pull the batting and fabric over the edges of the lid, using a staple gun to secure them. Work your way around the edges of the lid, pulling the fabric taut and stapling as you go.

6 Once you've finished stapling, cut off any excess fabric. If you want a more polished look for the underside of the box lid, cut a piece of fabric 1 inch smaller (on all sides) than the lid and staple this in place.

7 If you have children, or would like to ensure that your lid is secure, you can install safety hinges, which will keep the top from sliding or slamming down on small fingers.

In a time where e-mail, text messages, and social networking updates seem to rule our communication world, it can be wonderfully refreshing to send a real letter, and sealing it with wax adds a wonderful, old-world touch. Designer and artist Kimberly Munn used a simple wooden dowel and wood-burning tool to create this personalized, budget-friendly wax seal (which she sweetly customized for Design*Sponge!). Whether you carve an image, your company's logo, or just an initial, a wax seal is a great way to ensure that people won't forget a letter from you.

DESIGNER
Kimberly Munn

COST
$30

TIME
1—2 hours

DIFFICULTY
★ ★ ★ ★

MATERIALS

Wooden dowel
(½–1½ inches in diameter,
depending on size of design)

Sandpaper

Ruler

Paper

Pencil

X-Acto knife

Tape

Wood-burning tool
with a fine tip

Stain

Sealing wax

Matches

Vegetable oil

Paper towels

Envelope

Tip

Measure the diameter of the wooden dowel—don't rely on the diameter written on the package or tag. If you are familiar with buying wood products, you know that the item you bought—whether it's a 2 × 4, a piece of plywood, or a dowel—is never the exact size it is sold as.

INSTRUCTIONS

1 Prep the dowel by sanding the end you plan on using as the seal. Smooth out the little dings and scratches, or they will show up in the wax impression.

2 Measure the exact diameter of the wooden dowel and design a seal to fit, either on paper or using a computer application. Keep it relatively simple unless you have a lot of experience with wood-burning tools.

3 Make a stencil by printing the final design and cutting it out with an X-Acto knife. The stencil doesn't have to be perfect, but it does need to capture the structure of the design.

4 Flip your stencil so it reads backward and secure it to the dowel end with tape. Trace the design onto the dowel end. Remove the stencil and flesh out the design if needed.

5 Carve out the design with the wood-burning tool, using the fine tip to capture small detail. To create a seal that leaves an even, smooth impression in the wax, it is important to maintain the same relative depth while carving.

6 Seal the wood with stain, and set it in a warm place to dry overnight.

7 Gather the sealing wax, matches, oil, paper towels, and an envelope (with letter inside). Lay the envelope on the work surface facedown. If the flap doesn't lie flat, weight it down. Then light the sealing wax and give the flame a chance to strengthen before dripping wax onto the envelope flap. Keep an eye on the diameter of the wax puddle in relation to the diameter of the seal. It may take practice to figure out how much wax is needed.

8 While the wax sets up (approximately 15 seconds) dip the seal tip in oil to keep the wax from sticking to it. Blot the excess oil on a paper towel, being sure to wipe down the edges of the seal. Then press the seal gently but firmly into the wax. Let the wax dry completely. To remove, wiggle the seal back and forth gently until you feel it release from the wax.

project

CUBBY END TABLE WITH CHAIR LEG BASE

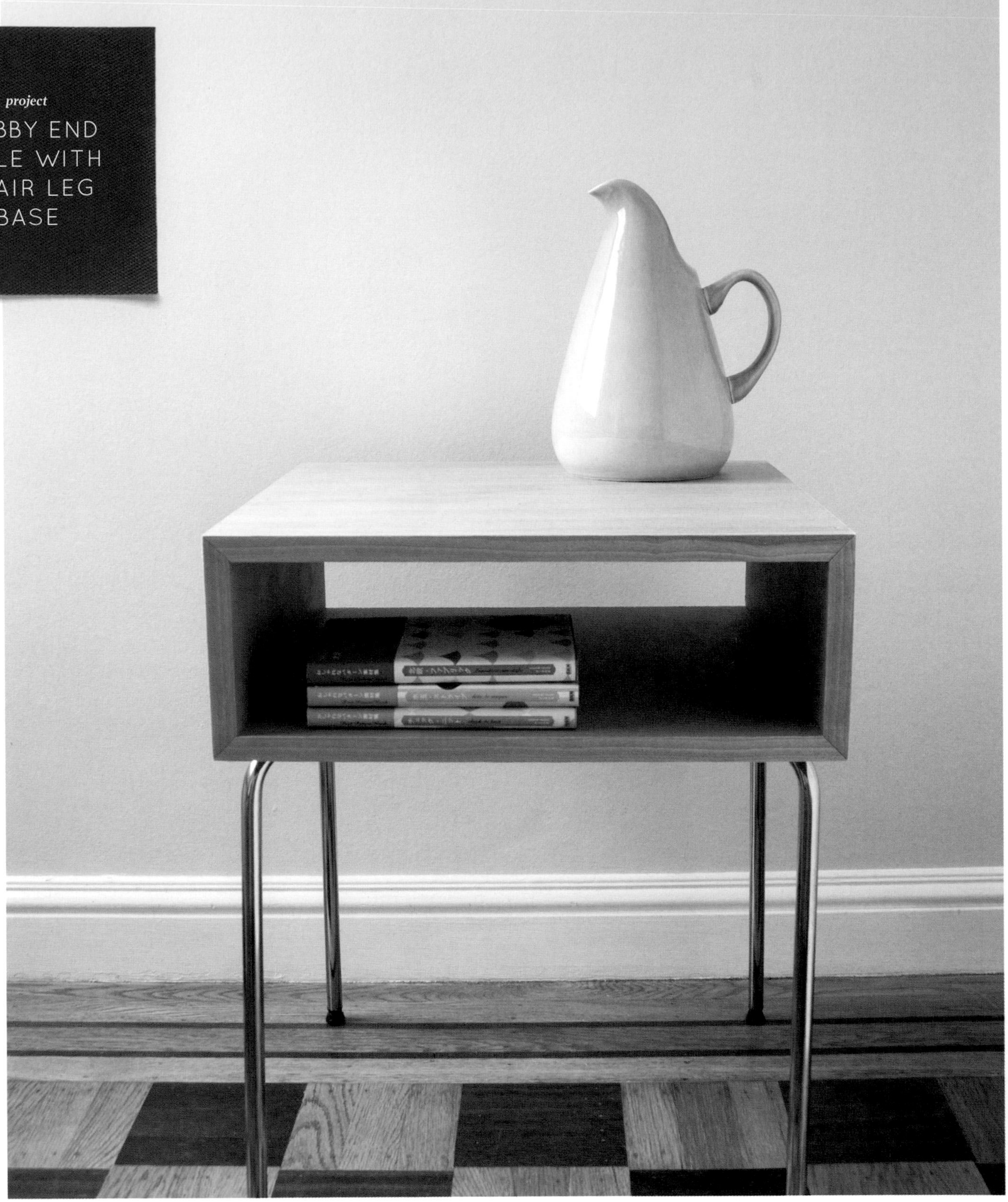

Cats can be picky about where they choose to sleep (min always choose someplace I need to be working, like my keyboard or a stack of papers), so giving them somewhe able and cozy to sleep can be worth the extra effort. When photo Kimberly Brandt found a mini vintage trunk at a thrift store, she would make the perfect bed for her cat, Marizpand, who prefers tight spaces. With a little bit of love and a splash of pattern from Butler Midwest Modern fabric, Kimberly has turned her once sh into a stylish sleeping spot for her cat.

The great thing about having the fabric affixed with Velcro is to remove and wash! I would love it if pets didn't make messes, b This way the beautiful fabric that you choose can stay beautiful!

<hr/>INSTRUCTIONS<hr/>

1 Line the inside of the trunk with kraft paper. Cut to size and affix with spray a

2 Adhere the soft half of the sticky Velcro just below the rim of the trunk and cor the perimeter.

3 Measure the trunk opening carefully, adding about 1½ inches on all sides for the Cut the fabric to size. Stitch the Velcro right along the edge of the fabric on the one corner-to-corner length at a time. The "stickiness" of the Velcro can make t bit tough if you're not using an industrial machine. If you find it difficult to stit switch to good old-fashioned needle and thread.

4 Turn the fabric to the wrong side and fold each corner at a diagonal so it is lined ½-inch space that you've left. Pinch in the corners and stitch about 1 inch in alor as for a pillow. Stitch the corner so it folds in. (Try this with a piece of paper firs hang of it.) You are creating a fabric "lid" which will be Velcro-ed over a bed of ba

5 Fill the case with your choice of filler; we used a synthetic batting, but a hypoalle would work fine if you have sensitive pets. Once the trunk is overflowing with bat the fabric to the Velcro in the trunk, being careful to smooth wrinkles around the

6 To keep the trunk open for your kitty's safety, affix L-shaped brackets either next place of the hinges. Your local hardware store can help you determine the correct s on the weight of your trunk lid.

SAFETY NOTE: Spray adhesive is pretty toxic, so you'll want to wear a mask and open your windc spray. Spray in short spurts and let your room fully air out before proceeding.

<hr/>

DESIGNERS
Derek Fagerstrom
and Lauren Smith

COST
$20

TIME
4 hours

DIFFICULTY
★ ★ ★ ★

Design*Sponge editors Derek and Lauren are always finding cast-off chairs at their local San Francisco thrift store. Most of them they wouldn't want to bring home, let alone invite guests to sit on, but every now and then they find bits and pieces of individual chairs that they can adapt for other purposes. For this project, Derek and Lauren salvaged the legs from a metal chair to create a custom cubby end table to store magazines and books.

<hr/>INSTRUCTIONS<hr/>

1 Ask your local lumberyard to cut down a quarter sheet of plywood to the following dimensions:

> Two pieces (top and bottom) at 18 × 18 inches
> Two pieces (sides) at 18 × 5 inches

2 Remove the seat and back from a salvaged chair. Set aside any hardware from the seat (it may come in handy later). If your chair legs are dirty, be sure to clean them. Rust can be removed with naval jelly or by manually scrubbing with steel wool or a wire brush.

3 Apply a bead of wood glue down one of the long edges of each 18 × 5-inch side piece. Place them onto opposite ends of the bottom cubby piece. Make sure they are perfectly flush. Give them a few minutes to dry in place, then flip the piece over and predrill 2 holes through the bottom piece into each side piece. Insert wood screws in the holes to secure the pieces.

4 Paint the interior of the cubby now, before attaching the top piece. When painting the top piece, leave a ½-inch area along 2 sides unpainted so the paint won't show through the seams once the top is attached. Let dry.

5 Put wood glue along the top edges of the side pieces and set the top piece in place. Let dry for a minute, then predrill 2 holes through the top piece into each side piece and carefully secure the pieces using finishing nails and a hammer.

6 Center the cubby on the chair legs and mark the location of the chair's screw holes on the bottom of the cubby with a pencil.

7 Check to make sure the tabletop will be level. If it's pitched in one direction, place the level on top and lift until it registers level. Determine the necessary number of washers or shims needed to make it level and predrill through them. Then flip the piece over and, with the legs and proper number of washers or shims in place, insert a screw through them all and into the bottom of the cubby. Turn the table over and check again that it is level.

8 Set the table on its back and measure out 4 pieces of the iron-on wood veneer to cover the raw edges of the front of the cubby. Cut them to length using a utility knife. For a fancy effect you can miter the ends by cutting the veneer diagonally at the corners.

9 With an iron set on medium heat (no steam!), iron the veneer onto the top edge of the cubby. Continue with the remaining edges.

10 Give everything a quick once over with the sandpaper, followed by your preferred stain or oil.

MATERIALS

One-quarter sheet of
1-inch-thick birch plywood,
cut to the dimensions
listed in step 1

Salvaged chair with
metal legs

Wood glue

Drill

Wood screws

Paint (for interior of cubby)

Paintbrush

Finishing nails

Hammer

Pencil

Level

Shims or thick washers, to
level out the tabletop

Iron-on wood veneer tape

Ruler

Utility knife

Iron

Sandpaper

Wood stain or oil

Stain brush or rag

project

SUITCASE
CAT BED

project

STAMPED
FABRIC
CURTAINS

Brooklyn designer Clara Klein has always been attracted to designing with repetitive elements, so she decided to create a simple foam template for her own bedroom curtains. By designing and cutting the template herself, Clara was able to keep her costs low and create a one-of-a-kind look for her home that truly reflects her personal style and taste.

DESIGNER
Clara Klein

COST
$32

TIME
4 hours
(plus drying time)

DIFFICULTY
★ ★ ★ ★

~~~~~~~~~~~~ INSTRUCTIONS ~~~~~~~~~~~~

1   Design your pattern and trace it onto the craft foam, then cut around the tracing. Clean up the edges as needed.

2   Assemble and glue the foam template onto a piece of cardboard to create an oversized stamp.

3   Prepare the work surface by laying out the curtain fabric. Place kraft paper beneath the curtain or between the curtain and the lining, as some ink will bleed through.

4   Start inking the stamp. Clara used a soft watercolor brush to distribute the ink as evenly as possible (otherwise the imperfections will be visible when you hold the textile against the light). Then place the stamp ink side down on the curtain fabric and use the rolling pin to roll back and forth over the top to ensure even distribution of ink. Continue inking and printing.

5   When you finish the project, let it dry, then heat set the ink by ironing over it.

MATERIALS

Craft foam

Box cutter or utility knife

Craft glue

Cardboard for backing

Fabric to print on—Ikea curtains are nice because they are lined, so you don't see the back side of the print

Kraft paper

Soft watercolor brush

Screen printing ink

Heavy rolling pin

Iron

Monogrammed hankies may seem a bit old-fashioned or dated, but when done with fun, modern imagery, and sophisticated font choices, they can be a great gift for birthdays, holidays, or even weddings. Design*Sponge editor Kate Pruitt used freezer paper (a paper with one waxy and one plain side that allows you to transfer images onto another surface with an iron) to apply her monograms and chose images that would mean something to the recipient, like a pet's silhouette or a trademark pair of glasses. But you could choose anything you like, ranging from simple initials to the outline of a house for a great housewarming gift.

DESIGNER
Kate Pruitt

COST
$10

TIME
2 hours

DIFFICULTY
★ ★ ★ ☆

MATERIALS

Computer/printer

Prewashed fabric squares
(16 × 16 inches)

Ruler

Pencil

Thread and pins

Sewing machine
(or no-sew fusible
webbing if you prefer)

Scissors

Iron

Freezer paper

Craft/utility knife
and a cutting mat

Fabric paint

Small foam brush

~~~~~~~~~~~~~~~~ INSTRUCTIONS ~~~~~~~~~~~~~~~~

1   Design your pattern with the monogram letters and print out several copies to determine the right size for your handkerchief. Your handkerchiefs will be 14 inches square, so your design should probably be 2–3 inches. These copies can be black and white, because your design will be one color.

2   Use your ruler and pencil to mark a 14-inch square centered on the back of your fabric, so that you have a 1-inch border for your hem. Fold over ¼ inch on the back of the fabric and press, then fold over the remaining ¾ inch, press, and pin in place. Sew all the way around and cut any excess thread. Trim the hem and iron it flat.

3   Print your final design on a piece of freezer paper that is cut to standard 8.5 × 11 size. (It should feed quite easily through your printer.) Use the utility knife to carefully cut out the design and the letters. Go slowly and be very exact. Cut out anything you want to print on the handkerchief.

4   Heat up the iron and lay the freezer paper stencil on the right side of the handkerchief. Iron the paper carefully, going over it several times with mild pressure. The freezer paper will adhere to the fabric, creating a nice, clean line.

5   Once the freezer paper stencil is adhered, cut another piece of freezer paper slightly larger than the stencil design and iron it to the back of the handkerchief, underneath where the design will appear. This ensures that paint will not seep through the fabric.

6   Place a small amount of fabric paint on the foam brush and dab it over the design, covering the design entirely, especially all corners and edges. If you are using a light color, like white, you may need to do several coats. Allow each coat to dry before adding the next.

7   Once the paint has completely dried, peel the freezer paper off the front and back.

NOTE: These handkerchiefs should be washed according to the directions that come with the fabric paint. I usually recommend hand washing in cold water.

project
PEG-BOARD
POT RACK
Turn to page 24 to see the pot rack in Grace's home.

When it comes to my kitchen, I try to think like a sailboat designer, incorporating as many double-duty storage compartments as possible and making use of vertical as well as horizontal space. Inspired by Julia Child's classic pot wall, I decided to make use of an awkward small wall in the room by creating my own custom Peg-Board rack. Despite not being the most skilled woodworker around, I was able to create a simple frame, mount it to the wall, paint the Peg-Board a vivid orange to match our walls, and attach it to the frame. Now all of my pots, pans, and lids have a home without taking up valuable cabinet space.

DESIGNER
Grace Bonney

COST
$20

TIME
3 hours

DIFFICULTY
★ ★ ★ ★

MATERIALS

Peg-Board

Pencil

4 strips of wood
1–1½ inches thick
(I used small strips of found wood), cut to match the length and width of your Peg-Board

Screws

Screwdriver

Plastic tarp or cloth

Primer

Paintbrush or roller

Paint
(I used Benjamin Moore's Tomato Red)

Drill

Peg-Board hooks

~~~~~~~~~~ INSTRUCTIONS ~~~~~~~~~~

1   Place your Peg-Board on the wall where you would like it to hang and lightly trace an outline with a pencil.

2   Using your thin pieces of wood, create a "frame" on the wall, using the outline of the Peg-Board to guide you. This frame not only anchors the Peg-Board but also creates enough space behind it for the hooks to fit.

3   Use screws to attach each piece of wood until you have a rectangular frame on the wall along the inside lines of the traced Peg-Board. Be sure to use anchors if your walls are hollow or thin—the Peg-Board will support the weight of heavy pots and pans, so it needs to be secure.

4   Prime the Peg-Board while it's lying flat on a plastic tarp or cloth. Use a very thin coat so the holes don't fill with paint and clog. Let dry, then apply a thin layer of paint. Using a roller designed for smooth surfaces works nicely here. If any Peg-Board holes start to fill, use a pencil tip to clear out the excess paint. Let dry.

5   When the Peg-Board is dry, attach it to the wooden frame, drilling through the peg holes. Use as many screws as you need for the Peg-Board to feel secure. Paint over the screw tops to cover up the metal. Let dry.

6   Hang your pots and pans on the Peg-Board using Peg-Board hooks.

Small-space living often means that storage is limited, so it's great when a piece of furniture or decoration can serve dual purposes. Derek and Lauren used some of their favorite wool army blankets to create these comfortable floor pillows (quick and easy seating for unexpected guests) and used winter blankets and extra pillows as stuffing! Now when they change their winter bedding they can hide the heavier bedding in plain sight and have it double as comfortable seating for guests.

DESIGNERS
**Derek Fagerstrom
and Lauren Smith**

COST
$25 for 2 pillows

TIME
2 hours

DIFFICULTY
★ ★ ★ ★

MATERIALS

1 wool army blanket will yield
one large (28 × 28-inch)
and two small (18 × 18-inch)
pillows

Scissors

Measuring tape or ruler

Matching zippers, in lengths
that are as close to the final
width as possible

Pins

Sewing machine with
zipper foot

Matching thread

Duvet, comforter,
or pillow for stuffing

INSTRUCTIONS

1. Choose your placement (some army blankets have a decorative stripe on either end that looks great on a pillow) and cut out two squares per pillow that are 1 inch larger than your finished pillow all the way around. (Derek and Lauren cut out two 29 × 29-inch squares for the large pillow and two 19 × 19-inch squares for each small pillow.)

2. Center one side of the zipper along the bottom edge of the fabric square, with right sides together and matching raw edges. Pin the zipper tape to the fabric and sew, using the zipper foot. The stitch line should be as close to the zipper teeth as possible.

3. Unzip the zipper and sew the other side to the second fabric square, right sides together. If the zipper is shorter than the length of the fabric, stitch up the ends after the zipper is attached.

4. With right sides together, stitch up the remaining three sides of the two fabric squares, leaving the zipper side open. Trim corners and turn pillowcase right side out.

5. Fold the duvet into a square (or fold your pillow in half) and stuff into the pillowcase, zipping the open end when you're done.

There of you living in big cities may experience the curse of the teeny-tiny city bathroom. With space so limited, every surface and cabinet has to serve double duty. Derek and Lauren decided to create a shower curtain that would store both their toiletries and washcloths. Lightweight denim and grommets complete the look, which you can easily customize with pieces of ribbon, trim, or fabric patches.

DESIGNERS
**Derek Fagerstrom
and Lauren Smith**

COST
$30

TIME
3 hours

DIFFICULTY
★ ★ ★ ★

MATERIALS

Measuring tape or ruler

Fabric, with thread to match

Sewing machine

Iron

Tailor's chalk or pencil

12 large grommets and
grommet puncher
(available at fabric stores)

Scissors

Hammer

〜〜〜〜〜〜〜〜〜〜〜〜〜〜〜〜〜〜〜〜 INSTRUCTIONS 〜〜〜〜〜〜〜〜〜〜〜〜〜〜〜〜〜〜〜〜〜

BEFORE YOU START: Depending on the width of your tub and whether you'd like your shower curtain pulled taut or draping, calculate your fabric needs. Keep in mind that you may need to piece two lengths of fabric together to meet the tub length. Measure the length of your tub and the distance between your shower curtain bar and the floor. Add a couple of inches to the tub length measurement (more if you want the curtain to drape) and measure the width of the fabric you want before calculating how much you'll need. Remember to calculate extra for making the pouch.

To Make the Curtain

1   If necessary, stitch together two long pieces of fabric to meet the tub length measurement, and press the seam open. Measure and cut the fabric. It should be about 7 inches longer than you want the shower curtain and at least 2 inches wider.

2   Fold both sides under ½ inch and press, then fold under another ½ inch to hide the raw edge. Stitch up both sides using a sewing machine.

3   Fold the top edge under ½ inch and press. Fold under another 3 inches and press, stitching along the fold, about 3 inches from the edge. Repeat on the bottom of the curtain.

4   Using tailor's chalk or a pencil, mark the positions of 9 or 10 grommets along the top hem, then—following the instructions that came with your grommet puncher—snip small holes where the grommets will go, and hammer them into place.

To Make the Storage Pouch

5   To make a pouch like the one pictured, cut out a piece of fabric that measures 16 × 45 inches. Then cut a second piece that measures 16 × 12 inches and a third that measures 16 × 6 inches.

6   Fold under one raw edge along the top side (one of the 16-inch sides) of each of the two small pocket pieces and stitch.

7   Line up all three pieces along the bottom edge and pin together. (If the layers are too thick to fit into your sewing machine, remove one of them and continue.) Fold the raw edges under ¼ inch, press, fold over again ½ inch, and stitch all the way up both sides. Repeat on the bottom of the pocket, stitching through all layers.

8   Stitch one or two channels up the layered pieces to create pockets.

9   Finish the top of the long piece the same way you did with the shower curtain, adding 2 or 3 grommets, and hang on the outside of the shower curtain.

W e've all outgrown a silverware set or two, or lost a fork to a faulty dishwasher, so Kate decided to repurpose her worn-out silverware for a project *outside* the kitchen. By bending her silverware, she created hooks she can use as creative curtain tiebacks. Now even the humblest fork can have a new life in the kitchen.

DESIGNER
Kate Pruitt

COST
$13

TIME
1 hour

DIFFICULTY
★ ★ ★ ★

INSTRUCTIONS

1   Clean and polish all silverware.

2   Hold the fork or clamp the fork handle down to a table and use pliers to bend the tines so they are flat with the face of the fork. Place the mouth of the pliers as far down onto the tine as possible, so you are bending the entire shaft of the tines, not just the tips.

3   Clamp the flat face of the fork down to a table with a piece of scrap wood beneath it. Mark two small dots slightly to the right and left of the center of the fork face with a permanent marker. Use the drill with a ⅜-inch metal drill bit to drill holes at those two dots. Metal drill bits should go through your silverware without too much trouble, but it takes a little time, so be patient. Keep applying pressure and keep your drill vertical.

4   Now the fork is ready to be bent into a hook shape. Decide if you prefer the front or back design on the handle. If you prefer the back of the handle, clamp your fork with the face of the fork right side up. If you prefer the front of the handle, flip the fork over and clamp it down. Clamp the fork directly underneath where the fork stem becomes the fork face.

5   Use the pliers to grip the fork stem and bend it from its horizontal position to a vertical position. Your fork face is now at a right angle to the stem.

6   Unclamp the fork, then reclamp it to the table about 1½ inches down the handle from where you last clamped it. Repeat step 5, bending the handle from its horizontal position to a vertical position. You can experiment with trying to bend the fork in more curved shapes rather than right angles, but this is the cleanest shape you can get with these simple tools.

7   If you wish to paint the fork, lay it on a sheet of newspaper and spray with a coat of primer first. Let the primer dry and then spray with two even coats of color.

8   The fork is now ready to be attached to the wall. Drill into the wall through the two holes you drilled in the fork in step 3 and attach the fork to the wall with screws.

Variation: Spoon Hooks

If you want to use spoons for this project, you must drill one hole in the center of the spoon basin. Then follow the same steps for bending as with the fork, but you want the spoon basin to be facing up when you bend it, which means for spoon curtain hooks you will see the back side of the handle. Spoons will not secure well to a vertical surface if they are flipped over.

MATERIALS

Old silverware
(forks are best)

Two medium clamps

Needle-nose pliers

Scrap wood

Permanent marker

Drill with ⅜-inch
bit for metal

Newspaper (optional)

Spray primer (optional)

Spray paint (optional)

Tip

Forks work best for this project, but you can also use spoons (see Variation). Knives do not work because they are much thicker and do not bend easily.

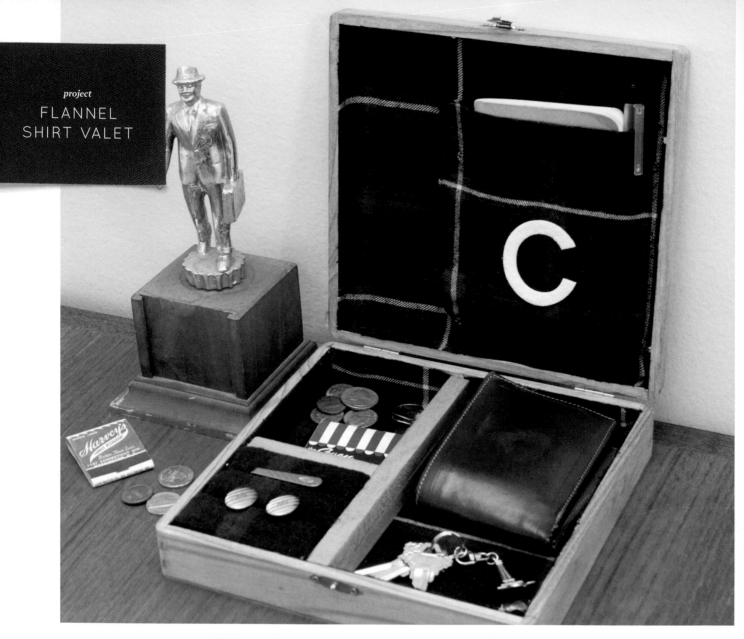

I can always count on Kate to come up with a clever project that involves reusing something I already have around the house. Kate used an old flannel shirt to create this valet as a gift for her boyfriend. This guy-friendly project was made by simply cutting the flannel shirt to fit the inside of the box and then adding some dividers to store smaller items.

〜〜〜〜〜〜〜〜〜〜〜〜〜〜〜〜〜〜〜〜〜〜 INSTRUCTIONS 〜〜〜〜〜〜〜〜〜〜〜〜〜〜〜〜〜〜〜

1   Stain or paint the wood with your desired finish. Allow to dry.

2   Measure the inside floor of the valet and the depth of the sides. If it already has dividers in it, measure the floors and sides of the separate compartments. You will cut one fabric rectangle to line each compartment.

3   Cut off the sleeves of your flannel shirt. Cut the largest flat rectangle you can out of the back of the shirt, cutting right against the seams and underneath the collar. Then lay out the rectangle with the right side of the fabric facedown. Use your ruler to draw the rectangle(s) for the compartments on the back of the fabric. Make the rectangle(s) follow the grid of the plaid. Add a ¼-inch allowance on all sides and cut out the shapes.

4   Paint a thin layer of glue on the floor of your valet, trying not to get any glue on the sides. If you have multiple premade compartments, only paint glue on one of them. Then carefully lay your fabric piece with the right side up onto the glued surface. Smooth out any wrinkles or bumps in the fabric and make sure the pattern is straight. Leave the fabric that will be glued to the side loose; you will glue it in the next step.

5   If your valet has premade compartments, repeat step 4 for each one. Then paint the inner sides of the valet or compartments with glue and smooth the fabric flaps into place, lining the interior of the valet. In the corners, use scissors to make a 45-degree snip in the extra fabric and fold the two flaps so they overlap slightly. Trim excess fabric from the corners. Let dry. Use the X-Acto knife to trim any excess fabric along the top edges.

To Make Your Own Dividers

6   Measure the height of the inside of the tray and cut a balsa wood strip to that measurement. Carefully trim the balsa strip to the length needed for the divider. When the balsa piece slides in snugly, it is ready to be attached. Stain or paint the balsa wood, if desired. Make very tiny pencil marks on both the top and bottom edges of the tray as guidelines for setting in the divider piece. Spread a thin line of hot glue along the bottom edge of the balsa strip and insert it into the valet, aligning it with the guide marks. Repeat this step to add subdividers.

To Create a Cuff Link Insert

7   Measure the compartment for the cuff links and cut a rectangular block of foam that is just as wide, but ¼ inch longer than the compartment. This is so when you fit the foam in, it has to compress slightly to create a snug fit for your cuff links. Then measure and use a marker to draw three lines equidistant from one another along the top of the foam rectangle. Use your ruler and X-Acto knife to slice through the foam along those lines. Slice about three-quarters of the way into the foam, not all the way through.

8   Cut a rectangle of the shirt that is as wide as the block of foam and twice as long, so the extra fabric can be tucked into the slices you made. Spread a thin layer of glue on the top of the first section of foam and lay the fabric onto it. Carefully spread glue onto both inside edges of the first slice. Fold the fabric down into it as deep as it will go, keeping the pattern straight. Repeat for the other slices. Wrap the fabric around so it overlaps the underside of the block of foam by an inch. Cut excess fabric and glue the flaps down to the underside of the foam block.

9   Spread glue on the base of the cuff link compartment and slide the foam block in, squishing the foam toward the center to allow room on the side to squeeze in a little hot glue. Then release the foam block so it settles into the compartment snugly. Clean any excess glue immediately with a cotton swab.

To Make the Pocket Detail

10 Cut the whole pocket out of the shirt, up to the edges of the pocket but keeping the sewn seams intact. Glue the back of the pocket to the inside of the valet anywhere you choose, making sure to cover the entire surface of the back of the pocket with glue and pressing firmly to fully adhere the pocket. Add a monogram detail or any special touches.

Every few months Design*Sponge editor Kate Pruitt would purchase a new scratch pad for her cat from a local grocery store. Upon close inspection she realized it was basically a box full of corrugated cardboard! Rather than spend more money on scratchers, Kate decided to find a new use for her old shipping boxes by creating a recycled cat scratcher with a decorative edge. Now her cat can scratch away, and Kate has found a new way to recycle old cardboard boxes.

DESIGNER
Kate Pruitt

COST
$30 or less

TIME
2 hours

DIFFICULTY
★ ★ ★ ☆

MATERIALS

Cardboard boxes
(all sizes, all kinds, at least
5 medium-sized boxes)

Ruler

X-Acto knife

Masking tape

Scrap paper, felt, or fabric
(optional)

Glue (optional)

~~~~~~~~~~~~~~~~~~~~~~ INSTRUCTIONS ~~~~~~~~~~~~~~~~~~~~~~

1 Choose a height for the pad (Kate's is 4 inches tall).

2 Measure and cut your cardboard in identical-width strips. Cut so that the ridges in the cardboard are going across the width.

3 Start rolling the cardboard in your hands and bending at each corrugation. The cardboard will start to curl naturally.

4 Tightly wind one strip into a cylinder and tape closed. This will be the core of your round.

5 Add another piece of cardboard at the edge where the first ended and secure it with two pieces of masking tape. Choose which side will be the top, and make sure that side is always even. It is less important if the other side is slightly uneven—it will still sit properly and the top will look perfect.

6 Keep adding until the pad is at least 1 foot in diameter. Tape each piece right next to the end of the last piece and keep the coiling tight.

7 Cut your paper or fabric to size and wrap it around the outside. Tape to secure.

8 Trace the bottom circumference of the scratcher onto the scrap paper or fabric and cut out the circle. Tape or glue to the bottom.

Tip

Catnip can be sprinkled onto the scratcher from the top— the fabric or paper liner on the bottom will keep it from coming through.

DESIGNER
Kate Pruitt

COST
$10

TIME
3 hours

DIFFICULTY
★ ★ ★ ☆

Inspired by a marble bust statue she saw in a magazine, Design*Sponge editor Kate Pruitt decided to create her own budget-friendly version to showcase her favorite jewelry. Using her computer to create a silhouette template (which you can download online at www.designsponge.com/templates), Kate created a wooden bust that is perfect for displaying on your dresser or countertops or for hanging on the wall.

~~~~~~~~~~~~~~~~~~ INSTRUCTIONS ~~~~~~~~~~~~~~~~~~

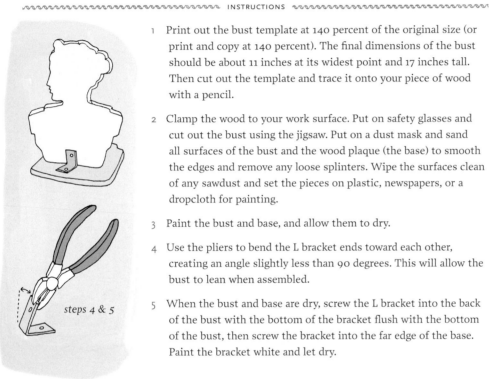

steps 4 & 5

1   Print out the bust template at 140 percent of the original size (or print and copy at 140 percent). The final dimensions of the bust should be about 11 inches at its widest point and 17 inches tall. Then cut out the template and trace it onto your piece of wood with a pencil.

2   Clamp the wood to your work surface. Put on safety glasses and cut out the bust using the jigsaw. Put on a dust mask and sand all surfaces of the bust and the wood plaque (the base) to smooth the edges and remove any loose splinters. Wipe the surfaces clean of any sawdust and set the pieces on plastic, newspapers, or a dropcloth for painting.

3   Paint the bust and base, and allow them to dry.

4   Use the pliers to bend the L bracket ends toward each other, creating an angle slightly less than 90 degrees. This will allow the bust to lean when assembled.

5   When the bust and base are dry, screw the L bracket into the back of the bust with the bottom of the bracket flush with the bottom of the bust, then screw the bracket into the far edge of the base. Paint the bracket white and let dry.

Variation: Wall-Mount Version

Instead of using a base, follow these steps to hang your bust on a wall.

1   Use 2-inch screws to secure a 1¾-inch-thick scrap of wood to the backside of the bust, centered in the chest area a few inches down from the neck. (Make sure the screws will not come through the front of the bust.)

2   Screw in two cup hooks on the right and left corners of the outermost top edge of the scrap piece of wood (farthest from the bust surface). The hooks should open downward.

3   Paint the whole attachment, and let it dry. Hang by two nails (or screws) on a wall.

MATERIALS

Bust template

Piece of wood at least ½ inch thick and 12 × 17 inches in measure

Pencil

2 table clamps

Safety goggles and dust mask

Jigsaw (with a fine tooth blade for detailed cuts)

9 × 12-inch wood plaque (these are available at craft stores)

Sandpaper

Plastic drop cloth

White paint

Paintbrush

4-inch metal L bracket (usually come in pairs at the hardware store)

Two pairs of pliers

Four ¾-inch screws

Screwdriver

Tip

The key to using a jigsaw is working on small areas. Don't try to cut along the entire outline of the template. Instead, cut away at the outline in small sections, coming at the edges from all different angles to get the best, cleanest cut around the shape. This means you will be making very small cuts, especially around the lips and nose, but if you work slowly and carefully, you'll get good, clean lines. Adjust and reclamp the cutout for better cutting angles as needed.

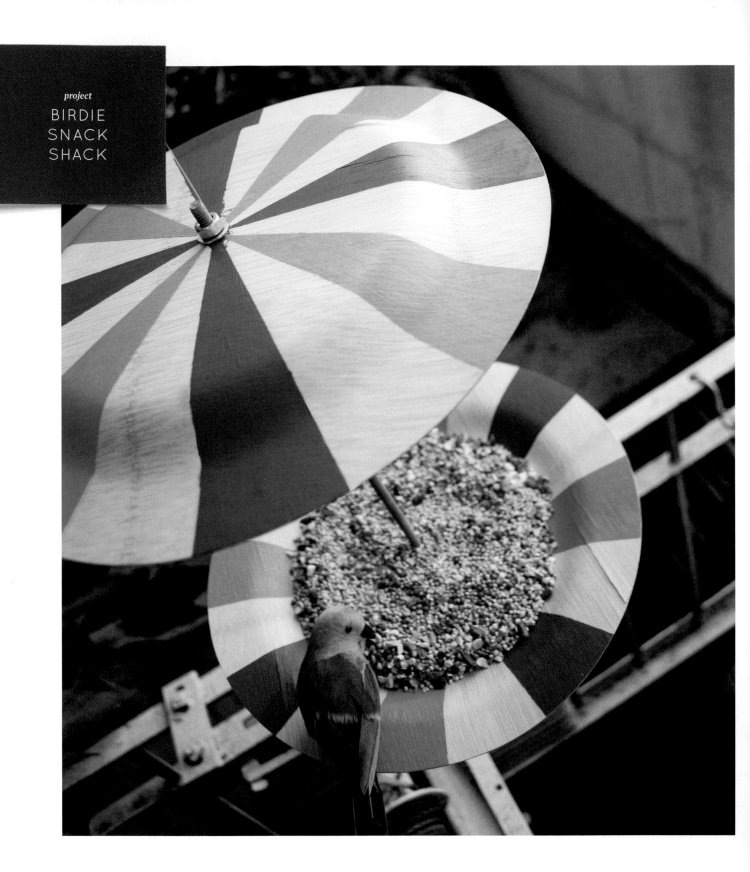

Who says birds can't enjoy a day at the amusement park? Design*
Sponge editors Derek Fagerstrom and Lauren Smith decided to
create a carnival-colored bird feeder out of two bamboo dinner
plates, a piece of threaded rod, and a pinecone. Inexpensive and easy to make,
this custom bird feeder now serves as a miniature snack stand for Derek and
Lauren's backyard birds.

DESIGNER
Derek Fagerstrom
and Lauren Smith

COST
$10

TIME
1 hour

DIFFICULTY
★ ★ ★

~~~~~~~~~~ INSTRUCTIONS ~~~~~~~~~~

1   Drill a hole through the center of each plate.

2   Mark, tape off, and paint a design on the bottom of one plate and the top of another (Derek
    and Lauren also painted the all-thread with orange paint). If desired, put a clear coat of
    polyurethane on the plates to protect them from the elements.

3   Once the paint is dry, sandwich each plate with washers and nuts, and attach one to the top
    and one to the bottom of the threaded rod.

4   Tie a piece of monofilament or twine to the top of the bird feeder for hanging (in particularly
    wet or snowy areas, hang it under an eave or awning) and fill the bottom plate with bird seed.
    For an extra special treat, coat a pinecone with peanut butter and roll it in bird seed, then
    attach it to the bottom of the feeder with monofilament.

MATERIALS

Drill with ⅜-inch drill bit

2 plates
(we used 11-inch bamboo
dinner plates from Bambu)

Ruler

Pencil

Blue painters' tape

Acrylic paint (nontoxic)

Water-based polyurethane
(optional)

Paintbrush

12-inch piece of
¼-inch threaded rod
(available at
hardware stores)

Four ½-inch nuts
and washers

Monofilament or twine

Bird seed

Pinecone (optional)

DESIGNER
Kate Pruitt

COST
$30 or less

TIME
2 hours

DIFFICULTY
★ ★ ★ ★

D esign*Sponge editor Kate Pruitt was bored with the prefab, garden-store bird feeders she always saw in her town, so she decided to create her own. Using wooden bowls from Ikea, sisal rope, and a soda bottle, she designed a playful acorn-shaped bird feeder for her backyard. When the birds have finished, Kate can create a new birdseed mold and hang it again.

MATERIALS

Soda bottle
(the base should fit inside
the bowl nicely; you can also
use a terra-cotta pot for this)

Scissors

Drill

Cooking oil spray

Sisal rope

1 packet of gelatin

Birdseed mix

Wood bowl

2 pieces of ¼-inch wooden
dowel, the same length as
the bowl diameter

INSTRUCTIONS

1 Wash and dry the soda bottle. Cut 4 inches from the base with scissors. Then drill a hole in the bottle cap that you can fit the rope through.

2 Lubricate the inside of the bottle with the cooking spray to help the bird seed mold slide out easily. Then slide a length of rope through the bottle cap leaving 5 inches poking out of the cap and 12 inches coming out of the other opening.

3 Make the gelatin according to the directions, using ice-cold water so it will set up quickly. Add bird seed a little at a time to the gelatin and mix so the seed is completely coated and starts to bind together. (This mold used 2–3 cups of birdseed and a half packet of gelatin. Don't use too much gelatin; the birds don't like it.)

4 Fill the bottle with the bird see mix, using one hand to hold the rope in the center of the bottle and the other to pack the birdseed firmly in around the rope. When the mold is full, pack it down again. Place it in the fridge for a couple of hours to set, then take it out and let it dry for a couple of hours. When it's ready, tap the bottle gently to release the seed. Taking off the bottle cap will help, and you can gently push from that end while pulling from the other end to release the shape.

5 At the round end of the birdseed mold, carefully unravel the rope to obtain two strands. Use the strands to tie the two dowels onto the bottom of the mold in criss-cross formation as a bird perch. Snip off any extra rope.

6 Drill a hole in the center of the wooden bowl. Tie a knot an inch or two above the flat end of the birdseed base and slide the wood bowl onto the rope upside down. Tie another knot right above the bowl and then make a large knot at the top for hanging. Snip any extra rope.

DESIGNER
Kate Pruitt

COST
$17
(for ten place settings)

TIME
1—2 hours

DIFFICULTY
★★★☆

Inspired by British designer Lisa Stickley's china table linen series, Kate Pruitt decided to design her own version. To celebrate the spring weather, Kate focused on a floral theme, printing each image onto inkjet transfer paper and then ironing it onto her napkins and place mats. The key to success with this project is to use simple, high-resolution images that can be cut into one clean shape. If florals aren't your thing, consider using simple letters to create a monogram or a custom place mat for a birthday party.

INSTRUCTIONS

MATERIALS

Photos of food, dishes, figurines, plates, etc.— anything you want, but make sure it is high-resolution

Computer

Inkjet printer transfer paper

Inkjet color printer

Napkins and place mats (these were from Ikea and cost less than a dollar each)

Iron

Scissors

1   Upload your photos to your computer and adjust the size to your liking. Make a couple of black-and-white prints on 8½ × 11 paper to check that you like the size and detail on your photos. You want your images to be something you can cut all the way around to have a freestanding object.

2   When the images are ready and sized, print them in color on the transfer paper according to the directions on the package. Use the highest quality setting on your printer. If you don't have a printer at home, a local print shop can print images for you.

3   Allow the transfer prints to dry. Meanwhile, iron all of the wrinkles out of your place mats and napkins on high temperature with no steam. Allow these to cool.

4   Cut out your shapes from the transfer prints. Trim all excess off, cutting right up to the edge of your subject. Lay the transfer paper down on the fabric and iron it according to the directions.

5   Continue following the transfer instructions for cooling, peeling off the backing, and setting the image.

NOTE: Transfers print in reverse, so if you wish to work with text, you must reverse the image on your computer before printing.

W hen it comes to vintage clothing, Amy Merrick is Design✻ Sponge's resident expert. Her collection of dresses and accessories is legendary, so it was no surprise that her clothes would eventually inspire a project. Amy used leftover bits of fabric to create fabric-covered hangers for her favorite vintage finds. Even the saddest wire hanger will feel proud after being covered with a colorful patterned fabric.

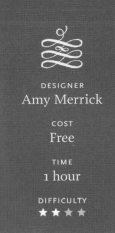

DESIGNER
Amy Merrick

COST
Free

TIME
1 hour

DIFFICULTY
★ ★ ★ ★

~~~~~~~~~~~~~~~ INSTRUCTIONS ~~~~~~~~~~~~~~~

1 Trace a hanger onto a piece of scrap paper to make a pattern. Add ½-inch seam allowance to the top of the pattern and 1½-inch allowance on the bottom.

2 Trace the pattern onto the fabric twice and cut out the pieces.

3 Hem the bottoms by turning them up ¼ inch and stitching. Pin right sides together and stitch along the top, leaving a ½-inch slot open in the center to slip the hanger through. The bottom stays open so you can remove the hanger if needed.

4 Turn the cover right side out and iron it. I made a small bow to hand stitch at the opening because I'm girly like that.

MATERIALS
—————

Wire hanger

Scrap paper

Ruler

Fabric measuring at least 14 × 9 inches

Scissors

Sewing machine

Thread

Pins

Iron

I
f you've got a black thumb like I do, a terrarium can be a great way to bring something green into your home without the maintenance level of larger plants. Tassy Zimmerman, of Sprout Home nursery and floral studio in Brooklyn, created this terrarium as the perfect miniature landscape for those with limited space, gardening skills, or the time needed to care for trickier plants.

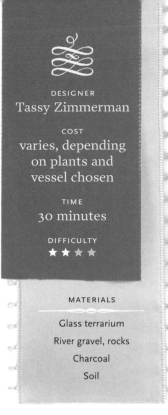

DESIGNER
Tassy Zimmerman

COST
varies, depending on plants and vessel chosen

TIME
30 minutes

DIFFICULTY
★ ★ ★ ★

MATERIALS

Glass terrarium

River gravel, rocks

Charcoal

Soil

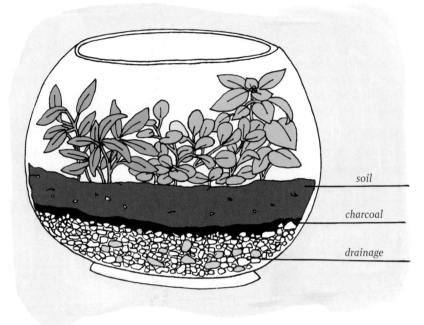

soil

charcoal

drainage

〜〜〜〜〜〜〜〜〜〜〜〜〜〜〜〜〜〜 INSTRUCTIONS 〜〜〜〜〜〜〜〜〜〜〜〜〜〜〜〜〜〜

1   Select a container. Before choosing a container, you must decide what you wish to grow in your terrarium. All plants in a terrarium should have similar light, moisture, and other environmental needs. If you want to grow sun-loving plants in natural light, use an open terrarium. If you want to grow plants that require high humidity, the container should be closed. For any container, it's advisable to choose slow-growing plants.

2   Add 1 to 4 inches of drainage material to the terrarium. Crushed river gravel works well, but any small stones or bits of broken pottery will do. Top this with a thin layer of charcoal.

3   The kind of soil used will depend on the type of plants you wish to grow (cacti/succulent soil vs. potting soil). Use enough soil so that you can dig a hole for the root ball of the plants. For example, if you are adding a fern that has a 4-inch root ball to the terrarium, you will need to add at least 4 inches of soil. Generally speaking, the depth of the drainage material, charcoal, and soil should equal about one-third of the terrarium's height.

4   Make sure any necessary pruning is done prior to placing the plants in the terrarium, and that the plants are free of insects and disease. Set the largest plants in the terrarium first, followed by the smaller plants. Groundcover should be added last. Don't forget to have fun with it and add some small animal figurines.

DESIGNER
Halligan Norris

COST
$50—$90

TIME
5—6 hours

DIFFICULTY
★ ★ ★ ☆

A good friend of Halligan's told her that when she was growing up her family didn't have a lot of extra money to spend on furniture Instead of saving for new pieces around the house, her clever mother used found electrical spools as coffee tables! The friend's story of her mom's resourcefulness inspired Halligan to reinterpret this idea with a new spin as a round library.

~~~~~~~~~~~~~~~ INSTRUCTIONS ~~~~~~~~~~~~~~~

MATERIALS

Construction spool
(try your local junkyard, thrift shops, curbs, and eBay)

Electric sander or sandpaper
(80 and 220 grit)

Duct tape

Scissors

Trammel point

Pencil

Compass

Drill

¾-inch spade bit

Ruler

¾-inch dowels
(length and number based on the size of your spool)

Band saw or handsaw

Dead blow mallet or hammer

One quart of primer paint
(optional)

One quart of paint,
color of your choice

Paintbrush

Clear spray paint sealer
(available at your local hardware or home improvement store)

Three rolling casters (Ikea sells great affordable casters) and mounting screws

Screwdriver

1 Sand the spool to remove all dirt and splinters. Be careful—the splinters on these things can be nasty.

2 To figure out where to place the dowels, use the duct tape to put an X over the center of the spool's hole. Eyeball the middle of the tape X, and place the end of your trammel point there, rotating it to draw a guideline 3½ inches from the edge of the spool. Don't remove the tape; you will need it again later.

3 Use a compass to mark drilling points approximately 6 inches apart along the guideline, depending on the diameter of your spool. (Mark a spot on the guideline and place the point of your compass—set 6 inches open—on it, then move the other arm of the compass to mark the next spot. Keep going until you reach your starting position.)

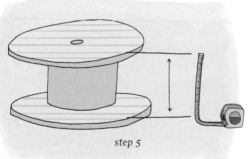

step 5

4 Drill holes through the top of the spool using a ¾-inch spade bit.

5 To figure the length to cut the dowels, measure the length of the distance from the top surface of the spool to the top surface of the base.

6 Cut dowels to length and sand ends to remove any splinters.

7 Drive the dowels into the holes using a dead blow mallet or a hammer. The dowels should be very tight and sturdy when driven down to touch the spool base.

8 To make the tabletop's decorative painted circle, use your tape X and trammel point to draw a guideline 4½ inches from the edge of the table.

9 Paint base of spool, top of spool, and the dowels. I recommend starting with a coat of primer, followed by two layers of the desired color.

10 After the paint has dried, seal the entire table with a clear spray, sanding with 220 sandpaper in between coats.

11 Space the three casters evenly in a triangular pattern, mark the holes with a pencil and use a drill to screw them into place. I used some from Ikea that came with instructions.

Design*Sponge editor Kate Pruitt had been mulling over this chair bench idea for quite some time before committing to its construction. The hardest part was finding three mismatched chairs with the same seat height, and the rest involved ½-inch MDF, some clamps, decorative fabric, and 2-inch-thick foam. "I absolutely love how this turned out, and I adore the mismatched quirkiness of it."

1   Use the drill to remove one left and one right arm from each of the armchairs. Use pliers to remove any broken or old screws. Then clean, sand, and stain or paint the chairs, as desired.

2   Assemble the chairs in the bench arrangement with the fronts aligned and the front legs touching. (There may be space between the chairs toward the back of the seats but this is all right.) Measure the space between each chair cushion at the front and back of the chairs and record these amounts. Then remove the seat cushions. Strip the seats of all foam and fabric to reveal the wooden seat pieces. These pieces will be the templates for your bench cushion.

3   Lay the piece of fiberboard or MDF on the ground. Place the seat cushion templates onto the fiberboard in the same order as the chairs, with the front of the templates flush with the fiberboard's front edge. Space the templates using the distances measured in step 2.

4   Trace the three shapes on the fiberboard with a marker and remove the cushion templates. The back of your bench cushion will not be a straight line if the chairs are different depths. (If you prefer to have an even, straight back on the cushion, a small portion of the deeper chair seat may show when the cushion is in place.) Mark this side of the seat template as the top.

5   Once the shape is completely drawn out and all measurements have been double-checked, clamp the fiberboard down. Wearing safety goggles, cut out the cushion shape with the jigsaw, cutting along the outer side of the lines as a precaution. When finished, lay the cushion shape on the chairs to check the fit. Remove any extra material if needed.

6   Lay the seat foam on a clean surface and place the wooden cushion shape on it, top side up. Trace the shape of the seat onto the foam with a permanent marker. Remove the wooden shape and cut the foam with a box cutter, following your traced lines carefully. Check that the foam and wooden seat match. Mark the top of the foam with an X.

7   Lay the upholstery fabric facedown on a clean work surface and put the foam and seat facedown on top of it. Pull the fabric firmly and staple it to the back at even, frequent intervals, making sure the foam stays exactly aligned with the seat shape. Cut slits in the fabric to accommodate corners, bringing the fabric over to the back in smooth folds. When finished, flip the cushion over and check how it looks. Restaple any uneven areas.

8   Place the bench cushion on top of the chairs, sliding it into place. Check that the chair fronts are aligned with the cushion front, and that the seat backs fit with the back of the cushion form. When everything is fitted, secure the cushion by screwing through the existing holes in the chair frames up into the fiberboard. You can use the original screws that you removed earlier, but these are often worn or rusted, so I recommend using new screws of the same size.

9   Use metal mending plates or 1 × 2-inch scraps of wood to reinforce the bench by connecting the seat frames where they meet, two at the back and two at the front. Secure them with several screws to each chair. The plates do not have to lie completely level to the ground and will not be seen underneath the seat, but they allow the bench to be moved and lifted more easily.

NOTE: It is important that you find chairs that have similar seat depths and are the same seat height when the cushions are removed. If the height is off by a fraction of an inch, you can compensate by using felt pads under the chair legs. When you are looking for chairs, you will observe that a lot of armchairs have arms that are simply held in by screws that you can remove very easily: one on the underside of the seat and one on the inside of the side of the chair. Choose this type of armchair for this project.

DESIGNER
Kate Pruitt

COST
$95

TIME
1 day

DIFFICULTY
★★★☆

MATERIALS

2 wooden chairs with arms;
1 wooden chair without arms
(see Note)

Drill

Pliers

Sandpaper

Stain or paint (optional)

Measuring tape or ruler

½-inch-thick MDF or
fiberboard measuring
24 × 60 inches
(size may vary based on the
size of the chairs)

Permanent marker

Clamps

Safety goggles

Jigsaw

2-inch-thick foam measuring
24 × 60 inches
(may vary based on the size
of the chair bench)

Box cutter or knife

Fabric for the upholstered
cushion measuring at least
36 × 68 inches
(may vary based on the size
of the chair bench)

Heavy-duty staple gun
and staples

Scissors

Screws (1⅝ inches)

4 metal mending plates

Inspired by the Canadian design team Loyal Loot Collective's popular log bowls, Kate decided to use some cut logs from a fallen tree in her yard to create lined wooden "jars" to hold small accessories like jewelry and cuff links. If you've never used a paddle bit on your drill before, this is a great project to start with—it's simple and straightforward and will leave you with the perfect little pocket for storing treasures.

DESIGNER
Kate Pruitt

COST
$25

TIME
2–3 hours

DIFFICULTY
★ ★ ★ ★

MATERIALS

Safety goggles

Logs
(about 4 inches in diameter
and at least 12 inches long)

Compound miter saw

Pen

Ruler

Table vise

Rag or towel

Drill

2½-inch paddle bit
(also known as a boring bit)

Sandpaper
(coarse and fine grits)

Wood sealant

Paintbrush

Two sheets of craft felt

Scissors

Hot glue gun
and glue sticks

~~~~~~~~~~~ INSTRUCTIONS ~~~~~~~~~~~

1   Wearing safety goggles, cut your logs to the desired height with the saw. If they are already at the desired height, use the saw to cut a flat, level base for them if they can't stand upright.

2   Make a mark 2–2½ inches down from the top of your log, which will be the height of the lid. Make a clean, straight cut along the mark with your saw.

3   Mark the center of the top of the log base with your pen. This is the center of the hole you will make for the cavity.

4   Tightly clamp the log base into the table vise with a towel around it to protect the exterior (you might want to recruit a very strong person for this).

5   Place the pointed tip of the paddle bit onto the center point and begin to drill into the log. When the hole fills with sawdust, pull the bit out and blow the sawdust out of the hole to clear it, then start drilling again. This takes some muscle and patience, because you are essentially drilling into a huge knot. Keep pulling in and out of the hole to clear the sawdust and check that you are drilling vertically rather than at an angle. Stand on a chair to get extra leverage. Stop drilling when the hole is about 2 inches deep.

6   Using the coarse sandpaper, remove rough splinters from the inside of the hole. When it feels like all of the loose wood bits are gone, go over it again with fine sandpaper. Also sand the tops and bottoms of the log lid and base. Then wipe the surfaces clean of all dust. Using a rag, apply a thin layer of sealant on all cut surfaces: the top and bottom of the base, the top and bottom of the lid, and inside the drilled hole. Let the sealant dry.

7   Measure the exact diameter of the hole and the depth of the sides. Cut a strip of felt that is as deep as the hole and long enough to wrap around the circumference of the inside with a little overlap. Also cut out a circle to fit into the base of the hole.

8   Apply hot glue to the base of the hole. Place the felt circle down and smooth it out. Apply hot glue to the wall of the hole, tilting the log so the glue doesn't drip onto the felt base. Lay in the felt strip so it covers the interior surface; smooth out any lumps or wrinkles. Use scissors to trim any excess around the top.

When simple container gardening isn't enough, sometimes a change of location and vessel can be just the ticket. Kate decided she wanted to create a quirky garden that she could move around easily, so she used an inexpensive thrift store find to create her custom "herb chair." Inspired by the popularity of vertical gardens and sprouting city rooftops, Kate felt that this project was a great small-scale expression of the trend.

DESIGNER
Kate Pruitt

COST
$25

TIME
1 day

DIFFICULTY
★ ★ ★ ★

MATERIALS

Wooden chair with no cross-brace bars underneath the seat

Wood sealant

Paint (optional)

Paintbrush

Plastic planter bowl and matching drainage dish

Permanent marker

Drill with ½-inch bit

Protective goggles

Jigsaw

Hot glue gun and glue sticks

3 bags of decorative moss (found at craft stores with floral departments)

Latex gloves

Scissors

2 small hooks or knobs

Plants

Planter soil

INSTRUCTIONS

1   Find a chair that has no cross-bracing or supports beneath the seat—just four legs and a simple seat that is at least 4 inches larger than the diameter of the planter bowl. The chair can have an upholstered seat or a wooden seat, but if the chair is upholstered, remove the seat from the chair base by removing the four screws that hold it in place. Use pliers to remove all the staples holding the upholstery on the seat and pull off all the fabric and foam, exposing the wooden seat piece. Reattach the seat piece to the chair.

2   Paint the entire chair with several coats of weather-protective sealant. If you wish to repaint the chair, do this first and then follow with the coats of protective sealant. Allow the chair to dry completely.

3   Flip your planter bowl upside down and place it on the seat of the chair. Trace its outline with a marker. Then draw a second circle directly centered within the first that is ¼ inch smaller in diameter.

4   Drill a hole in the center of that circle with the ½-inch drill bit, so that a jigsaw blade can fit into it. Wearing goggles, use the jigsaw to cut out the circle, beginning at the center point and working around in several cuts. When done, the planter bowl should fit into the hole exactly and the lip of the planter should lie level with the chair seat.

5   Drill small drainage holes in the bottom of the planter bowl if it doesn't already have them. Then slide the bowl into the hole in the chair, holding it in place to keep the bowl and seat flush. Screw through the lip of the bowl into the wood chair to secure it in three equidistant spots.

6   Flip the chair over and use glue to secure the matching drainage dish to the base of the bowl. This will allow water to drain, but keeps the dish connected to the bowl and the chair. Allow the glue to dry and flip the chair back over.

7   Wearing latex gloves, cover the seat and the rim of the bowl with the moss, using hot glue to secure the moss to the chair. Glue the moss over the rim of the bowl and continue about 2 inches down into the bowl. Use scissors to shape the moss.

8   Mark the desired location of your hooks on the back of the chair with a pencil. Attach your small hooks or knobs at those points either by screwing in the hooks or drilling an appropriately sized hole for the knobs.

9   Plant your garden pot with herbs or small flowers. Hang your garden gloves, snips, or other tools on the hooks. This chair can be placed indoors or outdoors.

Design*Sponge editor Kate Pruitt had a huge collection of scarves and vintage linens that were just waiting to be used. She felt they were worthy of a beautiful display and decided to turn them into an oval fabric banner that would be infinitely reusable for special occasions. Kate started with BON VOYAGE to celebrate a friend's move, but a simple HAPPY BIRTHDAY or HAPPY HOLIDAYS design could easily be reused year after year.

To Make the Banner Pieces

1   Iron all your scarves and fabric to get rid of any wrinkles or creases.

2   Decide on a shape for your banner pieces. They can be triangular pennants, ovals, circles, rectangles, anything you wish. Each piece should be about 4 × 6 inches or 5 × 7 inches; much bigger and spelling out messages will become very space-consuming. Draw or trace this shape onto the card stock or scrap cardboard to create a template.

3   Lay out your fabric for the backing facedown. Lay the muslin or canvas fabric over it. Lastly, lay the scarves on top with the front of the scarf facing up. Pin the three fabrics together in several spots to keep them in place. Lay the template on top of each scarf and trace the outline with a pencil or fine-point pen. The template should fit more than once on each scarf. You will need about 60 pieces for a full set of letters, or you can make as many as you need to spell a specific phrase, and add more to the set over time. Once the banner pieces are all drawn out, place a pin through all three fabrics in the center of each piece and carefully cut them all out.

4   Cut the ribbon into 120 pieces that are 10 inches long, cutting two pieces for each banner piece. Fold two ribbon pieces in half and pin each fold between the middle and bottom layers of fabric on the top left and top right sides of a banner piece. The folded ribbons should be pinned about ½ inch in and they should be spaced so that when the ribbons are tied to a horizontal line, the banner piece will hang down straight. Repeat for the rest of the banner pieces.

5   Starting with one piece, sew ¼ inch from the edge all the way around the piece. Make sure to sew over the fold of both ribbons. Repeat with the rest of the banner pieces, removing pins as you go.

To Apply the Letters

6   Now all the banner pieces are ready to receive their letters. The recommended breakdown for a versatile set of alphabet banner pieces is to make two of each consonant and three of each vowel and the consonants *R, S,* and *T.* You can do a combination of many things: felt appliqués, iron-on letters, embroidered letters, fabric-painted letters—anything you wish.

Attach the letters as follows:

For felt letters   Print out the letters from your computer and cut them out of the paper. Trace them reversed onto the felt and cut them out. Use hot glue or fabric glue to attach the felt letters to the banner pieces.

For iron-on letters   Follow the instructions on the package of iron-on letters, making sure you put a layer of fabric between the iron and the banner piece so the iron will not damage the possibly fragile scarf fabric.

For embroidered letters   Lightly draw the letter on the banner piece with a pencil and go over the outline with embroidery thread, starting from the back.

For painted letters   Lightly draw or trace the letter on the banner piece with a pencil. Go over the outline with fabric paint, using a small brush and working slowly.

7   Tie the banner pieces to the rope or twine in the desired order, and hang.

DESIGNER
Kate Pruitt

COST
$30

TIME
1 day

DIFFICULTY
★★★☆

MATERIALS

Vintage scarves, hankies, dish towels, fabric, etc. (about the yardage of 15 large scarves)

Iron

1 sheet of card stock or thin scrap cardboard

Pencil

2 yards of patterned fabric for backing

2 yards of medium-weight plain muslin, canvas, or quilting fabric

Pins

Scissors

34 yards of thin cotton or silk ribbon (⅛–¼-inch width)

Sewing machine

Computer and printer (for making letter templates)

10 squares of craft felt (or 1 yard)

Hot glue gun and glue sticks

Iron-on letters (optional)

Embroidery thread and needle

Fabric paint and small brush (optional)

Rope or twine, cut to desired length

Derek Fagerstrom and Lauren Smith decorated their new throw pillows with a customized typographic appliqué using their favorite fonts and various pieces of colored felt they had around the house. "We love that every font has a distinct personality, and wanted to use our favorites so each pillow would speak to our personal styles and typographic interests."

DESIGNERS
Derek Fagerstrom and Lauren Smith

COST
$20

TIME
2 hours

DIFFICULTY
★★★☆

MATERIALS

1½ yards linen

Computer/printer paper

Scissors

Four 8 × 10-inch pieces of different colored wool felt (ultrasuede or vinyl would also work—use material that doesn't fray when you cut it)

Straight pins

Sewing machine

Thread

Iron

Two 18-inch square pillow inserts

~~~~~~~~~~~~~~ INSTRUCTIONS ~~~~~~~~~~~~~~

1 Cut out linen pieces: One 19-inch square and two 19 × 15-inch pieces per pillow.

2 Find a font you like and print out templates from any design or word processing program on your computer. We printed two versions of each letter, one slightly larger than the other. Cut out paper templates.

3 Pin the letters to the felt pieces and carefully cut them out.

4 Line up one of your larger letters in the center of a 19-inch-square piece of linen and pin. Machine- or hand-stitch the letter in place.

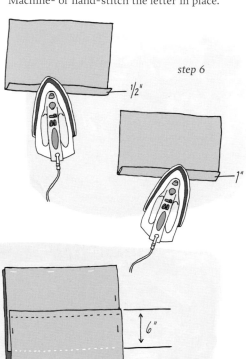

step 6

½"

1"

step 7

6"

5 Pin the smaller letter on top of the larger letter and stitch.

6 For the pillow back, on one long (19-inch) edge of each of the two 19 × 15-inch pieces fold over ½ inch and press with a hot iron. Fold over another 1 inch and press again. Then stitch along the edge with your sewing machine.

7 With right sides together, line up the two back pieces on the front piece so that the unfinished long edges are on opposite sides of the front piece and the finished edges overlap by 6 inches in the center. This will create a flap where the pillow can be inserted. Pin the pieces in position.

8 Stitch around all four sides of the pillow cover, and trim off excess material at corners before turning it right-side out. Insert pillow into cover.

E rik Anderson, a designer at Gerardot & Co., had always wanted to add some tiki-style torches to his patio to help keep the mosquitoes away, but wanted to find a more modern design that would suit his personal style. Unable to locate the perfect match in stores or online, Erik decided to create his own version from recycled wine bottles and inexpensive hardware-store fixtures.

DESIGNER
Erik Anderson

COST
$15

TIME
Less than 1 hour

DIFFICULTY
★ ★ ★ ☆

~~~~~~~~~~~~~~~~~~~ INSTRUCTIONS ~~~~~~~~~~~~~~~~~~~

To Assemble the Hanger

1 Decide where to mount the torch. Position the top plate connector to the mounting surface and mark the holes for where the screws will go. Predrill the screws and attach the plate connector.

2 Screw in the ⅜-inch/16 threaded rod until it stops (Channellock pliers are helpful for this part). Then thread the two hex nuts onto the rod and tighten one all the way down to the point where the rod meets the top connector plate. Leave the other hex nut at the outer end so it can be used to secure the split ring hanger.

3 Thread on the split ring hanger just far enough so that the rod is flush with the inside of the ring. Turn the second hex nut to snug it up against the split ring hanger.

To Assemble the Bottle

4 Carefully and tightly wrap the ½-inch end of the copper coupling with the Teflon tape. Keep each wrap nice and clean so that it creates a smooth, even surface. Continue building up the tape until the coupling fits very snugly into the opening of your bottle. Then insert the wick into the coupling until it sticks up about ¼ inch. (The Tiki brand replacement wicks are about ⅜ inch in diameter so they fit really well. Once they absorb the torch oil they're even tighter.)

5 Unscrew the split ring hanger on one side and position the bottle neck into the ring. Then flip the front half of the ring back into place and tighten the hanger evenly on both sides. You may need to loosen the other side to make sure both sides are even. Do not overtighten the hanger—you don't want to break the glass.

6 Use a funnel to fill the bottle with torch oil. (Erik uses Tiki's BiteFighter because it's clear and seems to do a good job of keeping the mosquitoes away.) Insert the coupling and wick into the top of the bottle and twist it snugly into place. Give the wick a few minutes to absorb the oil before lighting it. Use the copper cap to keep the wick dry when the torch is not in use.

SAFETY NOTE: This project is for outdoor use only. For safety reasons, use only fuel made specifically for outdoor torches. Tiki brand recommends that the wick never be set higher than 1 inch. Exercise the same discretion and common sense that you would with any small open flame.

NOTE: If you'd prefer that your hardware keep its shiny, unweathered look, you can give it several coats of clear polyurethane before you mount it. Personally, I think a weathered patina will add a nice element of character.

MATERIALS

Copper top plate connector (threaded for ⅜-inch/16 threaded rod)

Drill or power screwdriver

Two #10 × 1-inch zinc plated wood screws (if mounting the torch to wood)

⅜-inch/16 zinc-plated threaded rod (Erik bought a 3-foot-long rod and cut it down to eight 4½-inch rods using a hacksaw)

Channellock pliers (optional)

Two hex nuts (threaded for ⅜-inch/16 threaded rod)

1-inch split ring hanger (threaded for ⅜-inch/16 threaded rod)

½ × ⅜-inch copper coupling

½-inch-wide Teflon tape

Empty wine bottle (use any bottle as long as it's glass and the neck is 1 inch in diameter)

Tiki replacement wick

Funnel

Tiki torch fuel

½-inch copper cap

project

UPHOLSTERED OTOMI HEADBOARD

Turn to page 22 to see the headboard in Grace's home.

If there's one aspect of home design that I truly love above all others, it's upholstery. If my budget were unlimited I would collect all of my favorite fabrics and reupholster my couches, chairs, and benches on a regular basis. One of my favorites is Otomi, a hand-embroidered, animal-patterned cloth created by the Otomi people of central and western Mexico. These vibrant fabrics come in all sorts of colors, but I had my heart set on this one in vivid red that I found at Jacaranda Home. Determined to find a place for it in my home, I decided to use it to upholster a custom headboard I had a local carpenter cut. With a strong staple gun, a few sheets of foam, and inexpensive quilting batting, I finished the project during a long afternoon.

DESIGNER
Grace Bonney

COST
$200—$400

TIME
4 hours

DIFFICULTY
★ ★ ★ ☆

MATERIALS

Iron

Fabric

2-inch-thick foam
(size needed will
vary depending on
headboard size)

Headboard
(I had mine cut by a local
carpenter, but you can also
buy a precut rectangle of
plywood at Home Depot,
or trace a pattern and cut
it with a jigsaw to fit your
desired shape.)

Marker

Utility knife or electric knife

Batting
(standard quilting batting
is great; size needed will
vary depending on
headboard size)

Scissors

Dust mask

Spray adhesive

Staple gun and staples

Flush mount

〰〰〰〰〰〰〰〰〰〰〰〰〰〰〰〰 INSTRUCTIONS 〰〰〰〰〰〰〰〰〰〰〰〰〰〰〰〰

1   Iron the fabric and set aside.

2   Place the foam on the floor and lay the headboard on it. Trace the outline of the headboard with a marker and then cut the frame to size with a utility knife or electric knife. Repeat this step with the batting, cutting it 4–5 inches wider than the headboard wood all around. Then lay the fabric down, face up, and place the headboard on top. Adjust the headboard as needed to center the pattern, and then cut, leaving a 4–5-inch border all around.

3   Put on a dust mask or respirator and spray the foam with adhesive, then attach it to the front of the headboard. Let dry. Place your batting on the floor and lay the headboard on it, foam side down. Pull the batting to the back and staple it to the headboard at even, frequent intervals. Be sure to maintain an even tension as you work around the headboard. When finished, check the front. Restaple as necessary to eliminate uneven areas.

4   Once the batting is secure, drape your fabric over it, adjusting the position as needed. (I used spring plastic clamps to hold it in place.) Flip the headboard over so the fabric is facedown on the floor and staple the fabric into place, pulling it taut so you get a nice wrinkle-free finish. Check the front and restaple as necessary to eliminate uneven areas. Then cut away any excess from the back of the headboard to neaten up the edges.

5   There are a number of ways to attach the headboard to the wall or bed, but I prefer using flush mounts (just ask for them at your local hardware store, and check that they can handle the headboard's weight). They're easily screwed into the back of the headboard and onto the wall so the headboard simply slides into them.

SAFETY NOTE: Spray adhesive is pretty toxic, so you'll want to wear a mask and open your windows while you spray. Spray in short spurts and let your room fully air out before proceeding.

E veryone's got to wake up in the morning, so digital alarm clocks have become a part of our everyday lives. And unfortunately, they're not always the most attractive pieces of décor to have around the bedroom. Happy with her alarm clock's sound, but not with its appearance, Design*Sponge editor Kate Pruitt decided to create a faceted wooden cover to drop over it using sheets of inexpensive plywood veneer. Just print out the template Kate created (www.designsponge.com/templates), cut out the shapes from the veneer, and start folding to create a stylish cover for your everyday drugstore alarm clock.

DESIGNER
Kate Pruitt

COST
$10

TIME
1—2 hours

DIFFICULTY
★ ★ ★ ☆

MATERIALS

Alarm clock
(to fit this exact template,
it should be roughly
3 × 4 × 2 inches)

Ruler

Clock template

Scissors

Plywood veneer
(You can get this at craft
stores; Kate used two pieces
that were 5 × 10 inches, with
some left over.)

Spray adhesive

X-Acto knife and cutting mat

Low-temp glue gun
and glue sticks

~~~~~~~~~~~~~~~~~~~~~~~~~~~~ INSTRUCTIONS ~~~~~~~~~~~~~~~~~~~~~~~~~~~~

1   Measure your clock and size the template up or down to fit your clock's specifications. Print out the template twice, so you have a second copy for reference. Cut the first copy and glue the template to the plywood veneer sheet using spray adhesive.

2   Cut out the pieces. Also cut the shapes for the alarm button, the clock face, and the plug out of their larger facet pieces before you start assembling. Be *very* exact when cutting out this template, otherwise the facets will not fit together cleanly.

3   When you have all your facets cut, glue the pieces together with a low-temp glue gun. Hold each facet in place for 5 to 10 seconds to allow the glue to dry completely.

4   Once the pieces are assembled, slide the case over your clock to check the fit. Paint or decorate the case further if you wish. When you are finished, attach it to the clock using tape or a little glue on the back and front.

5   Plug in your clock and set the time! You can access the buttons (including the all-important snooze button) because the wood veneer is flexible enough to give when you press on it.

SAFETY NOTE: Spray adhesive is pretty toxic, so you'll want to wear a mask and open your windows while you spray. Spray in short spurts and let your room fully air out before proceeding.

W hen it came time to clean out a closet full of old, unworn clothes, Design*Sponge editors Derek Fagerstrom and Lauren Smith decided to reuse their favorite shirts for a quilting project. In addition to creating a custom design for a fraction of the cost of store-bought bedding, they also managed to free up some much-needed closet space.

DESIGNERS
Derek Fagerstrom
and Lauren Smith

COST
$20

TIME
3 hours

DIFFICULTY
★ ★ ★ ★

MATERIALS

15 men's shirts

Solid-color duvet cover

Ruler

Rotary cutter

Self-healing cutting mat

Pins

8 scraps of paper
numbered 1–8

Sewing machine

Iron

3 or 4 buttons

〜〜〜〜〜〜〜〜〜〜〜〜〜〜〜 INSTRUCTIONS 〜〜〜〜〜〜〜〜〜〜〜〜〜〜〜〜〜〜〜

1 Lay out the fabric squares on the floor in an 8 × 8 grid and arrange them into a pattern that you like. Pin a numbered scrap of paper (1–8) onto the first square of each of the eight rows so they stay in order as you stack them up and bring them to the sewing machine.

2 Using a ½-inch seam allowance, sew squares with right sides together to create strips 1–8. Press open all the seams with a hot iron.

3 Once all eight strips have been sewn, attach strip 1 to strip 2 using a ½-inch seam allowance, and press open the seam. Attach strip 3 to strip 4, press open seam, then attach to strips 1 and 2. Repeat with remaining strips.

4 With right sides together, attach the top (patchwork) piece to the bottom piece of your old duvet cover, leaving a 3-foot opening at the bottom.

5 Turn the duvet cover right side out, fold over the raw edge at the opening and stitch. Attach 3–4 buttons (from one of the shirts!) to the bottom piece. Use the buttonhole function on your sewing machine to create buttonholes on the opposite piece.

6 Insert your comforter or duvet, button it up, and settle down for a cozy afternoon nap!

NOTE: Derek and Lauren's duvet cover measures 80 × 80 inches, so they cut out 64 squares, each measuring 11 × 11 inches (32 from Derek's old shirts and 32 from the top piece of their existing duvet cover, which they took apart at the seams). They were able to get 2 or 3 squares from each shirt.

project

BUTTERFLY
DOME

Turn to page 47 to see the
finished product in Amy's
Brooklyn home.

DESIGNER
Jessica Oreck

COST
$200

TIME
2 days

DIFFICULTY
★ ★ ★ ★

I nspired by vintage French butterfly displays, Design*Sponge editor Amy Azzarito worked with her friend, nature documentary filmmaker Jessica Oreck, of Myriapod Productions, to create this stunning glass butterfly dome. The colors and patterns in the butterfly wings bring a beautiful jolt of color to any room, and can be customized to match any color palette you like. If real butterflies aren't in your budget, you can make a budget-friendly version using store-bought faux butterflies.

MATERIALS

Styrofoam or other cuttable, stiff foam at least 1 inch thick

Black jersey or velvet fabric

Spray adhesive

Staple gun (optional)

Hot glue gun and glue sticks

Bell jar

12 medium to large butterflies (www.butterflyutopia.com /unique_items.html) (see Tip)

Carbon steel wire (12 inches × ¹⁄₁₆ inch diameter) (www.mcmaster.com; product no. 8907k64)

Wire cutters

Superglue

step 2

~~~~~~~~~~~~~~~~~~ INSTRUCTIONS ~~~~~~~~~~~~~~~~~~

To Prepare the Base

1   Cut a circular piece of Styrofoam to fit inside the glass on the base of the bell jar. (Your bell jar may come packed in Styrofoam that is the perfect size for this purpose.)

2   Lay the Styrofoam on the black fabric and cut the fabric so that is 1½ inches wider than the Styrofoam all around. Attach the fabric to the Styrofoam with spray adhesive, folding the fabric over the edges. If the fabric is too heavy to be held with adhesive, staple it to the underside of the Styrofoam.

3   Using the hot glue gun, attach the fabric-covered Styrofoam to the bell jar base.

To Place the Butterflies in the Dome

4   Beginning with the larger butterflies, decide on the orientation (and placement), then insert the wire into each butterfly at that angle (use wire cutters to shorten the wire as needed). Add a drop of superglue at the point where the body of the butterfly meets the wire to secure the body. Be very careful handling the butterflies—the bodies are extremely delicate, and just brushing the wings will remove scales, causing the colors to become uneven. Repeat until all the butterflies are mounted on the wires.

step 4

5   Insert the wires into the Styrofoam base in the desired locations. If necessary, secure the wires using a dot of superglue at the point where they are inserted into the base.

6   Carefully place the glass dome over the base.

NOTE: Spray adhesive is pretty toxic, so you'll want to wear a mask and open your windows while you spray. Spray in short spurts and let your room fully air out before proceeding.

Tip

You can save a significant amount of money by ordering the insects unmounted. This means that you'll have to spread them open yourself. For more information: *www.thornesinsects.com*.

step 5

DIY BASICS

Whether you're an experienced crafter or brand new to the world of DIY, it's always good to brush up on the basics. Feeling comfortable around tools and knowing some

simple do-it-yourself skills will give you the confidence you need to spruce up your home (and furniture) with your own two hands.

In this minisection of the book, I'll be sharing some basic tips, tricks, and techniques for improving your furniture and home that will come in handy for years to come. Whether you're looking to update a desk from the flea market or sew your first pillow, this section will walk you through the steps and get you on your way to becoming your home's DIY pro.

In addition to my own essential basics, I've called upon some of my favorite upholstery experts to create a special subsection where you can learn how to make your own slipcovers and cushion covers. Sewing can seem daunting if you've never done it, but I hope you'll dive in and try making your own upholstery. It's one of the easiest ways to change a room's look and feel without spending a ton of money. Once you've mastered these techniques, you'll start seeing worn-out sofas and chairs with torn seat cushions as diamonds in the rough, just waiting to be polished and updated with a little DIY love.

1 Hammer
2 Standard screwdriver
3 Phillips head screwdriver
4 Reversible electric drill
5 Adjustable wrenches
6 Level
7 Utility knife
8 Tape measure
9 Pliers
10 Handsaw
11 Wire cutter
12 Wire stripper
13 Hot glue gun and glue sticks
14 Needlenose pliers
15 Staple gun and staples
16 Metal paint scraper
17 Paintbrushes

1 Toolbox

2 Duct tape

3 Electrical tape

4 Spray adhesive

5 Permanent marker

6 Scissors

7 Work gloves

8 Sandpaper

9 Safety goggles

10 Dust mask

11 Drop cloths

12 Vise grips

13 Sewing machine

14 Wood glue

15 Assortment of nails and screws

16 Superglue

17 Iron

step 3

step 4

MATERIALS

Plastic tarp

Gloves/goggles/
paint respirator
(to be worn at all times when
working with chemicals)

Paintbrush

Paint stripper
(You can find cans of
chemical paint stripper at
most hardware stores and all
home improvement centers.)

Metal paint scraper

~~~~~~~~~~~~~~~~~~~~~~~~~~~~~ INSTRUCTIONS ~~~~~~~~~~~~~~~~~~~~~~~~~~~~~

1   Work outdoors or in a small but open and well-ventilated space. Lay down a thick plastic tarp on your work surface.

2   After removing any hardware or valuable details like glass knobs from your piece, place it on the tarp.

3   Be sure you have on protective clothing and eyewear when you start stripping the wood. Using a paintbrush proportionate to your piece, apply a generous layer of stripper to the surface of your furniture. Following the directions on the can of paint stripper, wait for the product to take effect. This may take up to 30 or 45 minutes.

4   When the paint has started to soften, gently but firmly apply even pressure to the putty scraper and start to slide it against the surface of the furniture to remove the paint. Older wood can be easily damaged, so be careful not to nick or dig into the wood. You may need to repeat steps 3 and 4, particularly for stubborn finishes or multiple layers of paint.

5   Once you have finished, be sure to apply a coat of wood wax or sealant to protect the newly exposed surface of your furniture.

How to Strip Metal Furniture

1   Follow steps 1 through 4 above.

2   Lightly scrub with steel wool to remove rust spots and gently sand off any scratches. Follow these steps with a coat of metal polish or antirust sealant to protect the fresh metal surface.

HOW TO PAINT FURNITURE

step 2

step 1

step 3

MATERIALS

Sandpaper
(medium to light grit)

Damp cloth

Primer

Paintbrush

Paint

Polyurethane
(optional)

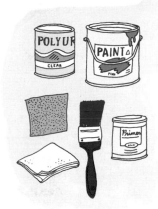

~~~~~~~~~~~~~~~~~ INSTRUCTIONS ~~~~~~~~~~~~~~~~~

1 If you're working with a piece of furniture that's already painted or has a slick finish, start by sanding all surfaces so that the paint will be able to adhere. When you're finished, wipe down your piece with a damp cloth to remove any dust.

2 Priming furniture is an essential step in ensuring a smooth finish. Coat the furniture with a thin layer of interior primer. Two thin, even coats of primer are always better than one thick coat of paint, which tends to dry unevenly. Let the piece dry.

3 Apply thin layers of paint to the surface of the furniture. As with the primer, it's better to err on the side of too little paint than too much. Thick paint will dry as a bumpy, sticky, and uneven surface. If you need to repeat with two or even three thin coats of paint, it's worth the extra effort.

4 Once your piece is dry, you can leave it as is or apply a thin coat of polyurethane or other sealant to protect the paint. This step isn't necessary, but goes a long way in making a piece look "finished."

HANGING WALLPAPER

MATERIALS

Plumb line

Ruler

Wallpaper

Cutting mat

Rotary cutter

Wallpaper glue

Paintbrush

Squeegee
(The kind you use on
your windows is fine
as long as it's clean.)

X-Acto knife

Damp cloth

1   Using a plumb line, lightly draw a straight line down the center of the wall with a pencil to create a reference point for hanging the first strip of paper.

2   To cut your wallpaper strips, measure the height of the wall, adding 4 inches. Lay the roll on a flat surface (such as a cutting mat), pattern side down. Measure your strips and cut using a rotary cutter (an X-Acto knife or even a pair of sharp scissors can also be used).

3   Prepare the glue according to the manufacturer's directions. Pay special attention to any directions about diluting with water if they call for thinning the solution.

4   Lay your wallpaper flat on your work surface and, with a paintbrush, apply a thin coat of wallpaper glue to the back, being careful not to get any on the patterned side of your paper.

5   Allow at least 5 minutes for the glue to become tacky. This is where most mistakes are made— if you apply the paper directly after coating it with glue, it won't adhere right away and will slide down the wall.

6   When the glue is tacky, apply the first strip of wallpaper, gently moving it into place against the reference line. There should be a 2-inch overhang at top and bottom. Step back to make sure the strip is straight, then, starting from the center and working out, use a squeegee to smooth out the paper and carefully remove any air bubbles. Be sure not to use too much pressure or you may tear the paper.

7   When moving on to the second, third, and fourth strips of paper, make sure the edges of each piece gently touch, but do not overlap—overlaps will only become more pronounced after the strips dry.

8   As you move along, carefully lining up your pattern, be sure to remove any excess glue with a damp cloth. The glue could dry and leave marks on your paper.

9   Once you are done hanging the paper, let it dry fully before trimming the overhang at top and bottom with an X-Acto knife. The paper can easily tear, rip, or bunch if you tug on it when it's not dry, so pour yourself a well-deserved glass of water (or wine) and wait patiently for the paper to dry fully.

NOTE: Wallpaper can be incredibly daunting if you don't prepare well up front. Before you start, be sure to clear your room completely of anything that could be in the way of hanging paper, or could potentially spill on, stain, or tear your paper. Wet wallpaper is sometimes very fragile, so be careful not to tear it on any shelves or sharp corners. Create a small workstation (in a well-ventilated area) on which you can place all your tools and hang your wallpaper while you wait for the glue to dry. This will ensure you work neatly, which will help you avoid tears or glue stains on the patterned side of your paper.

INSTRUCTIONS

1   Unplug your lamp and remove the bulb, harp, and shade. Turn the lamp on its side and remove any felt, metal, or cardboard covering the base. This should expose the point where the old wire comes out from the stem of the light through the base.

2   Unscrew the socket. If your socket will not unscrew easily you may need to remove the light switch.

3   Remove the old cord by pulling it from the bottom of the lamp base. Once it's removed you can thread the new cord up through the base and stem of the lamp. If it looks like it may be difficult to thread the new cord up, you can splice the new cord onto the old cord and pull it through that way. Simply strip one inch of the wire at the base of the old cord and the top of the new cord and twist the wires together. Cover their connection point with electrical tape. Pull the old cord up through the top of the lamp until at least six inches of the new cord appears above the lamp. Remove the electrical tape and detach and discard the old wire.

MATERIALS

Lamp

Screwdriver

Wire strippers

Electrical tape

Lamp cord plug

Lamp socket with switch

Underwriter's Knot

a

b

c

d

4   Using your new socket, pass the new cord (exposed wire end first) through the socket base (it may be easier to remove the socket base from the socket for this portion). To secure the wire, tie an underwriter's knot (see illustration) so you can separate the two strands of wire in the new cord.

5   Only one of the wire strands of your new cord is "hot." This is the wire you want to connect to the new socket base. To determine which wire is hot, simply look at the wire's texture. One side will be ridged or lined—that is the hot wire.

6   Loosen the screw on the side of your new socket and wrap the exposed end of the hot wire around it. Then tighten the screw onto the wire using a screwdriver. Make sure you don't have any excess exposed wire hanging outside the screw. If you do, loosen the screw and wrap the excess wire around it and retighten.

7   Now that the hot wire is wrapped around one screw, it's time to wrap the other, "neutral," strand around the other screw. Repeat the process in step 6 to attach.

8   Now that both wires are attached to the socket base, reattach the socket to the socket base (if you disconnected it in step 4) and pull the cord from the base of the lamp so the socket is pulled back into place on top of the lamp.

9   Using your screwdriver, screw the socket back into the base of the lamp.

10 If you removed felt, cardboard, or metal from the base of your lamp reattach it now or cut a new piece of cardboard or felt and reattach it with glue.

11 Replace the bulb, harp, and shade on your lamp and plug it in.

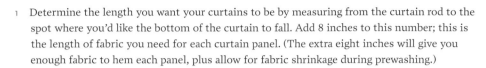

〰〰〰〰〰〰〰〰〰〰〰〰〰〰〰〰 INSTRUCTIONS 〰〰〰〰〰〰〰〰〰〰〰〰〰〰〰〰

MATERIALS

Fabric

Sewing thread to match fabric

Fabric scissors

Measuring tape

Straight pins

Sewing machine or
sewing needle

Iron and ironing board

1   Determine the length you want your curtains to be by measuring from the curtain rod to the spot where you'd like the bottom of the curtain to fall. Add 8 inches to this number; this is the length of fabric you need for each curtain panel. (The extra eight inches will give you enough fabric to hem each panel, plus allow for fabric shrinkage during prewashing.)

2   Determine the width you need. Most fabric is sold in widths of 45 or 60 inches. If you don't need a particularly full or gathered curtain, you may decide that one width of fabric is enough for your panel. If you prefer a more gathered look, you'll want the fabric to be anywhere from two to three times wider than the actual window width.

3   If your fabric is machine washable, wash and dry it to preshrink it before cutting and sewing. This is important: if you don't preshrink before sewing, the seams may pucker the first time you wash your curtains. Finally, before you start cutting or sewing, iron your fabric thoroughly. You'll need to remove all wrinkles and creases in order to measure and sew accurately.

4   Once you've measured, washed, and ironed your fabric, cut it to your desired measurements with fabric scissors.

5   Sew the side seams. Fold the fabric under 1 inch to the wrong side (back) of the fabric on one side, pressing as you go. Then, turn the fabric under another 1 inch and press again.

6   Pin this double-folded edge in place, inserting one pin every 4 to 6 inches. Always insert the pins perpendicular to the seam you will be sewing, with the heads to the right of the seam. This allows you to remove them easily with your right hand as you sew the seam.

7   Stitch a simple straight seam down the side, placing the stitch line about ⅛ inch from the interior folded edge of the hem.

8   Repeat steps 5–7 to hem the other side of the fabric.

9   To sew the bottom hem, fold under ½ inch of the bottom edge to the wrong side and press with the iron. Fold under 5 inches more and press; pin in place as described in step 6.

10 Stitch the hem approximately ⅛ inch from the interior folded edge. When sewing this seam, make it extra secure by backstitching at the beginning and end of the seam. To do this, sew the first 2 or 3 stitches of the seam, stop the sewing machine, press the Reverse Stitch button, and sew 2 or 3 stitches in reverse, then proceed to sew the rest of the seam. Repeat at the end of the seam. This process ensures that the seam won't unravel.

11 Sew the curtain rod pocket. At the top edge of the curtain, fold under ½ inch to the wrong side and press. Turn under another 2 inches and press again; pin in place as described in step 6. Stitch the seam approximately ⅛ inch from the interior folded edge, backstitching at the beginning and end of the seam, as in step 10, to secure. Slip the curtain onto your rod and hang.

NOTE: If you're new to sewing, start with a basic medium-weight fabric such as cotton or a cotton-linen blend. Its straightforward texture makes it easy to work with. Be sure to consider the necessary function of your curtains: Do you need them to protect your privacy or block light? Do they need to be machine-washable (a good idea for kitchens or windows that are frequently open, especially in cities where lots of dirt comes in through windows)? Do you want them to help keep out cold drafts, or do you merely desire a hazy sheer? All of these functions can be accomplished simply by choosing different types of fabric.

STAPLE-GUN UPHOLSTERY

One of the simplest ways to reupholster is with a staple gun. If you have a small stool, ottoman, or bench with a removable seat, you can easily change out the fabric without heading to the upholsterer.

〰〰〰〰〰〰〰〰〰〰〰〰〰〰 INSTRUCTIONS 〰〰〰〰〰〰〰〰〰〰〰〰〰〰〰

1   With a screwdriver, remove the seat or portion of your furniture that you'd like to reupholster. Carefully set aside the screws for reattaching the piece later.

2   Using needle-nose pliers, carefully remove all of the staples holding the original fabric in place. Be careful not to damage the foam underneath the fabric. If there is batting under the fabric, remove that as well.

3   Once you've removed the original fabric, examine the state of the foam. If it is in decent condition, proceed to the next step. If the foam needs replacing, order affordable pieces of foam on upholstery supply websites. If this is something you're sitting on, be sure to choose foam of at least a moderate quality and density so your seat doesn't sag or sink too much when someone is on it. (I typically work with 3- to 4-inch foam for small chair seats.) Cut your foam to fit your seat using a box cutter or electric knife. Make sure the edges are as clean as possible.

4   Cut a piece of batting (quilt batting is fine for casual projects, but if you have the budget, upholstery-quality batting—available online—is very nice) 4 inches larger (all around) than the foam.

5   Lay the new batting over the top of the foam and staple it to the underside of your seat, pulling it taut to ensure an even surface.

6   Cut the fabric 4–5 inches larger (all around) than the foam and batting layers. Lay the fabric on top of the batting-covered seat and start to pull and staple it to the seat. Be sure to keep an eye on where the screw holes for your chair are. If you staple fabric over them, it will be tough to find the spots to reattach your seat. It may sound silly, but I often cut small coffee stirrer straws and place them in the holes to mark where they are. That way I know where to stop when I'm stapling.

7   Once the fabric is stapled, cut off any excess, then flip the seat over and reattach it to your chair/bench/stool with the original screws.

MATERIALS

Screwdriver

Needlenose pliers

Foam
(if your chair's foam
needs to be replaced)

Batting

Scissors

Staple gun and staples
(Electric staple guns are
great, but a basic hardware
store staple gun will do.)

Fabric

MATERIALS

Measuring tape or ruler

Chalk

Fabric

Scissors

Sewing machine

Thread

Pins

Seam ripper

Heat 'n Bond fusible hem tape

I f you've been craving a custom slipcover, are a bit of a seamstress, and fancy yourself a somewhat hands-on and crafty person, you'll love this simplified technique for constructing a fitted slipcover for a basic chair, love seat, or sofa. Writer, designer, and upholsterer Shelly Miller Leer of Flipt Studio (www.fliptstudio.com) has been reupholstering and redoing furniture for more than fifteen years and is going to walk us through the principles of how to cut, pin, and fit a slipcover right on your furniture. Like most hands-on projects, there isn't one right way to construct a slipcover, so don't worry if you find yourself making adaptations along the way to suit your individual style.

Here are some basics before you get started.

A slipcover is made up of multiple fabric pieces stitched together to form a well-fitted cover. Because upholstered furniture has vertical planes, horizontal planes, and angled planes and/or contours and curves that need to be covered, flat pieces of fabric sometimes have to be gathered, pleated, darted, or "eased" to accommodate those sections. Easing fabric means to pull the fabric closer together without causing any visible puckering or gathering. To ease fabric, simply make three rows of stitching with your sewing machine and tug on the loose ends of the stitching until the fabric is condensed into a smaller area. Don't tug too hard or you'll get puckering in the fabric—the goal is to condense the fabric as much as possible without creating ripples.

Some basic sewing skills are needed to do this project. You will need to know:

· How to measure fabric
· How to cut fabric based on its lengthwise grain
· How to sew fabric
· How to make darts, gathers, and pleats
· How to ease fabric
· How to install a zipper (optional)
· How to make welt cording (optional)

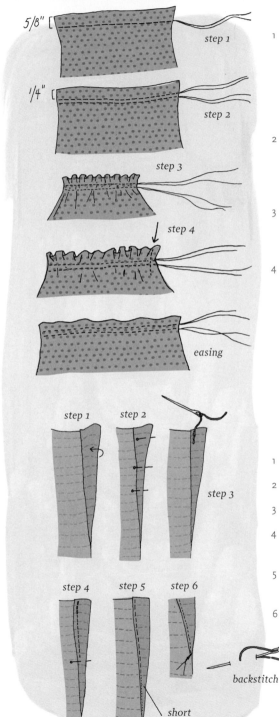

5/8"

step 1

1/4"

step 2

step 3

step 4

easing

step 1   *step 2*

step 3

step 4   *step 5*   *step 6*

backstitch

short stitches

How to Make a Gather

1 Using a wide stitch, sew one line of stitches across your fabric, ⅝ inch from the seam edge. Backstitch the first 2 or 3 stitches and leave 3 inches of thread after the last stitch at the end. (Don't backstitch.)

2 Sew a second line (above the first line), ¼ of an inch from the seam edge of your fabric. Backstitch as you did in step 1, leaving 3 inches of thread at the end.

3 Holding your fabric in place, tug on the top end of both 3-inch pieces of thread, creating a gather.

4 Spread the gather evenly across the fabric and sew a third line ⅝ of an inch from the edge of the fabric, this will keep the gather in place.

NOTE: For easing, repeat steps 1 and 2 for gathering. When you get to step 3 only tug the 3-inch threads slightly so you don't gather the fabric as much. Then repeat the rest of the steps.

How to Sew a Dart

1 Fold your dart.

2 Pin the dart.

3 Backstitch 2 or 3 times.

4 Sew most of the length of the dart, removing pins as you go.

5 As you get to the end of the dart, shorten your stitch length.

6 Hand knot the end of the thread.

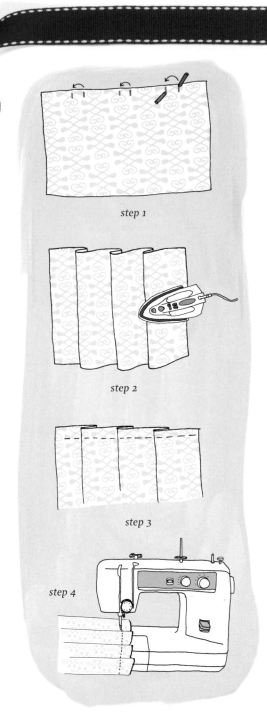

step 1

step 2

step 3

step 4

How to Make a Pleat

1. Mark the pleats on your fabric with tailor's chalk or a pencil, spacing them evenly apart.

2. Make the pleats by folding the fabric so that mark 2 lines up over mark 1, then press them in place lightly with an iron and pin at the top edge.

3. Stitch a basting line (a loose line made by setting your stitch size to the longest possible on your sewing machine) across the pleats to hold them in place. Remove the pins as you go.

4. Press in place again and then stitch across the top, just below the basting line, to hold the pleats in place.

MAKING A SLIPCOVER

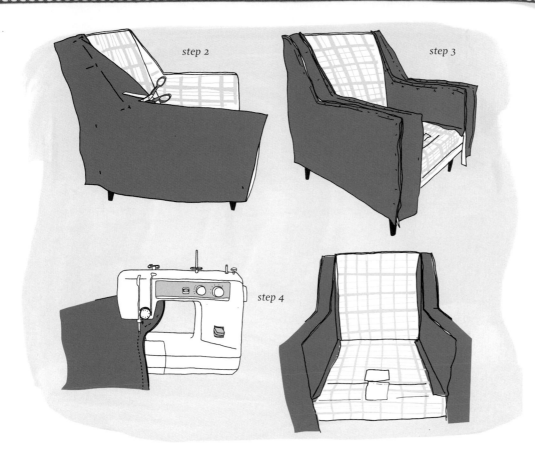

step 2

step 3

step 4

INSTRUCTIONS

1 Measure and sketch each section of the furniture to be covered. Determine if any two adjacent surfaces can be cut out as one piece, which will save you work.

2 Using the sketches as your template, cut each fabric section 2 to 4 inches larger than each surface measurement. If your chair has an attached seat cushion and/or back cushion, allow 2 inches extra at seams that will need to tuck down into the chair sides and back. (If the chair has a removable seat cushion or back cushion, see Notes.)

3 Place the three arm pieces (the top of the arms, the outside arms, and the inside arms) on the chair wrong side up and secure them with a few pins. Fit the pieces snugly, but not tightly, by lining up the cut edges and pinning them together. Place the pins parallel to the cut edges to indicate the stitch lines.

4 Remove the pinned pieces and stitch them together. Make sure to remove the pins before they go under the needle. Turn the pieces right side out and check the fit. If the arm pieces fit, cut the seam allowance so it measures ½ inch beyond all the stitch lines. If not, use a seam ripper to remove the stitching in the area that doesn't fit, repin it, and stitch it again.

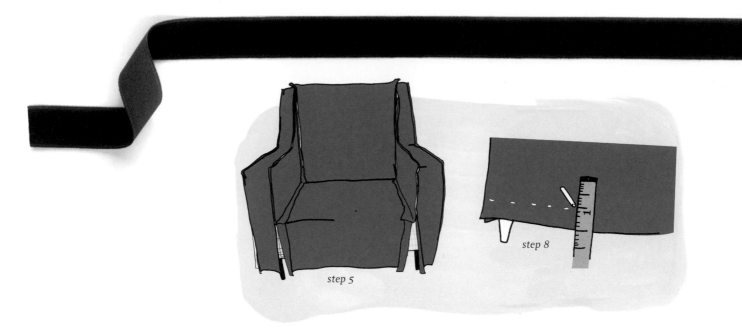

step 5

step 8

5   Fit, pin, and stitch the main piece (the long piece that runs from the top of the chair, down the inside back, and along the seat deck, front of the chair, and hem). Attach this to the arm sections. Turn the partially sewn slipcover (which now consists of the main front piece and both arms) right side out and place it on the chair to check the fit. If an adjustment needs to be made, remove the slipcover, and remove the faulty stitching. Put it back on the chair, refit, and pin. Repeat this process until this section fits the chair. Cut off the excess seam allowance to ½ inch beyond the stitch lines. Turn this big piece inside out again and put it back on the chair.

6   To attach the back section, match up the center marks and fit and pin to the top and back of the partially sewn, inside-out slipcover. Stitch the back piece into place. Note: If a zipper is to be installed onto one of the back seams, baste that seam closed. Adjust the seam allowance if you plan to use Velcro or ties as a fastener. If the slipcover is loose-fitting, no opening may be necessary.

7   Turn the slipcover right side out. If it fits properly, trim the remaining stitched seam allowances to ½ inch beyond the stitch lines.

8   Prepare the bottom hem by measuring and marking the edge to allow a 1-inch hem.

9   Using a zigzag stitch, sew the bottom cut edge of the slipcover. Next, fold the bottom edge up by 1 inch and press. Hem with Heat 'n Bond fusible hem tape, or stitch in place ¼ inch from the zigzagged edge. Remove the slipcover and press.

Not so long ago "green" textiles meant burlap and beige. These days you don't have to live like a mountain man to be eco-friendly. Green has gone from hippie to hip in a big way, giving us a vibrant range of chic, luxurious textiles that look as amazing as any conventional material, but they don't damage the planet and your health in the process. Nancy Mims of Mod Green Pod (www.modgreenpod.com) shared these tips:

There are two basic types of green textiles—the repurposed kind and the smart growth kind. "Repurposed" is when you reuse an existing material. This could mean you create bedding from old shirts (turn to page 269 to learn how!) or alter an old dress your grandmother gave you into a killer apron. In short, you're giving something old a new life and keeping it out of the landfill.

Companies are repurposing materials these days, too. Recycled PET plastics (things like plastic drink bottles) are now woven into soft and sturdy fabrics, perfect for heavy-use furnishings.

The other side of the green spectrum—new eco-friendly fabrics—consists of "smart growth" natural fibers, like cotton and hemp, grown organically without polluting pesticides and herbicides. And if they are manufactured organically, the nasty chemical baths that conventional textiles go through are also skipped. With conventional (nonorganic) cotton, toxins are added throughout the weaving, dying or printing, and finishing steps—toxins that later release fumes (called "off-gassing") into our homes and work spaces. Truly organic, natural fibers skip all of these nasty toxins to give you a clean product that won't off-gas into your home.

Here's what you should look for when shopping for green fabrics.

SUSTAINABLE NATURAL FIBERS. (Be sure that, in addition to the content, the fabric is manufactured with nontoxic, low-impact inks, dyes, and finishing agents.)

- Organic cotton
- Hemp
- Organic wool
- Organic linen
- Sustainable silk
- Nettles
- Seaweed

RECYCLED/DOWNCYCLED FIBERS

- Recycled PET bottles (postconsumer)
- Postindustrial recycled cotton (postindustrial)
- Recycled polyester (postindustrial)

Here are some companies that are making strides to offer great modern and green upholstery fabrics:

Mod Green Pod
www.modgreenpod.com

Q Collection
www.qcollection.com

Lulan Artisans
www.lulan.com

Oliveira
www.oliveiratextiles.com

Maharam
www.maharam.com

DesignTex
www.designtex.com

O-Eco-Textiles
www.oecotextiles.com

Rubie Green
www.rubiegreen.com

Kravet Green
www.kravetgreen.com

Live Textiles
www.livetextiles.com

Amenity
www.amenityhome.com

Harmony Art
www.harmonyart.com

N ow that you know some of the basics for home upholstery, Amanda Brown and Lizzie Joyce of Spruce Austin (www.spruceaustin.com), are going to walk us through the steps for creating final upholstery touches like fabric cording, fabric-covered buttons and button tufting, and cutting and wrapping a cushion.

MATERIALS

Measuring tape or ruler

Chalk

Fabric

Scissors

Sewing machine

Welt cord foot for your
sewing machine

Cording

Fabric Cording (Welt Cord)

Fabric-covered cording helps define lines and create a tailored look in your throw pillows and furniture.

~~~~~~~~~~~~~~~~~~~~~~~~~~~~ INSTRUCTIONS ~~~~~~~~~~~~~~~~~~~~~~~~~~~~

1   Measure how much cording you will need.

2   Using a ruler 1½–1¾ inches wide, draw lines diagonally (on the bias) on the fabric. Cutting these strips on the bias allows for maximum flex of the fabric and cording.

3   Mark the bottoms of all of the strips and cut them out.

4   Line up 2 strips of fabric with a marked end meeting an unmarked end. Cut the adjacent ends at a 45-degree angle.

5   Put the right sides of the fabric together and line up the cut edges so you have a ½-inch seam allowance.

6   Sew the ends together.

7   Repeat the steps above until all the strips are sewn to make one long length.

8   Make sure you have the single welt cord foot attached to your machine. Zipper foot attachments may also work.

9   Lay your welt cord in the middle of the fabric, folding the fabric snugly over the cord so the fabric edges meet. Sew along the right side of the cording. As you sew across the connections in the welt cord, spread open the seam allowance and sew over it to minimize bulk.

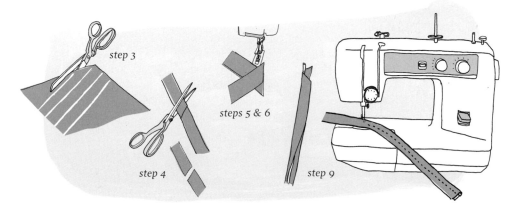

step 3

steps 5 & 6

step 4

step 9

Fabric Buttons and Button Tufting

Button tufting is a great way to add interest, dimension, and a touch of contrasting color to pillows, cushions, and furniture. Professional upholsterers have industrial button machines, but you can make your own fabric-covered buttons by following these steps!

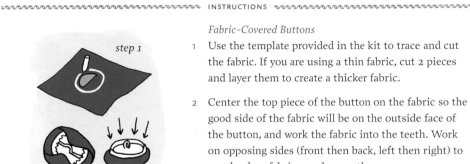

~~~~~~~~~~~~~~~~~~~~~ INSTRUCTIONS ~~~~~~~~~~~~~~~~~~~~~

Fabric-Covered Buttons

step 1

step 2   *step 3*

1 Use the template provided in the kit to trace and cut the fabric. If you are using a thin fabric, cut 2 pieces and layer them to create a thicker fabric.

2 Center the top piece of the button on the fabric so the good side of the fabric will be on the outside face of the button, and work the fabric into the teeth. Work on opposing sides (front then back, left then right) to evenly place fabric snugly over the cover.

3 Snap on the back of the button. Repeat with the second button.

Button Tufting

step 2

step 3

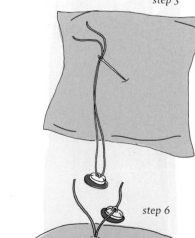

step 6

step 7

1 Cut a piece of doubled-over button twine long enough to go through the pillow/cushion and have a 6-inch tail.

2 Put one end of the twine through the button loop and then thread both ends of the twine through the needle.

3 Stick the needle all the way through the pillow/cushion at the desired spot, pulling the ends of the button twine through to the other side.

4 Remove the button needle.

5 Pull the ends of the button twine back and forth to make sure the twine moves freely through the pillow/cushion.

6 Loop one end of the twine through the loop of the second button.

7 Tie a slip knot in the button twine (see Note). Pull one side of the twine to tighten to the desired tension.

8 Tie a permanent knot and cut off the ends of the twine.

NOTE: To make a slip knot, holding one string in each hand, put the right string over the left string. Pass the right string behind the loop created, and then through the hole formed by the first crossover (see step 7 illustration). Pull tight.

MATERIALS

Button kit(s) for button size of choice (available at most craft stores; to tuft a cushion or throw pillow, one button is needed for each side of the piece)

Fabric

Scissors

Button twine

Button needle

Cutting and Wrapping a Cushion

Are your cushions solidifying? Leaking dust? Or providing no support? Follow these steps to revamp your old cushion inserts.

~~~~~~~~~~~~~~~~~~~~~~~~~~~ INSTRUCTIONS ~~~~~~~~~~~~~~~~~~~~~~~~~~~

1   Trace your old foam or cushion cover onto the new piece of foam.

2   Use an electric carving knife to cut on the lines. Be sure to keep your cuts straight up and down.

3   Use spray adhesive to attach Dacron to the surfaces and sides of the foam. Leave the zipper side free of any Dacron.

4   Trim off extra Dacron, stuff cushion into case, and sit pretty!

SAFETY NOTE: Spray adhesive is pretty toxic, so you'll want to wear a mask and open your windows while you spray. Spray in short spurts and let your room fully air out before proceeding.

MATERIALS

Upholstery foam

Permanent marker

Electric carving knife
or utility knife

Bonded Dacron

Scissors

Spray adhesive

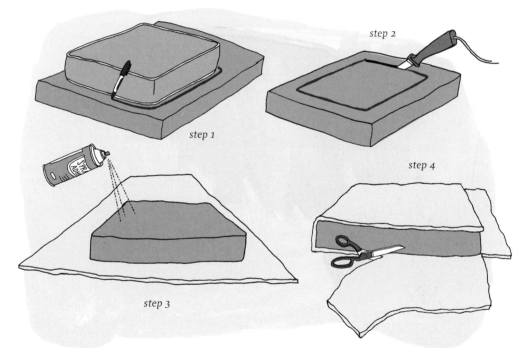

step 1

step 2

step 3

step 4

CHOOSING FABRICS FOR UPHOLSTERY

Finding great upholstery fabric is easier than ever these days. In addition to neighborhood upholstery shops, you can find fun and affordable upholstery fabrics online at Etsy *(www.etsy.com)*, J and O *(www.jandofabrics.com)*, eBay *(www.ebay.com)*, and Textile Arts *(www.store .txtlart.com)*.

You'll want to avoid choosing fabrics that are too thin, like drapery or bedding fabrics. Also, steer clear of anything too delicate or stretchy—it won't be able to stand up to the wear and tear of frequent use. Instead, look for:

- Canvas
- Chenille
- Heavy linen
- Velvet
- Leather
- Vinyl
- Wools

These fabrics all come in a variety of styles, colors, and textures that will give you the look and durability you need for upholstery projects.

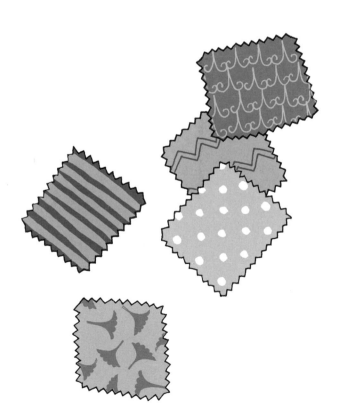

Pets and Fabric

Dogs and cats can be ruthless on your favorite upholstery fabrics. To protect your couches and chairs, stick to durable fabrics like leather, faux suede, and vinyl, as well as Crypton fabrics, which stand up to pet wear and tear. If you have larger dogs, consider outdoor or performance fabrics for extra protection.

To protect fabrics from cat scratching, try a double-sided tape like Sticky Paws brand to dissuade them from scratching. Place the tape on heavily scratched areas and cats will quickly learn to stay away from the fabric because their paws will stick (briefly and painlessly) to the tape.

Tips for Altering the Look of Your Furniture

THINGS TO DISCUSS WITH YOUR UPHOLSTERER

Cushion quantity and style

Skirt

Contrasting cording

Using multiple fabrics together

Upholstering parts of the furniture that were not previously upholstered, such as upholstering over broken cane or over an open back

Adding decorative tacks

THINGS TO DO ON YOUR OWN

Paint the frame

Add buttons to cushions

Change out the decorative trim

FLOWER WORKSHOP

Few things bring a room to life or add that last special something like a beautiful arrangement of flowers. My personal obsession with fresh flowers and potted plants

led me to add two floral columns to Design*Sponge and drag several of my editors along to countless flower arranging classes so we could learn more. For some people, flower arrangements can be somewhat daunting, but they can be easy, and exciting, to create.

In this section I'm going to walk you through some of the basic terms, tools, ideas, and guidelines for arranging flowers. Because I'm still learning, I got some expert help from Design*Sponge editor Amy Merrick. In addition to helping with the guidelines in the beginning of this section, Amy created ten beautiful arrangements that will illustrate key lessons in floral design, ranging from how to combine textures and vary heights, to using unexpected materials and vessels for your arrangements. By the time you try her ten

basic arrangement styles, you will feel confident enough to pull together flowers for everything from a special holiday centerpiece to a bedside table bouquet. And, because we're all trying to keep costs down, Amy has kept a budget in mind for these arrangements, and has listed some savvy sources.

I also invited Design*Sponge contributor Sarah Ryhanen to create a series of flower arrangements inspired by the homes in Sneak Peeks. The arrangements vary from the simplest single-stem groupings to dramatic centerpieces using driftwood. For each project, Sarah walks you through the flowers and supplies you'll need and teaches you how to re-create the look. Hopefully, these will inspire you to look to your own home for ideas when creating special arrangements.

UNDERSTANDING FLOWER TYPES

Flowers are typically broken down into three basic categories:

- *Line flowers:* Tall, sculptural blooms that add structure to an arrangement. These flowers are often strong enough (both visually and physically) to stand on their own in a vase, but can also be used to add height to a group arrangement.
  EXAMPLES: gladiolus, molucella, snapdragon, stock, bells of Ireland

- *Mass flowers:* Full, round flowers that bring weight to your arrangement. Twirl the flower in a circle—if it looks the same all the way around (like a hydrangea) it's a mass flower. Just as the name implies, mass flowers look great gathered together in a large group. They can also be used to fill larger holes in an arrangement.
  EXAMPLES: hydrangea, rose, carnation, tulip, gerbera, sunflower

- *Filler flowers:* These blooms are often underrated. And if you are going for affordable bouquets, that's a good thing because you can often find these flowers for next to nothing at flower shops—and sometimes in your own backyard. Think of filler flowers as mostly stems, perhaps with a few leaves or flowers. They can help to create a base for a flower arrangement or give a bouquet a fuller look. Or try using them on their own: Some filler flowers are pretty enough to stand alone.
  EXAMPLES: ferns, Queen Anne's lace, heather, hypericum berries, aster, wax flower

UNEXPECTED ELEMENTS

To add texture and color to a flower arrangement, consider adding the following:

- *Fruit:* Small lemons, oranges, or berries on their branches can add wonderful pops of color to an arrangement. If using citrus fruits, attach them to floral sticks.

- *Herbs:* Try a small-leafed herb like purple basil in your arrangement, or add height, line, and a wonderful smell with a fragrant plant like rosemary or lavender.

- *Succulents:* Attach these plants to floral sticks. Use a bit of floral wire to keep them in place.

TOOLS OF THE TRADE

Professional florists have all sorts of fancy tools at their disposal, but these basics are what you'll need for home arranging:

- *Scissors:* Florists are very protective of their cutting shears for a reason: The sharper the blades, the better the stems will cut.

- *Vessels:* Having a wide range of vases and vessels on hand means you're more likely to experiment with different flowers and arrangements. Think outside the box: Try a variety of vase shapes (tall, short, round, etc.), vintage jars (mason and jelly jars are perfect for simple arrangements), tea tins (make sure they are water-tight), and trophies (such a fun shape to work with).

- *String:* When working with smaller arrangements, tie the stems together with string to keep everything in place. Butchers twine works fine for this.

- *Frogs:* Floral frogs are a great way to anchor flowers and a good alternative to floral foam, which is usually petroleum-based and therefore not great for the environment. Frogs are inexpensive, can be found in a variety of different materials, and are perfect for securing individual flowers in an arrangement. Balled-up chicken wire is a good alternative to a frog.

- *Extras:* Floral tape, floral sticks, floral foam, and floral wire are helpful for controlling your arrangements, but aren't necessary for most.

floral frog

floral wire

floral tape

floral sticks

CUTTING AND PRESERVING FLOWERS

The way you cut flowers can have a big impact on the lifespan of your arrangement. Remember to:

- *Always cut flowers with a very sharp pair of scissors or a knife.* If you use a knife, be sure to cut through the stem in one stiff motion rather than sawing back and forth. The faster and cleaner the cut, the less likely you are to damage the stem and prevent water from getting to the flower.

- *Always cut on an angle.* A 45-degree angle is what you are aiming for. This will create more surface area than a straight-across cut, allowing more water to be absorbed by the flower.

- *Cut under water.* Trim flowers under the tap or as close to water as possible. The longer you wait between cutting and placing your flower directly into water, the sooner your flower will wilt.

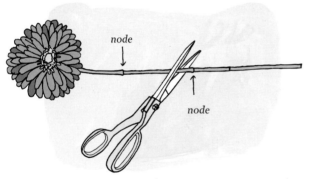

- *Cut between stem nodes or joints.* When cutting flowers in the wild (or in your garden), be sure to trim above the nodes and joints, which are the points at which new leaves or flower buds grow. These resemble little knobs on the stems.

- *Change the water every day.* Opinions are divided over whether preservative powders and mixtures (those little packs of white powder—mostly sugar and bleach—that get stapled to your cut flowers) really work. In truth, the best way to keep your flowers alive for as long as possible is to change the water every day. If you use a clear glass vase you're more likely to notice when the water looks murky. Keeping flowers in a cool place will also prolong their life.

FLOWER ARRANGING TIPS

When it comes to flower design, there are many different styles and methods. At Design*Sponge, we throw most of the rules out of the window and stick to a few key ideas. If you follow these guidelines (which are based on traditional Western flower design principles), you'll learn to create strong, balanced arrangements while staying true to your particular tastes and style.

- *Group flowers in odd numbers.* Arranging in uneven numbers is always more pleasing to the eye. If you're working with a small number of flowers, consider using three stems in a vase rather than four. If you're making a larger arrangement, try to cluster flowers in threes within the arrangement to create strong areas of color and texture.

- *Create a range of heights.* Using a combination of filler, line, and mass flowers will help to vary the heights in your arrangement, which will make the display more visually appealing. An arrangement will often have three tiers: lower, creeping flowers (jasmine and ivy vines are great for this), followed by the main flowers (roses, peonies, tulips, and other blooms that are medium height and add mass), and finally the top tier blooms that contribute height and structure (branches are great for this purpose).

- *Contrast textures.* A variety of textures always makes for a balanced arrangement. For example, pairing lacier flowers (maiden's hair ferns, Queen Anne's lace) with full, soft flowers (peonies or roses) will create a romantic, feminine arrangement that is pleasing to the eye.

- *Choose hues carefully.* Color has weight. Darker flowers often seem to be heavier and more prominent in an arrangement. Rather than placing a dark flower at the bottom of an arrangement (where the eye will be drawn downward) consider putting it up higher, where it will attract attention to other interesting flowers in the arrangement.

CREATING A BASIC ARRANGEMENT

Now that you know your flower types, how to cut and preserve flowers, and some basic floral design tips, you're ready to create an arrangement! Here are some simple steps to get you started.

- *Create a base.* Most people want to head straight for their show-stopper flowers when creating an arrangement. But it's best to first form a foundation for those blooms. Starting with your filler flowers, place them in the vessel so that their stems cross, creating a lattice that will act as a support system for the other flowers.

- *Add your mass flowers.* Peonies, roses, and round-faced flowers are now ready to be added. Insert them into the lattice you created. Make sure the flower heads are well supported by the filler flowers. For instance, the filler flowers can lean against the heavier flower heads to prevent drooping and snapping. When adding these flowers, remember to vary their location and height within the arrangement.

- *Add the taller flowers.* Tall stalks, branches, and leggier flowers should be added last, as accents to the main body of the arrangement. Vary their location and height to avoid creating a uniform tall wall above the mass flowers. Sarah at Saipua says these flowers are a way of adding "the feeling of movement" to an arrangement. For instance, a particularly leggy and twisted Ranunculus can add a playful and light note to a bouquet.

- *Spin your vase around.* It's perfectly fine if the back of your arrangement isn't as pretty as the front. But if you have extra flowers, consider spinning the arrangement around to see if there are any holes that need filling. Try adding small, odd-numbered groups of mass flowers to your arrangement. For example, if you have a large hole in the bouquet, instead of using a big peony to fill the space consider instead adding a group of three smaller mass flowers like Scabiosa.

SIMPLE AND STAGGERED ARRANGEMENT

LESSON
Using staggered heights to mimic natural growth

APPROXIMATE COST
$30

WE USED
Cosmos

ALTERNATIVES
Ranunculus, nigella, Scabiosa, daisies

VASE
Fluted vase

OTHER MATERIALS
Small frog (optional)

INSTEAD OF LEAVING YOUR flowers all at the same height, try cutting the stems at varying lengths to create a simple arrangement that is reminiscent of flowers growing in the garden.

~~~~~~~~~~~~~~~~~~~~~ INSTRUCTIONS ~~~~~~~~~~~~~~~~~~~~~

Starting at the high point, roughly twice the height of the vase, and working down, hold flowers up to your vase to check placement before you clip their stems and place them in your container. Because cosmos have a natural flexibility and the mouth of this vase was wide, I used a small flower frog to hold the flowers in the center upright. This staggering technique can be used in all types of vessels and works with all kinds of flowers.

BUD VASE
ARRANGEMENT

LESSON

Using one large
focal flower as an
arrangement in itself

APPROXIMATE COST
$15

WE USED
Tree peony, chocolate
cosmos, Bradford
pear foliage

ALTERNATIVES
Dahlias, peonies,
amaryllis for the face flower;
branches, dusty miller,
lambs ear for the foliage

VASE
Glass bud vase

ONE GORGEOUS, FULL-FACED FLOWER combined with
a little bit of foliage is sometimes all you need to create a show-stopping
arrangement. When money and time are tight, it's easiest to let a beautiful
flower speak for itself.

〜〜〜〜〜〜〜〜〜〜〜〜〜〜〜〜〜〜〜〜〜 INSTRUCTIONS 〜〜〜〜〜〜〜〜〜〜〜〜〜〜〜〜〜〜〜

Place your foliage in the bud vase. Add your large flower, keeping in mind that it will look most
natural if its center rests on the mouth of the vase. Include a cluster of wispy, small flowers to
add interest.

LOW, NATURAL ARRANGEMENT

LESSON
Using floral foam to create a low, cascading arrangement

APPROXIMATE COST
$35

WE USED
Hydrangea, dahlias, passion vine, astilbe, geranium, cosmos, Bradford pear branches

ALTERNATIVES
Garden roses, ivy, Scabiosa, hosta leaves, lilac

VASE
Bowl, low-footed urn, or compote

OTHER MATERIALS
Floral foam

CREATING A CASCADING ARRANGEMENT in floral foam is a surprisingly easy way to showcase a few standout flowers. These arrangements look especially pretty in bowls, footed urns, and compotes.

INSTRUCTIONS

Cut down a block of floral foam to fit in your vessel and soak in water for 10 minutes (do not use foam for dried flowers). Place foam in your bowl, hole side down, and fill with water (I used a liner in my terra-cotta urn as it wasn't watertight). Use your hydrangea and branches to create a natural, soft coverage of your foam, then add your few largest show flowers. Place any gesture flowers and trailing vines last. When using foam, if you remove a flower from its place, you will need to retrim its stem before using it again. Consider the placement of each flower carefully, as too much moving of stems will fill the foam with holes and cause it to crumble.

WE USED
Baby's breath

ALTERNATIVES
Wax flower, carnations, chamomile

VASE
Decorative tea tins

OTHER MATERIALS
Clear silicone caulk (optional), twine

OFTEN-OVERLOOKED FILLER FLOWERS CAN make adorable arrangements clustered en masse. To create a cheeky centerpiece, use a variety of tea tins repurposed as vases. Even grocery-store coffee cans act as impromptu vessels when you need to create something colorful, fun, and inexpensive.

∿∿∿∿∿∿∿∿∿∿∿∿∿∿∿∿ INSTRUCTIONS ∿∿∿∿∿∿∿∿∿∿∿∿∿∿∿∿

Test your tins to make sure they don't leak. If they do, smooth some clear silicone caulk (available at the hardware store) over all of the inside seams and allow to dry. Next make a small but dense bouquet of baby's breath in your hand by clipping off the side shoots of flowers on each stem to have more manageable pieces. Once you have created a dome shape to fit your tea tin, tie off the stems with twine and place in water.

BRANCH ARRANGEMENT

LESSON
Using only branches
to create a large,
dramatic display

APPROXIMATE COST
$30

WE USED
Burning bush branches

ALTERNATIVES
Dogwood, crab apple,
Russian olive, Bradford pear
branches, spirea

VASE
Footed cup vase or
chalice-style vase

OTHER MATERIALS
Chicken wire

WHEN YOU NEED SOMETHING large and dramatic but don't want to fork over serious money, try making an arrangement with only branches. Flowering branches look beautiful in the spring, and colorful foliage and fruiting branches are perfect for fall.

〰〰〰〰〰〰〰〰〰〰〰〰〰〰 INSTRUCTIONS 〰〰〰〰〰〰〰〰〰〰〰〰〰〰

Clip a medium-sized square of chicken wire to ball up and place in the bottom of your urn (this will act as your support). Starting with the largest branches first, place them in the urn so that the chicken wire holds them in place. Continue to add more branches as you turn the vase to create a full and round arrangement that can be viewed from all angles.

UNEXPECTED ELEMENT ARRANGEMENT

LESSON
Focusing on textural greens and natural elements instead of flowers in arrangements

APPROXIMATE COST
$25

WE USED
Artichokes, ferns, geranium leaf, rosemary, passion vine, Scabiosa buds

ALTERNATIVES
Succulents, crab apple, cockscomb, wild grasses, basil

VASE
Large water or juice cup (we used a Jadeite cup)

OTHER MATERIALS
Bamboo skewers (optional)

THINK OUTSIDE THE BOX when it comes to materials for your arrangements. Fruits, vegetables, herbs, and houseplant cuttings can make fun, unexpected mixed arrangements and can cost less than their floral counterparts. Now your backyard garden can add to your centerpiece as well as your dinner.

~~~~~~~~~~~~~~~~~~~~~~~~~~~~ INSTRUCTIONS ~~~~~~~~~~~~~~~~~~~~~~~~~~~~

Place your bulkiest element first—I used two artichokes on the stalk. If you're unable to find fruits or vegetables still on the stalk, you can push bamboo skewers through the centers to create makeshift stems. Continue to add fronds and leaves to create a lush mixed arrangement.

HAND-TIED
BOUQUET

LESSON
Making a small
hand-tied bouquet
with three main
types of flowers

APPROXIMATE COST
$25

WE USED
Anemones, Amensia roses,
spray roses, begonia leaf,
Scabiosa

ALTERNATIVES
Ranunculus, dahlias,
peonies, cosmos, foliage

VASE
Mason jar

OTHER MATERIALS
Rubber band, ribbon

USING JUST A FEW kinds of flowers and a pretty ribbon, a simple
hand-tied bouquet makes a sweet gift or display when placed in a mason
jar. The addition of a velvet ribbon elevates the arrangement enough to
make it perfect for a homespun wedding. So if the price of wedding flowers
seems overwhelming, consider tying your own bouquet to keep costs more
reasonable.

INSTRUCTIONS

Starting at the top center, make a loose dome shape by spiraling the stems in the same direction.
Clustering one type of flower together adds a natural, effortless look. Add a single pretty leaf
to offset the bouquet and while holding it loosely in one hand, send a few small gesture flowers
(leggy blooms that mimic growth or movement) down the center. Use a rubber band to secure the
stems, tie a pretty ribbon around it, and clip the stems to the same length.

WILDFLOWER ARRANGEMENT

LESSON
Creating a loose, just picked from the field—style arrangement

APPROXIMATE COST
$35

WE USED
Dahlias, Bradford pear, astilbe, cosmos, wax flower

ALTERNATIVES
Roses, foliage, Queen Anne's lace, Scabiosa, sedum

VASE
Large glass cup

BY MIXING TEXTURES AND types of flowers, creating a loose, natural arrangement is a snap. No matter what season it is, you can always choose from an array of inexpensive leaves, branches, and filler flowers. Select a range of textures and colors and you'll have an arrangement that feels beautiful, organic, and effortless.

~~~~~~~~~~~~~~~~~~~~~~ INSTRUCTIONS ~~~~~~~~~~~~~~~~~~~~~~

Create a frame for your arrangement by placing branches in your vase first. Add in your filler flowers, such as sedum or wax flower. Then cluster together several of your fuller flowers to create a focal point. Last, add a few gesture flowers to create natural movement.

DOME
ARRANGEMENT
LESSON
Creating a compact
arrangement
APPROXIMATE COST
$50

WE USED
Dahlias, hocus pocus roses,
garden roses

ALTERNATIVES
Peonies, hydrangea, lilac

VASE
Wide cynlinder vase
(we used a mercury
glass vase)

DOME-SHAPED ARRANGEMENTS ARE A classic, goof-proof option for a centerpiece. Mixed flowers in tonal colors make a great dressed-up arrangement, while using only one type gives a simple, casual look. Don't fret if your dome shape is less than perfect: a naturally rounded shape will look just as elegant.

~~~~~~~~~~~~~~~~~~~~~~~~~ INSTRUCTIONS ~~~~~~~~~~~~~~~~~~~~~~~~~

Starting along the lip of your vase, place flowers in a spiral pattern so that the stems cross one another as you go around the circle. Continue to spiral upward, varying flower types to create a dense arrangement with texture.

SEASONAL
TABLESCAPE

LESSON
Using natural
elements combined
with small
arrangements and
single stems to create
a tablescape

APPROXIMATE COST
$50 (including
pumpkins)

WE USED
Garden roses, geranium
leaves, rosemary,
persimmons on the branch,
amaranthus, cinderella and
baby boo pumpkins

ALTERNATIVES
Crab apple branches, hosta
leaves, ferns, basil

VASE
An assortment of bottles, a
teacup, and/or small vases

OTHER MATERIALS
Chicken wire

MAKING A FESTIVE AND memorable centerpiece is as easy as combining natural elements like these heirloom pumpkins with a simple mix of bottles, stems, and miniature arrangements. Rather than going overboard with cornucopias and larger pieces, you can get the same effect by grouping smaller arrangements around a central focal point.

~~~~~~~~~~~~~~~~~~~~~~~~~~~~~ INSTRUCTIONS ~~~~~~~~~~~~~~~~~~~~~~~~~~~~~

Find a complementary mix of bottles and vases to create a tablescape. To make a small arrangement in a teacup, cut a small square of chicken wire, ball up, and place inside to act as the support for the flowers. A combination of one type of flower, two types of greens, and one type of branch makes a quick and simple small arrangement. By adding bottles of varying heights filled with branches and leaves, the tablescape is complete.

VINTAGE
BOTTLES FOR
THE AVID
COLLECTOR

page 60

INSPIRATION
Amy Merrick's
Brooklyn apartment

APPROXIMATE COST
$10

WE USED
Ranunculus

ALTERNATIVES
Look for wildflowers with
twisting and turning
stems: Queen Anne's lace,
echinacea, daisies, or garden
roses with leggy stems
would all look lovely. The key
is to keep them at different
heights, combining open
flowers with closed buds.

VASE
A mix of narrow-necked
vintage bottles in a range
of sizes (try eBay, Craigslist,
thrift stores, and junk shops
for inexpensive bottles)

DESIGN*SPONGE EDITOR AMY MERRICK has such neat
collections of everything—her house is like a beautiful curio cabinet. Sarah
was inspired to use old medicine bottles (like the ones Amy collects) to
elevate a few simple stems of Ranunculus to specimen status. The best thing
about this type of floral arrangement is that you can save money by focusing
on only a few special blooms, rather than a full bouquet. Try using a mixture
of different bottle colors and heights to give more visual interest to the
arrangement.

INSTRUCTIONS

Place a single bloom in each vase and use a range of vases in varying heights. Be sure to consider
the unopened blooms as well. Their tiny buds often act as bits of sculpture next to the open
blooms.

BIRCH-WRAPPED ARRANGEMENT

INSPIRATION
Genifer Goodman
Sohr's Nashville
cottage

APPROXIMATE COST
$50 to $100

WE USED
Tree peonies, boronia,
Leucadendron, pepperberry,
pomegranates, and
chocolate cosmos

ALTERNATIVES
Any combination of
trailing vines (such as ferns
and wild vines), berries,
round fruits (try citrus),
and flowers (garden roses).
Consider spray painting the
citrus a metallic color for
a richer feel.

A tip about birch bark

As birch trees age, they
discard layers of their bark,
leaving it on the forest floor.
The texture is divine—
papery and very malleable.
The best time to grab it is
in the fall—but please don't
attempt to cut bark off a
living tree!

SARAH LOVED THE LOG cabin walls in designer Genifer Goodman Sohr's home so much that she was inspired to create an arrangement that would fit a woodsy cabin theme. Using naturally fallen birch bark, she created a custom vase and an arrangement to fit the home's red and pink theme. The best part about this arrangement? You can simply slide the birch bark off the vase when you're done and reapply it to a different vessel for a new bouquet.

INSTRUCTIONS

1 Using a 6 × 6-inch cylinder (a large tin can will work nicely), wrap a piece of birch bark around the perimeter. The birch pieces have a natural curve to them, so it should be very easy to wrap around a simple cylindrical vase.

2 After wrapping, cut the strip of birch down with a knife or razor blade so that it matches the height of the vase. Secure with hot glue, or tie with twine to hold it in place.

3 For the arrangement, loosely gather your main elements (tree peonies and boronia) and place them in your birch vase. Attach the fruit to floral sticks and add in the remaining elements piece by piece until you have an arrangement that feels balanced, but still loose—like something you'd put together when staying at a cozy log cabin.

STUDY IN WHITE AND GREEN

INSPIRATION
Bonnee Sharp's
Dallas home

APPROXIMATE COST
$30 to $50

WE USED
Geranium leaves,
Ranunculus, tillandsia (air
plants), tulips, Amaranthus

ALTERNATIVES
This arrangement is all
about the color palette. To
create a similar green and
white look at a lower cost, try
white (or a combination
of white and green)
carnations or spray roses.
Basil leaves would work well
as filler foliage. Ivy, jasmine,
or another trailing element
can replace the Amaranthus.

OTHER MATERIALS
Floral foam, floral wire,
floral sticks (optional)

SARAH LOVED THE MANY shades of green in textile designer
Bonnee Sharp's bedroom and decided to capture all of that verdant color in
a more condensed form. By using a compote as a vase, she elevates this little
study from easy to elegant. Simple tricks like changing the height of the
container—whether this means using a taller vessel or standing a shorter one
on a stack of books—can have a dramatic effect.

INSTRUCTIONS

1   Place a 2-inch cube of soaked floral foam in a shallow compote or similar raised container.
    Add the geranium leaves and Ranunculus to create a base for the air plants.

2   Using floral wire, attach the air plants to floral sticks or the stems of other flowers and bend
    them into the desired position.

3   Once the air plants are in place, fill any remaining holes in the arrangement with tulips and
    Amaranthus.

DRIFTWOOD ARRANGEMENT

INSPIRATION
Linda and John Meyers' Portland, Maine, home

APPROXIMATE COST
Most of these things you can find in your yard or the woods—just be sure you have permission to gather them.

WE USED
Black Queen Anne's lace, morning glory vines, Leucadendron, begonia leaves, and agonis

ALTERNATIVES
A mix of wildflowers, vines, and leaves gives this loose arrangement its character. Save money by substituting a mix of native plants from your area. Queen Anne's lace is often found growing wild in fields: Keep an eye out for this plant when you're driving around town (but don't take anything growing in a protected area or on private property).

VASE
Piece of driftwood that has natural openings in it

OTHER MATERIALS
Floral foam

EVERYWHERE YOU LOOK IN designers Linda and John Meyers' house there seems to be something interesting hidden. It's dense with dark, layered colors, like a whimsically patterned forest. Sarah wanted to create an arrangement that felt as dramatic, so she used a large driftwood log to act as the base for this colorful arrangement. When creating a centerpiece for your next dinner party, consider using something unexpected as a container, like a piece of driftwood or a hollow log—it will get your guests talking and will inspire you to create an arrangement that is more free-flowing and natural.

INSTRUCTIONS

1   Using a piece of driftwood (if you don't have access to any, try eBay for affordable pieces), stuff a 5-inch cube of soaked floral foam (the size of the foam will depend on the piece of wood you use) into a hole to act as the base of the arrangement.

2   Starting with the larger stems and working toward the smallest, place your flowers into the foam. This arrangement is meant to be loose and flowing, so don't be afraid to let pieces hang where they may.

NOTE: Because of the lack of a water reservoir, this arrangement won't last as long as others—but it will make an impressive centerpiece for a party or special event.

FRAGRANT ARRANGEMENT

INSPIRATION
Carol Neiley's
Lyon apartment

APPROXIMATE COST
$20

WE USED
Peach garden roses,
tuberose

ALTERNATIVES
This arrangement is all about
color and fragrance. When
going small like this, it's
worth splurging on a nice
flower or two, but if you want
to keep costs even lower you
can replace the roses with
similarly colored carnations.

VASE
A long-necked vase that
flares at the opening

THE FRENCH ARE SERIOUS about flowers—and are known to pay particular attention to the fragrance of their blooms. The pale peach color in Basic French owner Carol Neiley's bedroom helped determine the color of this fragrant nosegay set in a petite parfait glass. We have a feeling Carol's French neighbors would approve of this fragrant bunch.

━━━━━━━━━━━━━━━ INSTRUCTIONS ━━━━━━━━━━━━━━━

To create this simple arrangement, start by using primary flowers clustered in threes. The main ingredient here is a set of three garden roses; the secondary flower, tuberose, is added behind as an astute pair. Don't be afraid to leave things simple—sometimes less is more when it comes to fragrant flowers. You don't want to overwhelm the room with scent, so stick to a small number of fragrant blooms.

ARRANGEMENT OF RED TONES

INSPIRATION
Su-Lyn Tan and
Aun Koh's red door
in Singapore

APPROXIMATE COST
$40

WE USED
Roses, rose hips,
grasses, Ranunculus

ALTERNATIVES
Carnations now come in a
stunning array of colors.
Pick an assortment of
various reds and purples to
create a similar arrangement
at a lower price.

VASE
A red vase or container
with a narrow neck

Tip

When working with one
color in an arrangement it's
best to focus on variations
in shade, texture, and size.
Look for plants, leaves,
vines, and flowers that
represent a wide range of
your color and you'll create
an arrangement with more
depth. To add a visual "pop"
try mixing in a small bit of
complementary color. In this
case, green enhances the
richness of the red blooms.

THE RED DOOR TO Su-Lyn and Aun's home really sets the tone for how we view its interior. Sarah wanted to mimic this intense color with an all-red arrangement, while showing how to work with different shades of the same color. Once you've chosen a red vessel to act as the main color, try working with a mix of reds, pinks, and purples that will be enhanced by the vivid red of the base.

INSTRUCTIONS

1   Start with your favorite, or a particularly interesting, bloom and place it in the center of your palm (see Note). Working outward from there, continue to add blooms, making sure to vary the height of each flower as you go. For this arrangement, Sarah kept the stems long so she could keep adjusting the blooms before placing them in the vase. This is a great technique if you're working with a vessel that has a small opening.

2   When you're done, trim the stems and place the flowers in your vessel. Then fluff and tweak a few stems outward to give the arrangement a fuller feel.

NOTE: Sarah made this arrangement in her hand, keeping the stems rather tight in her fist as she worked to account for the small opening in the ceramic vessel.

BOX OF SUCCULENTS

INSPIRATION
Tara Heibel's
Chicago home

APPROXIMATE COST
$50 to $100

WE USED
Succulents, Echeveria,
Agonis, silver brunia,
hanging Amaranthus, seeded
eucalyptus, Ranunculus,
and umbrella fern

ALTERNATIVES
This bouquet features
trailing flowers combined
with heavier, sculptural
blooms. Try replacing the
filler and trailing flowers with
ferns, wild berries, and vines.
Many of those elements can
be found for free in your
backyard or in local fields.
Small spray roses work in
place of the Ranunuculus.

VASE
A low, wide vase or container
works best here. A small
wooden box would make
a great alternative.

OTHER MATERIALS
Chicken wire, wooden
floral sticks

A GARDEN DESIGNER AND owner of Sprout Home, Tara Heibel's home is filled with all *sorts* of interesting green plants. As a fellow florist, Sarah was drawn to Sprout Home's textural and unusual arrangements and decided to create one that reflects the modern feel of Tara's home and floral style. Don't be afraid to work succulents and other types of greenery into your arrangements at home—varying shades of green can be just as beautiful as (and much less expensive than) colorful flowers.

INSTRUCTIONS

1   Place a sheet of chicken wire inside an aluminum cube (plastic, ceramic, or wood will work just as well). You can find chicken wire at most hardware stores or home improvement centers.

2   Wire the succulents to the wooden sticks so you can place them in the chicken wire just like the other flowers in the arrangement.

3   Once the succulents are wired, put them in the vase (use the chicken wire to hold them in place). Then fill the open spaces with the other flowers and greens to make a layered, lush composition.

BEFORE & AFTER

At Design*Sponge, we love few things more than rescuing a piece of furniture bound for the trash and giving it a new life. Whether you paint something, add new hardware,

or embark upon a major renovation, the process of before and after makeovers is a popular one with both our editors and readers. A weekly makeover column was launched in 2007 to celebrate the amazing transformations we were receiving from readers, and quickly became a site favorite. I'm thrilled to share fifty great projects in this chapter of the book.

Each project is broken down by cost, time, and difficulty so you can get a feel for whether a certain makeover method is right for you. While I've chosen to include a few large-scale makeovers that were lucky enough to have big budgets, the majority of projects here were submitted by readers just like you, working with limited time, real-world budgets, and an average set of construction skills. From repainting chairs to transforming vintage suitcases into side tables, there's a project here for everyone. I hope these makeovers will inspire you to check out your local yard sales, thrift stores, and even curbsides as potential sites for finding projects for your home, rather than places to retire furniture in need of a little TLC.

Every Thursday at Design*Sponge, there is a recurring debate in the comment sections of the Before & After posts about whether it's "right" to alter a vintage or antique piece of furniture. People seem to fall into two clear (and vocal) camps: those who believe an artist or designer's original piece should never be changed, and those who feel alterations are fine as long as they mean giving the object a new life in someone's home. My editors fall into different positions on the "to change or not to change" spectrum so I decided rather than tell people what is right or wrong, I'd try to share some helpful tips for identifying pieces of furniture or design that are handmade, of high quality, or are of notable financial value. Whether you choose to paint after that is entirely up to you!

SIGNS OF HANDMADE OR HIGH-QUALITY CRAFTSMANSHIP

- Dovetail joints
- Solid hardwood (as opposed to veneer)
- Corner blocks (which provide long-term support for furniture)
- Equal fronts and backs (high-quality items should have the same attention paid to both the front and back pieces of the furniture)
- Drawer runners (wooden or metal drawer runners provide extra stability)

ADDITIONAL TIPS FOR ASSESSING YOUR USED FURNITURE OR ACCESSORIES

- *Look for stamps, labels, and ID tags:* Manufacturers in different fields often stamp or mark their work to ensure authenticity.
- *Assess damage:* Clearly the less damage your object has, the better, but sometimes cracking or discoloration can indicate a time period in which something was made, possibly adding value to your object. Be sure to ask the seller what they know about the source of any imperfections on their pieces.
- *Understand the market:* If you have an eye on a specific style or piece, do a little research to get a feel for the trademark characteristics of your desired find. It never hurts to do a search on eBay, 1stdibs, or Craigslist to see if you can find similar items. Experienced antique or vintage dealers will often sell pieces online and can tell you what signs to look for in specific types of furniture (and what you might expect to pay for them).

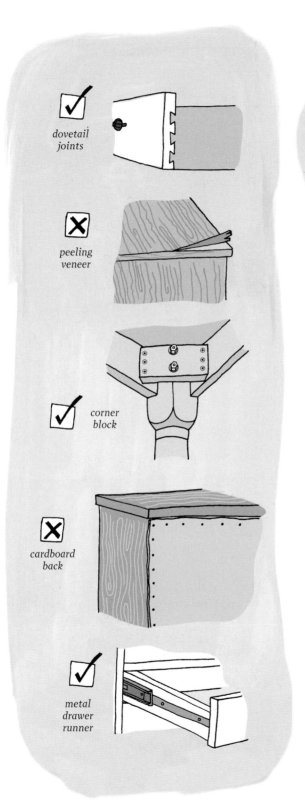

dovetail
joints

peeling
veneer

corner
block

cardboard
back

metal
drawer
runner

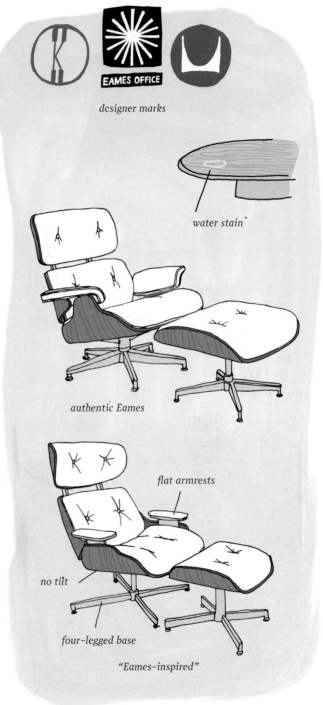

designer marks

water stain

authentic Eames

flat armrests

no tilt

four-legged base

"Eames-inspired"

COST
$6

TIME
3 hours

DIFFICULTY
★ ☆ ☆ ☆

after

I love when I hear from readers or artists who choose to update something that I probably wouldn't have given a second look. Design*Sponge readers Matt and Beth Coleman, of Lancaster, Pennsylvania, bought a $2 down-on-its-luck thrift store scale on a whim and decided to attempt a makeover. A coat of Sun Yellow spray paint from Krylon instantly revived the frame, and a sheet of cork contact paper replaced the damaged black rubber. The couple now has a unique scale to dress up their bathroom.

before

COST
$45

TIME
1 hour and 45 minutes

DIFFICULTY
★ ★ ★ ★

after

before

Maui-based graphic designer John Giordani loved his stainless-steel cabinets, but wanted to add some spice to the boring brown color. Inspired by a Mark Rothko painting, John decided to paint the cabinet with a Kilz spray-paint-and-primer-in-one. Now that the look is colorful and fresh, the cabinets have become a cheerful conversation piece in John's home.

COST
$10

TIME
8 hours

DIFFICULTY
★ ☆ ☆ ☆

after

Newlywed couple K. C. and Sara Giessen wanted to decorate their Atlanta home with new furniture but were faced with a tight budget. So this clever couple opted to transform their hand-me-down table into a one-of-a-kind dining centerpiece. After cutting a plate-and-utensils template by hand, Sara painted a reverse stencil design on the tabletop in a vibrant neon green color. When the stencil was dry the final result was a colorful new table with playful spots for plates and silverware.

before

COST
$271

TIME
4 hours

DIFFICULTY
★ ★ ★ ★

after

When interior designer and stylist Lauren Nelson first brought this wooden chair to her Cambridge, Massachusetts, home, her boyfriend was not excited about its prospects. But Lauren said, "Trust me, it has potential." After cleaning, sanding, and repainting the frame, Lauren used a bold purple and white fabric from Stout Brothers to give it a crisp, clean look. Lauren's boyfriend now agrees it is their favorite chair in the house.

before

COST
$15

TIME
1 hour

DIFFICULTY
★ ☆ ☆ ☆

after

Most people pass by lumberyards on their way home and don't look twice, but blogger Michelle Hinckley, of Oro Valley, Arizona, saw it as a chance to create an interesting—and affordable—side table. After picking up a $5 log stump, Michelle painted the entire piece a smoky gray color and topped it off with a $10 mirror from Target. When everything was dry and in place, Michelle had a brand-new, stylish side table for under $20.

before

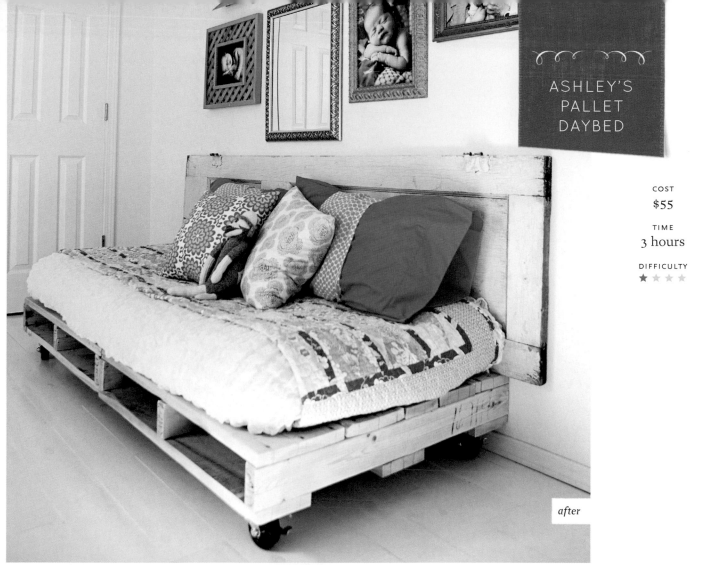

COST
$55

TIME
3 hours

DIFFICULTY
★ ☆ ☆ ☆

after

before

Not everyone would look at a wooden pallet and see furniture for their daughter's playroom, but photographer Ashley Campbell saw the potential in this humble piece of wood. Looking to keep things "cozy and cuddly," Ashley added wheels (with locks) to the pallets, and then bought a comfortable mattress and piles of bedding and pillows from Target and Ikea to create this colorful daybed for her home in Broken Arrow, Oklahoma. To complete the salvaged look, Ashley turned an old door into a makeshift headboard.

SAFETY NOTE: Wooden pallets are often treated with chemicals for industrial use. For more information about pallet safety, see *www.ehow.com/ way_5729154_wood-pallet-safety.html*.

COST
$32

TIME
10 hours

DIFFICULTY
★ ☆ ☆ ☆

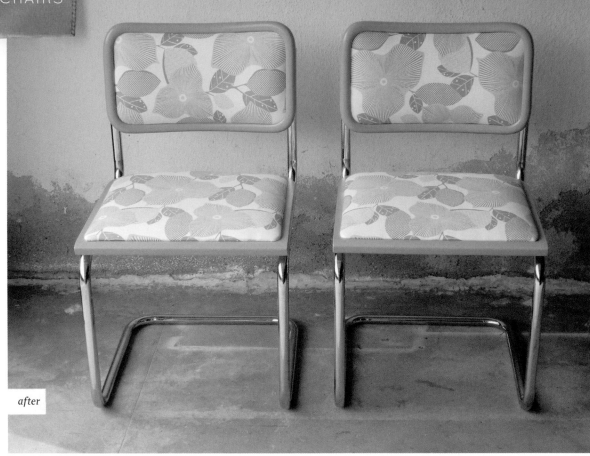

after

One of the common elements among before and after makeovers is the sense of nostalgia that draws people to damaged furniture. In this case, architect and designer Carmen McKee Bushong found herself taking these metal tube chairs home because they reminded her of a pair from her childhood. Determined to give them an update, Carmen repainted the wooden frames yellow, upholstered the seats in a bold floral print from Amy Butler, and gave them a new life in her Los Angeles home.

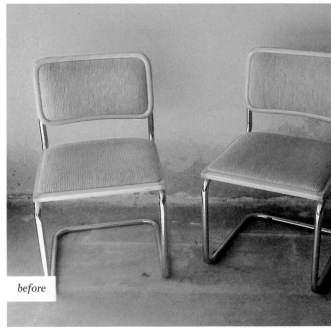

before

COST
$30

TIME
1 hour

DIFFICULTY
★ ☆ ☆ ☆

after

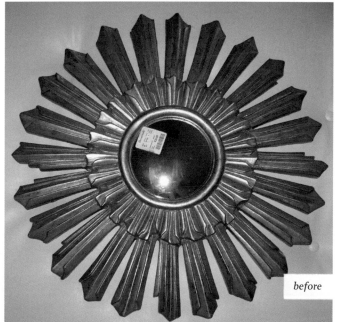

before

Blogger and all around crafty lady Michelle Hinckley is a big fan of sunburst mirrors, but not the high price that often comes with them. So when she found this $29 version at a HomeGoods near her home in Oro Valley, Arizona, she immediately scooped it up. Determined to create her own sunburst look on a lower budget, Michelle used a ninety-seven-cent pack of bamboo skewers from her local grocery store to create a custom sunburst design. Once the skewers were glued in place, both frame and skewers got a coat of black and silver paint to give them an antiqued effect.

COST
$30

TIME
2 hours per desk

DIFFICULTY
★ ☆ ☆ ☆

after

Though the saying is cliché, it really is true that one man's trash is another man's treasure. Oregon crafter and mom Tanya Risenmay Smith stumbled upon these vintage school desks and immediately jumped at the chance to turn someone else's junk into cherished new pieces for her children. After carefully removing the rust from each desk, Tanya sprayed the frames with a white primer to prep them for a coat of glossy apple red and pink spray paint. Once they dried she coated the tops with blackboard paint, giving the kids a new place to learn and play.

before

COST
$44

TIME
3 hours

DIFFICULTY
★ ☆ ☆ ☆

after

before

Artist Shirin Sahba adores vintage trunks, so she was ecstatic when her husband spotted this piece at a local secondhand shop. Though it arrived at their Vancouver Island home in pretty bad shape, Shirin saw potential and decided to update her find with a little do-it-yourself love. Shirin cleaned and repainted the frame using an eye-popping coral red and now loves that "everyone who walks into the house is drawn to it right away!"

COST
$20

TIME
1 hour

DIFFICULTY
★ ★ ★ ★

after

Estate sales can be great places to pick up inexpensive design items. Blogger Michelle Hinckley of Three Men and a Lady found this $15 gold mirror at an estate sale and brought it home with her for an office project. Michelle removed the mirror from the frame and replaced it with an old corkboard she'd been saving, and secured a piece of burlap fabric to the cork board with spray adhesive and staples. The mirror's frame got a new coat of white paint, and then the cork and burlap board was reattached. The chic new memo board was then hung from a ribbon in Michelle's office in Oro Valley, Arizona.

before

COST
$45

TIME
2.5 hours

DIFFICULTY
★ ☆ ☆ ☆

after

before

Headboards are a great way to bring bold color or pattern into your room without too much of a commitment—especially when your headboard is a budget-friendly folding screen! Tuscaloosa, Alabama, artist Brooke Premo won an intricately designed folding screen at an auction she attended. After a little sanding and a coat of bright blue-green paint, Brooke refurbished this auction find into the headboard she had always wanted.

COST
$100

TIME
8 hours

DIFFICULTY
★ ☆ ☆ ☆

after

One of my favorite ways to update a piece of furniture is to give it a bright pop of color in an unexpected place. Design*Sponge reader Nicole Haladyna, who specializes in updating older furniture in Austin, Texas, did just that with her desk. After painting the body a sophisticated gray hue, Nicole played up the desk's dual personality by contrasting the mature exterior with a playful orange interior.

before

after

COST
$16

TIME
2 hours

DIFFICULTY
★ ☆ ☆ ☆

before

Wooden pallets are some of the most versatile and easy-to-find building materials around. Mom-on-the-go Karen Brown, of Malden, Massachusetts, was looking for a way to keep her older daughter's nicer books out of her toddler's reach, so she decided to solve her problem with a great afternoon do-it-yourself project. Using a wooden pallet she found on the street, Karen cleaned and dried the frame, sanded the surface, and coated it with a wax polish (Fiddes Wax in Rugger Brown) to give it a modern, beachy feel.

SAFETY NOTE: Wooden pallets are often treated with chemicals for industrial use. For more information about pallet safety, see *www.ehow.com/ way_5729154_wood-pallet-safety.html.*

COST
$2,500
(includes new
furniture and
supplies)

TIME
3 months

DIFFICULTY
★ ☆ ☆ ☆

after

Graphic designer Jenny Enfield Dean and photographer
Joe Miller both travel a lot for work. When they moved
in together, they collaborated on the interior design of a
home that would be a nice haven to come back to. Over the
course of three months, they gathered an eclectic mix of
furniture, including new and vintage pieces. They both also
created original artwork to decorate their space. The result
manages to feel modern, with bold and graphic touches,
while also conveying an inviting warmth and cozy feeling.

before

ORLANDO'S
STRIPED
FLOORS

COST
$60

TIME
16 hours

DIFFICULTY
★ ★ ☆ ☆

after

before

Los Angeles—based artist and designer Orlando Dumond Soria's floors were getting him down, until he decided to swap out the dingy old floors for a chic new striped look. Using only inexpensive black and white self-adhesive linoleum tiles, a box cutter, and a pencil, Orlando cut the tiles by hand to create a striped design that only cost $60. It's hard to believe that something so stylish could come from linoleum, but Orlando's project is proof that a high-end look really can come from budget-friendly, low-end materials.

COST
$60

TIME
15 hours

DIFFICULTY
★ ★ ☆ ☆

after

When Lori Dunbar removed the carpet in the sunroom of her Wisconsin home, she decided, both literally and figuratively, to let the sun in. Lori used a customized blend of sunshine yellow Behr porch paint and her own custom-designed template to bring a fresh look to her room. While the carpet had weighed down the space before, Lori's whimsical new patterned floor gives it a sense of lightness that is right at home on a sunporch.

before

COST
$3,000
(including new
furniture and
accessories)

TIME
1 (long) weekend

DIFFICULTY
★ ★ ☆ ☆

after

before

We've all dealt with awkward room layouts before, and designer Jason Martin's guest bedroom in Los Angeles was no different. Determined to overcome the room's less-than-desirable layout, Jason placed his desk at the end of the bed so he could make the most of the space and have the room do double duty as guest bedroom and office. To bring color to the room, Jason covered the back wall with inexpensive curtains from Ikea. To finish the look he added furniture from his own design studio, Jason Martin Designs, and inexpensive accessories from Crate and Barrel that matched the room's palette of warm browns.

after

COST
$40 plus wallpaper
($7 per square foot)

TIME
8 hours

DIFFICULTY
★ ★ ☆ ☆

Like many of our homes, Design*Sponge editor Amy
Merrick's apartment doesn't get as much light as she
would like. Looking to create an urban oasis reminiscent
of the flowers surrounding her at Brooklyn floral studio
Saipua (where she works), Amy decided to center her office
makeover around a reproduction C. F. A. Voysey wallpaper
pattern. Originally created in 1926 and now produced
by Trustworth Studios in Plymouth, Massachusetts,
the Apothecary's Garden wallpaper Amy chose fills her
office with playful images of flowers, birds, and insects.
While she may not have a garden in her backyard,
Amy comes home to one in her office every day.

before

COST
$80

TIME
1 day

DIFFICULTY
★ ★ ★ ★

after

Few patterns give the look and feel of freshness quite
like a good stripe. This bench makeover from Diana van
Helvoort utilizes a bold striped pattern to give an old bench
a new look. As the owner of a ribbon and crafts shop in
Munich, Diana has an eye for great design, and knew that
this bench, left on the side of the road, had the type of
good construction that would never feel outdated. After
hauling it home, Diana sanded the bench, primed it, and
gave it a coat of bright white paint. Once the paint dried,
she covered the seat and back in a colorful striped fabric
and added grosgrain ribbons from her shop for extra detail.

before

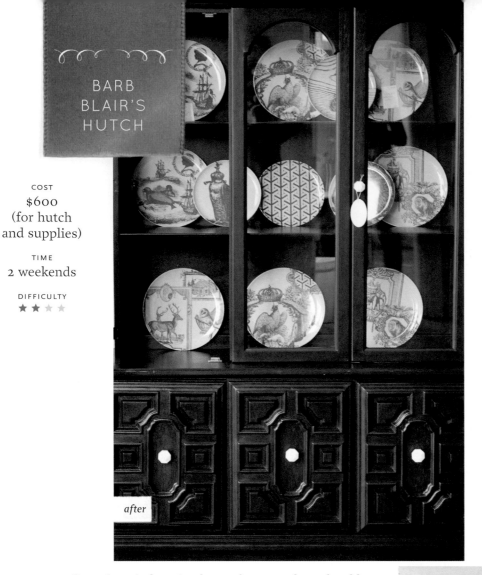

COST
$600
(for hutch
and supplies)

TIME
2 weekends

DIFFICULTY
★ ★ ☆ ☆

after

Sometimes it doesn't take much to transform the old
into the new. Barb Blair, owner of Knack Studio in
Greenville, South Carolina, understood this concept when
she transformed a worn hutch into a sleek new piece
with a coat of Ebony paint by Ralph Lauren, and fresh
new hardware. "All it took was a few small changes—
like removing the gaudy hardware and replacing it with
something more sophisticated—to bring this piece into
the modern day, and hopefully into a new home."

before

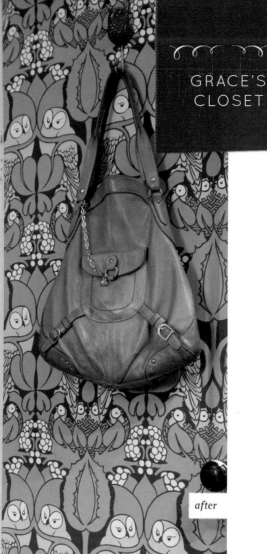

COST
$200

TIME
4 hours

DIFFICULTY
★ ★ ☆ ☆

after

before

Though I've shown my home on Design*Sponge before, I've always managed to cleverly leave out one part of the apartment: my closet. With our limited amount of space it had sadly become a stash-everything-and-run spot where shoes, clothing, office supplies, and crafting materials were piled up when company came. Determined to turn my closet into a tiny jewel box of color and pattern rather than a dark hole for clutter and trash, I used a roll of Whoot, from Trustworth Wallpaper, to cover not only the door and walls, but the clothes bar as well. Treating the closet like an extension of my personal space—and less like a place to hide clutter—made me more careful about what I kept inside and how I chose to store it. Now, rather than throwing myself up against the closed door when guests come, I open the door proudly and show them my tiny woodland-themed closet.

COST
$55

TIME
4 hours

DIFFICULTY
★ ★ ☆ ☆

after

Artist Lucinda Henry of Shakti Space Designs in Portland, Oregon, decided to get her blog audience involved in her makeover project by taking a vote on which finish she would use. When the polls had closed, the voters favored using Kittrich Walnut Woodgrain contact paper as the final decoration. After painting the body of the dresser white, Lucinda designed a floral pattern and cut each flower shape from the woodgrain contact paper, applying it to the front of the dresser. The stick-and-peel contact paper gives the illusion that a luxe dark wood is peeking out from underneath—but it's really just an everyday cabinet.

before

COST
$650
(including dresser
and supplies)

TIME
9 hours

DIFFICULTY
★ ★ ☆ ☆

after

before

Decorative paper can be one of the most affordable—and fun—ways to update an old piece of furniture. Barb Blair of Knack Studios in Greenville, South Carolina, used a vibrant floral paper from Papaya to update the panels on this dresser, after painting the frame with a peachy milk paint finish. If a full paint job isn't in the cards for your furniture, consider an update like Barb's using gift wrap, colored stationery, or wallpaper—you can buy small sizes and keep your budget low, but still give your furniture a high-end, decorative look.

COST
$40

TIME
5 hours

DIFFICULTY
★ ★ ☆ ☆

after

Looking for a large-scale planter solution can be expensive, but Austin-based furniture designer Chad Kelly knew he could create something more reasonable and fun with a standard filing cabinet. "I saw a similar cabinet-turned-planter in a store and it cost $600! But I knew I could do it myself for far less." Chad found the perfect Anderson Hickey filing cabinet on Craigslist for only $30, and used Rustoleum Sunburst Yellow protective enamel spray paint for the vibrant color. After building plywood boxes to fit inside the cabinet, Chad filled them with plants purchased from local nurseries.

before

COST
$150

TIME
5 days

DIFFICULTY
★ ★ ☆ ☆

after

before

Gray and yellow is one of the most popular color combinations we see on Design*Sponge, so we were thrilled to see Knoxville homeowner Libby Gourley use this classic combo as part of her kitchen makeover. An avid cook, Libby was set on updating her 1970s kitchen so that she would enjoy spending time in the room making meals for her family. To keep costs low, Libby focused on using paint to give the room a modern feel. Inspired by the food found in her kitchen (an egg, to be specific), she used a sunshine yellow and bright white paint combination to make her cabinets pop against the soft gray walls. Playful kitchen accessories bring an added dash of color to the room, completing the "appetizing" makeover Libby desired.

NIGHTWOOD'S
PROVENCE
SIDEBOARD

COST
$10

TIME
12 hours

DIFFICULTY
★ ★ ☆ ☆

after

Well-known for their rustic furniture makeovers, Brooklyn-based designers Nadia Yaron and Myriah Scruggs, of Nightwood, decided to transform this vintage sideboard into a chic, modern piece. Using salvaged pieces of oak, chestnut, pine, and walnut (all purchased for under $10), Nadia and Myriah designed a unit that was "casual and rustic while still having a touch of elegance."

before

COST
$25

TIME
3 hours

DIFFICULTY
★ ★ ☆ ☆

after

Dumpster diving is a popular pastime for dedicated before-and-after artists. Designers Jason and Martina Ahlbrandt found these black office chairs in a local Dumpster and decided to bring them home for a little upgrade. Originally Jason thought they'd be great for patio chairs, but Martina had the brilliant idea to combine them to create a custom bench. After removing the seats and backs, Jason and Martina spray-painted the frames silver and joined them together with five 1 × 4 wooden boards, creating a brand-new, five-foot-long bench for their backyard in Nashville.

before

349

ERIC'S IKEA DRESSER

COST
$85

TIME
9 hours

DIFFICULTY
★ ★ ☆ ☆

after

When it comes to furniture makeovers, few stores hold as much possibility as Ikea. Full of affordable, basic furniture just waiting to be customized, Ikea provides endless inspiration. Eric Teng, managing partner of the branding and advertising firm DMD Insight in New York City, is one of my favorite "Ikea-hackers." Erik purchased a Rast dresser from Ikea for less than $40 and decided to give it a luxe look by creating a contrasting light and dark finish. After sanding the dresser, Eric applied a stain (MinWax's Dark Walnut) to the body of the dresser. Once it dried, Eric painted the drawers a glossy white and added new hardware from Home Depot. He described the final look as "luxe, unexpected, and extraordinary," and we couldn't agree more.

before

COST
$42

TIME
1.5 hours

DIFFICULTY
★ ★ ☆ ☆

after

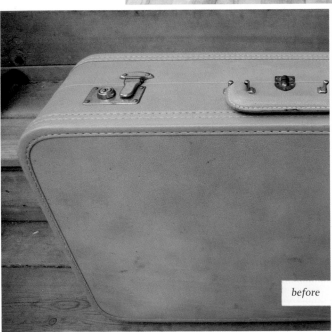

before

Suitcase makeovers are a huge part of the Before & After column at Design*Sponge. We've seen them turned into everything from entryway consoles and bedside tables to hanging storage. Artist Keeley Durocher decided to turn one of her favorite suitcases into a table, celebrating the fact that this world-traveling piece of design had finally come home to rest. By attaching a set of four tapered table legs from Waddell to the bottom of the suitcase, Keeley was able to create a sturdy table structure. Once the two pieces were connected, she painted the top and bottom with a glossy black spray paint to create a unified piece. Now this clever little suitcase table stands below a mirror in Keeley's Ottawa home, ready to hold household accessories and memorabilia from Keeley's travels.

COST
$5

TIME
about 2 hours

DIFFICULTY
★ ★ ☆ ☆

after

Graphic designer Christy Kilgore has an eye for color and loves to combine complementary hues for maximum impact. So when she found a metal box and table base on the side of the road in Charleston, Illinois, she decided to bring them home for a makeover. Working with outdoor spray paint (Krylon's Pumpkin Orange and Blue Ocean Breeze), Christy decided to paint the top and bottom different colors and combine them to create a side table that would bring bright color into her home—as well as some extra storage.

before

COST
$114
(including cost
of dresser)

TIME
20 hours

DIFFICULTY
★ ★ ☆ ☆

after

before

Furniture rehab partners Lauren Zimmerman and Nick Siemaska both work in creative fields in Boston, with Lauren in advertising and Nick working as a musician. Being surrounded by the arts in their everyday lives inspired this talented team to branch out and start making over furniture in their spare time. With this project, Lauren and Nick used contrasting shades of gray paint to give this aging dresser a new life. After removing a stubborn coat of varnish on the dresser's exterior, Lauren and Nick filled and sanded the drill holes in each drawer left by the original hardware. A coat of gray-blue paint was applied to the frame (Glidden's Wood Smoke) and a lighter gray (Glidden's Natural Linen) was used as an accent on the dresser's side and drawer fronts. After the paint dried, Lauren and Nick drilled new holes for orange pulls they found at a local salvage shop.

COST
$300

TIME
a few weekend
afternoons

DIFFICULTY
★ ★ ☆ ☆

after

Designer and decorative artist Brett McCormack knows his way around a can of paint. Looking to update his prewar New York City apartment, he turned to paint to create the serene, sophisticated feel he desired. Using a mix of paints, he created a faux marble top for his table, achieving a high-end look for a fraction of the cost. With black and brown spray paint, Brett updated and coordinated a pair of $1 tag sale lamps to mimic the look of oxidized iron. "I love the visual weight they have and wanted to emphasize their unique silhouette." He also painted the apartment's floors a light gray color (Benjamin Moore's London Fog) to give the appearance that the furniture was "floating on a cloud."

before

COST
Part of a $20,000 home renovation

TIME
3 months

DIFFICULTY
★ ★ ★ ☆

after

Industrial designer and design and process manager for Heath Ceramics, Christina Zamora recently completed the partial renovation of her Oakland, California, home. Looking to create a fully functional, minimalist kitchen, Christina worked closely with her builder, Jon Norton, to customize every detail of her new kitchen, from the kiln shelves (used as a kitchen island) screen-printed with oxides on the front to the backsplash/counterbox that serves as extra storage. The result is a space that works for Christina's family and blends effortlessly into their modern home.

before

COST
$50 to $75
(for cutting
the metal)

TIME
1.5 hours

DIFFICULTY
★ ★ ★ ☆

after

For Jessica Lynch, a daily hike can prove to be an inspiration for a DIY project. After finding a large piece of scrap metal in the woods near her home on Guemes Island, Washington, Lynch got the idea to cover her fireplace with this free find. She power-washed the metal and had a contractor cut the piece to a perfect fit. "I'm really attracted to this worn piece of metal with its rivets, dents, and faded paint colors, and knew before I even built my house that it was going to make its way somewhere into the plans."

before

COST
$1,000
(including the
dresser and
materials)

TIME
40 hours

DIFFICULTY
★ ★ ★ ☆

after

before

In Boston's Jamaica Plain neighborhood, the restoration team
of Chroma Lab—Alicia Cornwell and Tony Bevilacqua—made
this 1940s dresser "seaworthy" with a sleek ocean-themed
design. To convert the drawer pulls from two holes to one,
they used wood putty to fill half the holes and then sanded
them smooth. They used a custom blend of seven shades of
blue paint from Benjamin Moore and Mixol Universal Tint to
paint a wave pattern that transformed this dresser into one of
their most talked-about pieces.

COST
$360

TIME
5 days

DIFFICULTY
★ ★ ★ ☆

after

Starting off as a quick and simple project, Scott Goldberg's chair makeover quickly became a *much* more involved process. "I literally pulled out every rusted staple, repaired and refinished all the wooden parts, screen-printed my own fabric, and replaced all of the nonreusable components with better and longer-lasting materials." From his home in Venice, California, Scott customized the fabric pattern based on the work of local designers Robert Kaufman and Victoria Vu. He used Elmer's wood glue, low-density foam, and stainless-steel hardware to complete the look. Talk about a total transformation.

before

COST
$50

TIME
20 hours

DIFFICULTY
★ ★ ★ ☆

after

before

Designer Kara Ginther, of Kara Ginther Leather in Madison, Wisconsin, was given an antique suitcase as a gift. It was love at first sight. Knowing her way around a leather tool or two, Kara decided to update the suitcase by carving and painting it to add her own story to the suitcase's rich history. Inspired by nineteenth-century bandboxes, Kara sketched a design directly onto the leather, carved it, and then painted the design with latex paint.

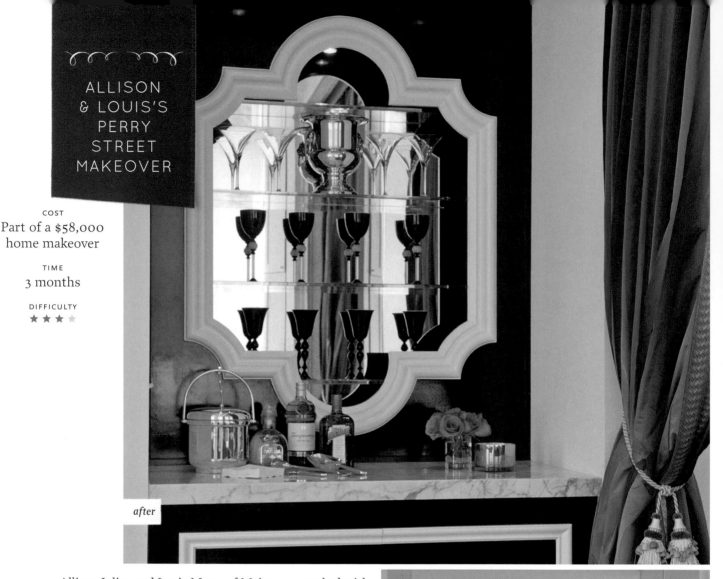

COST
Part of a $58,000
home makeover

TIME
3 months

DIFFICULTY
★ ★ ★ ☆

after

Allison Julius and Louis Marra of Maison 24 worked with
John Hummel and Associates to make over a historic
home in Manhattan's West Village. The apartment,
formerly owned by an artist who enjoyed the space for
its abundance of natural light, was to be transformed
into a pied-à-terre for Dawn and John Hummel, a West
Coast—based couple who wanted to have a private oasis
to come home to on frequent trips to New York. Allison
and Louis's design plans focused around two key elements:
the couple's love of Dorothy Draper's modern baroque
style, and a request by Mrs. Hummel to incorporate her
favorite color, hot pink. The apartment's bar area was
transformed with Draper-inspired details like a bright pink
curtain and contrasting white and black molding details.

before

COST
Part of a
$65,000 full home
renovation

TIME
4 months

DIFFICULTY
★ ★ ★ ☆

after

before

When it comes to renovating victorian homes, Design*
Sponge readers seem to be divided equally into groups
that either "love it!" or "hate it!" I tend to fall into the "love
it!" camp, especially when you're dealing with a 1970s-era
bathroom remodel that could use a little love. Marites Abueg
and Keith Morris of The Abueg Morris Architects in Berkeley
decided to take on this local project, creating a modern yet
classic retreat that included custom cabinetry from San
Francisco designer Thomas Wold, new flooring made from
reclaimed barn siding, and a sleek new bathtub/shower
combination that gives the homeowners more usable space.

COST
$13,000 in addition
to $36,000 for
new cabinets and
appliances

TIME
Renovation
completed over
3 months

DIFFICULTY
★ ★ ★ ★

after

The majority of makeovers we feature on Design*Sponge
are focused on keeping budgets low, but when I came
across this kitchen makeover from Melbourne-based
artist Neryl Walker and art director Tim Haynes I
couldn't resist sharing it. Neryl and Tim were lucky
enough to win a contest called "Australia's Most Desperate
Kitchen," which gave them more than $36,000 in new
cabinets and appliances! As if that wasn't enough, Neryl
and Tim decided to put their design skills to use and
spend some of their own money (and time) to redo
the ceiling, floors, and electrical system on their own.
When the final plate was put back in place, Neryl and
Tim were thrilled to see that their 1970s kitchen had
gone from dark and small to bright, open, and airy.

before

COST
$750

TIME
1 weekend

DIFFICULTY
★ ★ ★ ☆

after

before

Before and after projects always have special meaning to the owner, but this one, in Woodstock, New York, has a particularly deep significance. Using salvaged wood posts and materials from a glider found at a local yard sale, Gene Gironda created a beautiful backyard pergola for his then-girlfriend, Linda. Not only was the pergola a romantic gift, but it later acted as the centerpiece at their garden wedding. Linda explained, "I will always remember our wedding when I look at the pergola. We love to relax under it together with a glass of wine and wave to our neighbors as they walk by."

TIFFANY'S COUCH

COST
$220
(for sofa and supplies)

TIME
10 hours

DIFFICULTY
★ ★ ★ ☆

after

Reupholstery can be one of the toughest makeover jobs, but nursing student Tiffany Misao Nelson forged ahead with a full couch makeover as her first-ever upholstery project. Having recently taken some sewing lessons, Tiffany decided to be brave and apply what she had learned to her living room sofa. With the help of online tutorials, she used a pretty patterned fabric from a local shop to recover her couch and create a clean new look. Thrilled with the final result, Tiffany now has the confidence to tackle all sorts of upholstery projects around her home in San Antonio, Texas.

before

COST
Part of a $200,000
full-home
renovation

TIME
Work finished
over the course
of one year

DIFFICULTY
★ ★ ★ ☆

after

before

As much as Design*Sponge readers love individual furniture makeovers, few things can top the impact of a complete home renovation. The gut renovation of this 1970s oceanfront home near Portland, Oregon, was completed by Lois MacKenzie and Pamela Hill of Otto Baat Design. "The house had great architectural bones and such huge potential for opening up the space, yet everything about the interior felt dark and introverted. Our vision was to create an intimate, modern environment juxtaposed with the dramatic beauty of the Oregon coastline outside." Focusing on a gray, yellow, white, and red color palette, Lois and Pamela used a mix of high-end (wallpaper from Tres Tintas) and low-end (Ikea) furnishings to finish the top-to-bottom makeover.

COST
$35

TIME
2 days

DIFFICULTY
★ ★ ★ ☆

after

Every now and then I come across a furniture makeover that really sticks with me—and this piece from Colorado artist Olga Kaydanov has remained one of my favorite projects since I first posted it on Design*Sponge in 2008. After inheriting her grandmother's dresser, Olga decided to transform it by creating a do-it-yourself sunburst pattern using small wooden dowels. That's right—each tiny piece of wood was placed and glued by hand to give the effect of sunbursts on the dresser's sides and drawers. After staining the entire piece a dark ebony hue, Olga cut wooden dowels in different lengths and placed each one by hand to create the custom pattern. Despite the many hours that it took to create the look, Olga was thrilled with the final result—and the fact that she'd created a look that was uniquely hers.

before

COST
N/A
(renovations made
over time using
a mix of new and
old furniture)

TIME
Series of changes
made over one year

DIFFICULTY
★ ★ ★ ☆

after

For graphic designer Caroline Popham, home
makeovers aren't always about replacing the old
with the new. After moving into her London home,
she decided to bring a mix of older furniture and
lighting into her space to create a fresh, new look.

After finishing major changes like replacing the
home's roof and plumbing system, Caroline repainted
all of the walls and brought in a wide range of furniture
and accessories, from antique markets, hardware
stores, and thrift stores to create a look that spoke to
both the age of the home and her personal style.

before

COST
Total $3,000
(try eBay for
discounted suzanis)

TIME
1 week at the
upholsterer

DIFFICULTY
★ ★ ★ ★

after

Suzani fabrics are incredibly popular in home décor right now, but unfortunately can come with a pretty high price tag. After falling in love with a dramatic pair of suzani-upholstered wingbacks at the Soho Hotel in London, photographer Pilar Valtierra knew she wanted to re-create the look on a more reasonable budget. After picking up a pair of affordable wingback chairs on Craigslist and scouring Los Angeles for a pair of affordable suzanis, Pilar was able to work with a local upholsterer, Ames Ingham, to create her dream chairs. By using preowned chairs and finding a pair of mismatched suzanis, Pilar was able to get the look she wanted—for less.

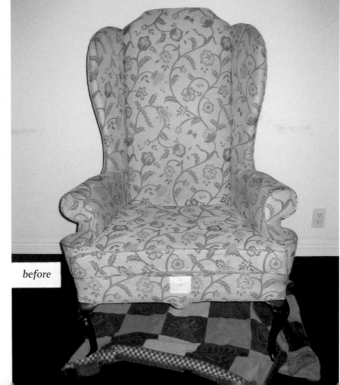

before

COST
$1490

TIME
One week

DIFFICULTY
★ ★ ★ ★

Amy's Tips for Upholstery

Collect magazine photos
to illustrate the look you're
trying to achieve.

Decide which direction
you'd like the fabric to run
and if you'd like the cording
in the same fabric or in a
contrasting color.

If you want tufting, you'll
need to specify how deep
you'd like the buttons and
the style of tufting.

When the upholsterer
comes to pick up your piece,
be certain to show him or
her the photos and make
sure you discuss all the
points on your list.

after

before

Design*Sponge editor Amy Azzarito loved her sofa when it
came home in 2004. But that was before she brought home
two kittens, who also loved the sofa and its loopy fabric.
In fact, they loved it to shreds. But because she believed in
the sofa's good bones, Amy wanted to try a makeover. She
decided to go with a velvet fabric from Joe's, in Manhattan,
because velvet is made of cut thread with a short, dense
pile, which makes it difficult for cats to hook into and pull
on. In addition to a fabric change, Amy also asked her local
upholsterer, DAS Upholstery in Brooklyn, to make the tufting
more visible. "I was able to get a completely custom look and
the smooth fabric doesn't interest the kitties' claws at all."

COST

Part of an overall $70,000 conversion

TIME

Part of a 3-year DIY renovation/conversion

DIFFICULTY
★ ★ ★ ★

after

It takes an open (and creative) mind to see a raw space like this one and imagine a warm home for your family. But designer Drew Allan did just that, converting this Depression-era brakeshop in Cincinnati into a colorful home for his wife, Sarah, and their daughter, Junia. After major renovations to the floors, walls, and ceiling, Drew kept the interior decoration budget-friendly by using curbside furniture finds and bold paint colors to fill the space and give it warmth. Drew even used discounted Lowe's wallpaper to highlight the beautiful exposed beams on the upper portion of the wall.

before

COST
N/A
(part of a
full-home gut
renovation)

TIME
10 months

DIFFICULTY
★ ★ ★ ★

after

before

As soon as Mary Welch and Jeremy Pyles of Niche Modern lighting in Beacon, New York, spotted this early nineteenth-century factory building they knew it was the right space for their family. Undeterred by the raw dirt floors and boarded windows, Mary and Jeremy explained that they could still "feel the majesty of the space, as though it were a living creature, even in its roughest state." Though they may have bitten off more than they could chew at first, the finished project—a sleek modern home for their growing family—leaves them with absolutely no regrets. Focusing on a renovation that went from the top of the space (which got new ceilings and lighting from Mary and Jeremy's lighting company) to the bottom (new flooring and a second floor which houses the couple's master bedroom), this designing duo was able to create a dream home that reflected their personal style.

371

ANTIQUES &
FLEA MARKETS

Alameda Flea Market
Alameda, California
(first Sunday of every month)
www.antiquesbybay.com
This flea market is legendary among Bay Area locals, designers, and our Design*Sponge editors in San Francisco. You'll find a fantastic selection of vintage housewares—just be sure to arrive early!

The Antiques Garage/West 25th Street Market/Hell's Kitchen Flea Market
New York, New York (every Saturday and Sunday)
www.hellskitchenfleamarket.com
In addition to furniture and vintage fashion, you'll find unexpected objects like small frames, old hotel keys, and vintage sporting equipment.

Bell'occhio
www.bellocchio.com
We love Bell'occhio for vintage trims and knickknacks

Brimfield Antique Show
Brimfield, Massachusetts
(May, July, and September; dates vary)
www.brimfield.com
The Design*Sponge team heads to this antiques fair as often as we can—it's our favorite shopping destination for vintage and antique home goods.

Craigslist
www.craigslist.org
The utility of Craigslist can vary depending on your location, but if you're vigilant you can score some great deals on vintage furniture and lighting.

eBay
www.ebay.com
We love eBay for everything from tableware and clothing to furniture and jewelry. Be sure to set up eBay watch lists for items you're hunting for on a regular basis.

Ethan Ollie
www.etsy.com
Beautiful vintage pieces at reasonable prices. Great resource for art, glassware, vessels, lamps, and other trinkets.

Factory 20
www.factory20.com
Factory 20 is based in Sterling, Virginia, but they have a well-curated collection of vintage and antique furniture and décor available through their website.

1stdibs
www.1stdibs.com
An online marketplace representing some of the best antiques dealers in the world. Prices can be high, but the quality almost always justifies the cost.

Fyndes
www.fyndes.com
Fyndes is an online gallery and shop that showcases a mix of antique and contemporary designs from artists across the globe.

Goodwill
www.goodwill.org
Like the Salvation Army, Goodwill shops are a great place to source inexpensive vintage goods. The quality of the collections varies based on your local stores, but they're great jumping-off points for before-and-after projects and decorating.

Hindsvik
www.etsy.com
A beautiful collection of vintage pieces from stylish Canadian couple Daniel and Valeria. Always has a great selection of industrial and rustic vintage objects ranging from crates and furniture to books and art prints.

The J. Peterman Company
www.jpeterman.com
When you think of J. Peterman, you may imagine his goofy fictionalized character on *Seinfeld,* but this website actually carries a stunning collection of one-of-a-kind antiques and collectibles.

Old Goode Things
www.ogtstore.com
Old Goode Things specializes in unique vintage and antique items. In addition to great furniture, it also carries beautiful lighting and antique hardware like doorknobs and pulls.

Ruby Lane
www.rubylane.com
A great online collection of vintage and antique collectibles.

Salvation Army
www.salvationarmyusa.org
The strength of the selection at these stores depends on your local shop, but they're still great places to start when searching for affordable vintage furniture and accessories.

Scott Antique Market
www.scottantiquemarket.com
This Atlanta market is legendary for its amazing collection of vintage and antique sellers. In addition to monthly shows in Atlanta, they also set up a show in Columbus, Ohio, during the fall and spring. Check their website for the full schedule.

Surfing Cowboys
www.surfingcowboys.com
This Southern California shop carries a fantastic collection of midcentury modern furniture, and it ships across the country.

BED & BATH

Amenity
www.amenityhome.com
Nature-inspired bedding that oozes California cool.

Area, Inc.
www.areahome.com
Modern bedding that walks the line between masculine and feminine.

Brook Farm General Store
www.brookfarmgeneralstore.com
Their closely edited collection of bedding is simple, clean farm style at its best.

Cabbages & Roses
www.cabbagesandroses.com
We love their country-chic line of bedding and fabrics. If you like soft floral designs, this is your shop.

The Company Store
www.thecompanystore.com
Affordable, good-quality bedding and towels in a wide range of styles.

Dwell Studio
www.dwellstudio.com
Playful patterns for both adults and children. We love their classic Draper stripes.

Finn Style
www.finnstyle.com
An online site for Finnish home décor.

Garnet Hill
www.garnethill.com
This catalog is a sheet lover's paradise. They also stock a great collection of plush towels and other housewares.

Inmod
www.inmod.com
This modern design e-boutique has a wide range of bedding and even lets you design your own custom pillow and duvet. They also have a great range of lighting and furniture.

John Robshaw
www.johnrobshaw.com
Beautiful block-printed Indian textiles, including bed linens, duvet covers, quilts, and throw pillows.

L.L. Bean
www.llbean.com
Great for classic flannel and cotton ticking-stripe bed linens.

Lulu DK for Matouk
www.luludkmatouk.com
This sophisticated and colorful bedding is worth the splurge if you want to create a modern, grown-up bed.

Macy's
www.macys.com
Don't overlook this department store, which carries great bedding and towels. Look for Calvin Klein and Donna Karan bedding and bath towels.

Matteo
Los Angeles, California
www.matteohome.com
Soft, neutral linens that are perfect for layering with textured bedspreads and quilts.

Olatz
New York, New York
www.olatz.com
Olatz Schnabel (whose husband, artist Julian Schnabel, designed this gorgeous store) creates classic European-style linens that are the ultimate in luxury. We love her Palermo style with its wide, colorful borders.

Twinkle Living
www.twinkleliving.com
Playful bedding in a range of colorful geometric and floral patterns.

CRAFT & DO-IT-YOURSELF SUPPLIES

Ace Hardware
www.acehardware.com
For building materials and crafting supplies like stencils and metallic spray paint.

Cute Tape
www.cutetape.com
This shop carries a great selection of Japanese Washi tape and other decorative tapes that are great for crafting or decorating packages.

Dick Blick
www.dickblick.com
From paper goods and scrapbooking materials to fine-art supplies, Dick Blick is a one-stop shop.

Filz Felt
www.filzfelt.com
A great resource for high-quality 100 percent wool felt in a huge range of colors, available in pieces and also yardage.

Impress
Multiple locations in Washington State
www.impressrubberstamps.com
For custom rubber stamps and a wide range of premade stamp designs.

Kate's Paperie
Locations in New York, New York, and Greenwich, Connecticut
www.katespaperie.com
Our go-to shop for out-of-the-ordinary paper supplies, pens, and pencils.

Letterbox Co.
www.letterboxcostore.bigcartel.com
This shop stocks a fantastic collection of craft supplies and trinkets, from colorful baker's twine to vintage scissors and amber bottles.

Martha Stewart Craft Supplies
www.eksuccessbrands.com /marthastewartcrafts
Martha is the queen of craft and her line of decorative papers and hole-punch tools is a favorite among our DIY team.

Metalliferous
www.metalliferous.com
If you're making jewelry or other crafts requiring metal, this will become your new favorite site. They carry raw silver materials and base metals, along with beads and vintage metal pieces.

CRAFT & DO-IT-YOURSELF SUPPLIES (continued)

~~~~~~

Michael's
www.michaels.com
A crafter's nirvana that stocks everything from ribbons and glue guns to frames and scrapbooking supplies.

M&J Trimming
New York, New York
www.mjtrim.com
If I could live inside one store for the rest of my life, it would be M&J Trimming. They have every ribbon, trim, bead, and crystal you could imagine.

Paper Source
www.paper-source.com
Paper Source is a great one-stop shop for decorative papers, crafting tools, and rubber stamps.

Pearl Paint
Locations in New York, New Jersey, Florida, and California
www.pearlpaint.com
Beloved by artists, this store carries art supplies from paints and brushes to canvases, tapes, and clay.

Ponoko
www.ponoko.com
Rather than supplies, Ponoko actually provides services to turn your craft and design dreams into reality. You can submit your project plans here and choose from 2-D or 3-D services like laser cutting and electronics to finish your ideas. Ponoko will make the parts and ship them to you for assembly. Ponoko also has an online shop where you can buy and sell goods made with the site's services.

Rockler Woodworking & Hardware
www.rockler.com
For any kind of wood project big or small, this store has everything you could need. Also great for finding cabinet hardware and wood knobs.

Talas
www.talasonline.com
Talas carries a wide array of bookmaking supplies.

Tinsel Trading
www.tinseltrading.com
Along with M&J Trimming, Tinsel Trading is a mecca for DIY and craft enthusiasts. They stock an amazing collection of everything from glass glitter and ribbons to fringe, beads, and buckles. They also stock a nice array of fabric.

FABRIC

~~~~~~

High-end fabrics are often sold to the trade only (to decorators, architects, and designers, for instance), but the following stores sell directly to the public without a "nondesigner" markup.

B&J
www.bandjfabrics.com
B&J stocks one of our favorite hard-to-find fabric lines, Liberty of London. Their collection also includes fine laces, brocade, and faux fur.

Henry Road
Studio City, California
www.henryroad.com
Designer Paula Smail's colorful fabrics—including gold floral patterns—are perfect for upholstery or home décor projects.

Kathryn M. Ireland
West Hollywood, California
www.kathrynireland.com
This Los Angeles–based interior and textile designer creates amazing fabric patterns, including some inspired by Moroccan and African textiles.

Kiitos Marimekko
New York, New York
www.kiitosmarimekko.com
It's hard to beat the classic Finnish design house Marimekko's colorful fabrics. This is the brand's New York concept store, offering a wide range of their designs by the yard.

Lewis & Sheron Textile Co.
http://lsfabrics.com
Based in Atlanta, Lewis & Sheron carries a wide range of fabrics online, including a nice selection of colorful ikat prints.

Lotta Jansdotter
www.jansdotter.com
Lotta's sweet prints are perfect for clothing and home décor accessories.

Mod Green Pod
www.modgreenpod.com
Colorful patterns printed on organic cotton, and wallpaper in coordinating designs.

Mood Fabrics
Los Angeles, California, and
New York, New York
www.moodfabrics.com
Many people know Mood from its recurring role as *Project Runway*'s fabric supplier, but they're also a fantastic source for the rest of us. Mood carries a huge range of fabrics for clothing, crafts, and upholstery.

Purl Soho
New York, New York
www.purlsoho.com
In addition to an amazing array of fabrics from contemporary designers like Amy Butler and Joel Dewberry, Purl also stocks craft supplies, embroidery and needlepoint supplies, and crochet tools.

Rubie Green
www.rubiegreen.com
Michelle Adams's organic cotton fabrics come in a wide range of chic, colorful patterns.

SoSo Vintage
www.etsy.com
A good curated collection of cheery vintage fabrics for small projects.

Spoonflower
www.spoonflower.com
Spoonflower allows you to custom print your own fabric and have it sent back to you for projects or to sell. It's a fantastic resource for independent designers or buyers looking for something unique.

Studio Bon
www.studiobon.net
Designer Bonnee Sharp's fabrics are both fun and sophisticated. Look for her brown and black patterns on off-white linen.

Textile Arts
www.txtlart.com
A great range of fabrics from Scandinavian designers like Marimekko and Jungsbergs. Marimekko oilcloth fabric is moisture repellent.

FURNITURE & MORE

Anthropologie
www.anthropologie.com
From dishware and rugs to lighting and wallpaper, everything here is beautifully curated. Don't miss: decorative hardware in a wide range of styles, and wallpaper—including many peel-and-stick designs!

Ballard Designs
Locations in Florida, Georgia, and Ohio
www.ballarddesigns.com
This well-known home furnishings catalog is great for decorating basics like slipper chairs and upholstered headboards, as well as for accessories like mirrors and storage pieces.

Branch Home
www.branchhome.com
This online shop carries a wide range of eco-friendly design, from bedding and tea towels to toys and dishware.

CB2
www.cb2.com
This chain is like the cool younger sister of Crate and Barrel. Great finds: lighting and desktop accessories.

Chairloom
www.chairloom.com
Designer Molly Worth breathes new life into old chairs and sofas by upholstering them in bright, modern fabrics.

Design Public
www.designpublic.com
From tableware to children's design, all shipped directly from designers to your home.

Etsy
www.etsy.com
This wonderful designers' and crafters' marketplace just keeps growing and getting more incredible by the day. We love to shop the site for vintage napkins, plates, and serving ware. For textiles, try these Etsy shops: Skinny Laminx (skinnylaminx.etsy.com), WonderFluff (WonderFluffShop.etsy.com), and Swanky Swell (swankyswell.etsy.com).

Ikea
www.ikea.com
We're master Ikea-hackers at Design*Sponge so we visit frequently to pick up ridiculously cheap tables and chairs that can easily be transformed with paint and decorative details. Ikea also has a fantastic collection of budget-friendly by-the-yard fabric, some of which is available online.

Jayson Home and Garden
Chicago, Illinois
www.jaysonhomeandgarden.com
This Chicago favorite is a great source for everything from furniture to eclectic tableware. We love the Flea section of their website and check it regularly for one-of-a-kind vintage pieces like antique chandeliers.

Moon River Chattel
Brooklyn, New York
www.moonriverchattel.com
This antique and home store stocks both architectural salvage and new utilitarian objects. We love their beautiful glassware and tableware that combines classic design with a touch of vintage charm.

2Modern
www.2modern.com
Great contemporary furniture, lighting, and accessories.

Urban Archeology
Locations in Boston, New York, and Chicago
www.urbanarchaeology.com
For reproduction antique bathtubs and some of the best hardware around. We love their metal pulls.

Urban Outfitters
www.urbanoutfitters.com
Some very cute furniture and home décor at rock-bottom prices. Check out their trendy rugs: What they lack in plushness, they make up for with fun pattern and color.

Velocity Art and Design
Seattle, Washington
www.velocityartanddesign.com
Hip home décor. We love that they support local and independent designers.

Viva Terra
www.vivaterra.com
Eco-friendly home décor, including recycled railroad-tie furniture.

West Elm
www.westelm.com
A fantastic, ever-changing source for affordable, trend-conscious home décor. Great finds: their lighting collection, bedding, and rugs, and Parsons-style tables and bookcases.

Wisteria
www.wisteria.com
This catalog features an interesting mix of vintage and new furniture and home décor.

HARDWARE

Bauerware
San Francisco, California
www.bauerware.com
Funky knobs and pulls.

ER Butler
www.erbutler.com
ER Butler makes high-quality custom hardware
for doors, windows, and furniture. They specialize
in early American, federal, and Georgian period
styles.

Eugenia's
www.eugeniaantiquehardware.com
Eugenia's carries a wide range of one-of-a-kind
authentic hardware. Perfect for restoring older
homes to their original look and feel.

House of Antique Hardware
www.houseofantiquehardware.com
If you're craving something that feels antique,
they carry a great selection of reproduction
hardware.

MyKnobs.com
www.myknobs.com
This website has a huge collection of knobs,
pulls, door hardware, and everything else in
between. I love their twig and branch-style pulls.

The Hook Lady
www.hooklady.com
A stunning collection of hooks, including a wide
range of vintage and antique styles. We love their
collection of unusual hooks, ranging from bats and
tiny hands to pigs and mermaids.

LIGHTING

Barn Light Electric
www.barnlightelectric.com
If you love the look of vintage barn lights you'll
love this affordable collection of metal and enamel
lamps. They're also a great source for cage
pendant lamps.

Lumens
www.lumens.com
Whether you're looking for modern or traditional,
indoor or outdoor lighting, this web retailer has a
light for your style and price range.

Niche Modern
www.nichemodern.com
Their lighting combines modern glass globes
with antique-feeling Edison bulbs for a truly
unique look.

1000 Bulbs
www.1000bulbs.com
If you need a lightbulb, this store has it. From
compact fluorescents and halogens to metal halide
and rope lights, 1000 Bulbs has them all.

Rejuvenation
Portland, Oregon, and Seattle, Washington
www.rejuvenation.com
Vintage-inspired lights as well as shades,
hardware, and lamp parts.

Schoolhouse Electric
New York, New York, and Portland, Oregon
www.schoolhouseelectric.com
A great collection of period lighting and glass
shades. Their guest designer collections include
both retro and contemporary designs.

Sundial Wire
www.sundialwire.com
Sundial stocks great lighting supplies, including
high-quality cloth-covered wire.

The Future Perfect
www.thefutureperfect.com
If you're looking for one-of-a-kind statement
pieces, David Alhadeff's The Future Perfect is the
best choice. The designs aren't cheap, but they
are guaranteed to bring a bold dose of design into
your home.

Y lighting
www.ylighting.com
Online retailer with a mind-boggling collection of
lamps (ceiling, table, floor, track, and more).

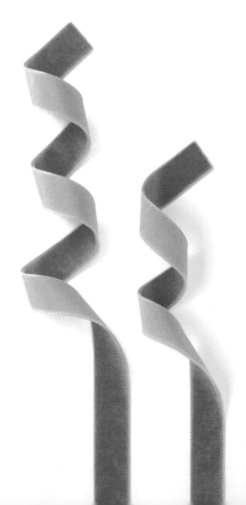

PAINT

~~~~~~~~~~~~~~~~~~~~~~~~~~~~~~~~~~~~

Behr
www.behr.com
Terrific bright hues that are perfect for sunrooms, children's rooms, or any space that needs a bright splash of color.

Benjamin Moore
www.benjaminmoore.com
I trust Benjamin Moore paints for almost all of my home projects. They have a great collection of grays.

California Paints
www.californiapaints.com
Wonderful eco-friendly paints with zero VOCs (volatile organic compounds) and an impressive historical paint selection.

Farrow & Ball
www.farrow-ball.com
The Rolls-Royce of paints. I would blindly trust just about any color they make. Their paints dry beautifully and come in unique colors, many of which are based on historic homes.

Hudson Paint
www.hudsonpaint.com
Some of the best chalkboard paint, including unexpected colors like Mercantile Red.

Martha Stewart Living Paint
Available at Home Depot stores across the United States
www.homedepot.com
Martha's paint colors are classic yet fresh, just like the style icon herself.

Montana Spray Paint
www.montana-spraypaint.com
One of the widest ranges of spray-paint colors around. Essential for any before and after makeover artist!

RUGS & FLOORING

~~~~~~

Angela Adams
Portland, Maine
www.angelaadams.com
Angela's nature-inspired rug designs are like artwork for the floor.

Bev Hisey
www.bevhisey.com
Bev's plush rugs are a celebration of bright color and pattern. They're definitely splurge-worthy.

Blue Pool Road
www.bluepoolroad.com
Peggy Wong's modern rug collection is perfect for adults' *and* children's rooms.

Dash and Albert
www.dashandalbert.com
Their lightweight cotton rugs are perfect for summer.

FLOR
www.flor.com
Carpet tiles in great colors and patterns that you can mix and match for a custom floor with a modern look.

Gan Rugs
www.gan-rugs.com
This Spanish design firm produces amazing, high-quality handmade luxury rugs. Their site provides links to local retailers.

Jonathan Adler
www.jonathanadler.com
Happy-chic rugs that perk up a room. Look for Jonathan's Greek Key and Pat Nixon patterns, which work equally well with both traditional and modern décor.

Judy Ross
www.judyrosstextiles.com
Our favorite: wonderful hand-embroidered runners in New Zealand wool.

Kea
www.keacarpetsandkilims.com
Their selection of kilim rugs is our favorite. They have a fantastic collection of *boucherouite* or "rag" rugs.

Madeline Weinrib Atelier
New York, New York
www.madelineweinrib.com
This showroom within the ABC Carpet & Home store in New York is filled with Weinrib's patterned rug designs, each of which is quite simply heaven in textile form. Her bold Suzani patterns are worth the splurge and her simpler flat-weave zigzag designs are a classic.

kitchens (*cont.*)
Foley & Sperduto, 106, 107
Gardener, 53
Goodman Sohr, 45
Grantham, 121
Heibel, 103
Hisey, 71
Marshall & Deskevich, 27
Marzolf, 117
Mehaffey & Hightower, 15
Merrick, 62, 63
Moore, 81
Naiman, 29
Ometz & Barfoot, 171
Pate & Taylor, 31
Peg-Boards, 24, 111, 222–23
Penney, 110
Phillips, 85
Reitmayer, 161
Robertson & Schulte, 41
Ryan & Emerson, 87
Ryhanen, 153
Schmidt, 35
Sharp, 55
Silverman & Bonnet, 19
Sims, 149
Tan & Koh, 159
Varian, 168
kitsch, 134
Klein, Clara, 219
Knoll, Florence, viii
Koh, Aun, 158–59, 312

L

ladders, 38, 78, 119, 142
Lasari, Romo, 149
Lee, Kin Ying, 6–7
library, Ryan & Emerson, 86, 87
lighting:
bentwood sconce, 208–9
bottle lamp & fabric shade,
184–85
DIY, 132
George Nelson bubble lamp,
75
glass wall, 99
mirrored lamp, 154
Murano glass, 167
Noguchi paper lamp, 91
outdoor planter pendant
lamp, 196–97
pendant lamps, 53
recycled wine bottle torch,
262–63
rewiring a lamp, 279

rooster lamp, 61
sconces, 91, 127
trouble lights, 118
Verner Panton, 147
wall-mounted, 35
wicker lamp, 146
living large, 65
living rooms:
Adams, 20, 21
Alhadeff, 33
Atkins-Hughes, 146, 147
Azzarito, 46, 47
Barratt, 136, 137
before & after, 370
Bolick, 79
Carlson & Clancy, 64, 65
Cassi, 151
Daoust & Baker, 90, 91
Dunker, 97
Engler, 93
Eyers, 57
Foley & Sperduto, 107
Fox & Dollahite, 123
Gardener, 51, 53
Gillis, 157
Goodman Sohr, 43
Gorder, 2, 3, 4
Grantham, 121
Hay, 37
Heibel, 102
Hisey, 68, 69
Ilasco, 164
Kelly & Alexis, 125
Marshall & Deskevich, 27
Mehaffey & Hightower, 12, 13
Meyers, 101
Moffitt, 75
Newkirk, 155
Norris & Smith, 112, 113
Ometz & Barfoot, 171
O'Neill, 9
Oschmann, 141
Pate & Taylor, 31
Penney, 109
Perna & Lee, 7
Phillips, 85
Robertson & Schulte, 39,
40, 41
Ryhanen, 152
Silverman & Bonnet, 19
Sims, 149
Stark, 94
Tan & Koh, 158
Thigpen, 128
Varian, 169
Walker, 73

Wood, 135
Lo, Joyce, 126–27
Loewy, Raymond, 19
log jars, 201, 254–55
Lowe, Edward, 11
Lynch, Jessica, 356

M

MacKenzie, Lois, 365
map-covered boxes, 188–89
Marra, Louis, 360
Marshall, Corbett, 26–27
Martin, Jason, 339
Marzolf, Maya, 116–19
McCobb, Paul, 23
McCormack, Brett, 354
Mehaffey, P.J., 12–15
mercury glass, 151
Merrick, Amy, 60–63, 191, 193,
245, 293, 340
message boards, 13, 332
Meyers, Linda & John, 100–101,
310
Miller, Jason, 33
mirrors, 37, 50, 51, 109, 111, 113,
151
sunburst, 329
Moffitt, Stephanie, 74–77
moldings, 41
monogram wreath, 242–43
Moore, Heather, 80–81
Morris, Keith, 361
Munn, Kimberly, 213
Murphy, Jennifer, 113

N

Naiman, Olga, 28–29
needlepoint, 139
Neiley, Carol, 16–17, 311
Nelson, George, 75, 92
Nelson, Lauren, 325
Nelson, Tiffany Misao, 364
Newkirk, Davy, 154–55
Newman, Carl & Christy, 104–5
Nightwood, 348
Noguchi, Isamu, 91
Norris, Halligan, 112–15, 251
Norton, Jon, 355

O

office, *see* home offices
Olson, Nick, 84, 85
Ometz, Shay-Ashley, 170–71

O'Neill, Rosie, 8–9
open space, 65, 143
Oreck, Jessica, 47, 271
Oschmann, Leslie, 140–41
Owen, Nicolette Camille, 10–11

P

pachinko machines, vintage, 103
paint magic (tips), 29
panel molding, 41
Pate, Wayne, 30–31
Pauchard, Xavier, 31
Pawlak, Zoe, 25
peacocks, 167
Peak, Elizabeth, viii
Pedersen, Bettina, 189
Peg-Boards, 24, 111, 222–23
Penney, Michael & Sara, 108–11
Perera, Kishani, 8, 9, 148, 149, 155
pergola, before & after, 363
Perna, Dan, 6–7
Phillips, Rebecca, 84–85
pillows, 13, 23, 35, 137, 139
appliqué, 260–61
bold patterns, 74, 97, 101
cutting & wrapping, 290
floor, 224–25
needlepoint, 48
tufting, 289
planter, before & after, 346
plate wall, 97
playrooms:
Ilasco, 165
Perna & Lee, 7
Tanya's desks, 330
Popham, Caroline, 367
porches, 95, 166
Premo, Brooke, 333
Pruitt, Kate, DIY projects, 177,
179, 195, 197, 199, 201, 205,
221, 229, 231, 233, 235, 239,
241, 243, 253, 255, 257, 259,
267
Pyles, Jeremy, 371

R

Reitmayer, Samantha, 160–61
Robertson, Jill, 38–41
Rothman, Julia, 67
rugs:
area, 73, 143
caring for, 83
kilims, 77
patterns, 82

reindeer hide, 91
Scandinavian, 91
shag, 101
striped, 136, 171
as wall art, 63, 82
Ruppel, Amy, 1
Ryan & Emerson, 86–89
Ryhanen, Sarah, 152–53, 293

S

Saarinen, Eero, 36
Sacks, Ann, 39
Sahba, Shirin, 331
Satterfield, Morgan, 162–63
scale, before & after, 322
Schmidt, Jacqueline & George, 34–35
Schueler, Kirsten D., 207
Schulte, Jason, 38–41
screens:
    folding, 139
    vintage, 167
Scruggs, Myriah, 348
sewing basics, 282–86
Sharp, Bonnee, 54–55, 309
shelving, 7
    Biblioteca, 127
    books, 37, 49, 53, 54, 56, 65, 78, 87, 113, 158, 335
    cabinets, 27
    Douglas fir, 169
    Ikea, 21, 93
    ladders to, 38, 78
    open storage, 11, 87, 143
    pipes, 162
    Po Cadovius wall system, 164
    skis, 15
    wall cubes, 13
shirt quilt, 268–69
shower curtain with storage pouch, 226–27
sideboard, before & after, 348
Siemaska, Nick, 353
silhouettes, 120, 135
Silverman, Adam, 18–19
silverware curtain hooks, 228–29
Sims, Molly, 148–49
sitting rooms:
    Caleo & Karol, 145

Sims, 149
skull, 136
Smith, Adam, 112–15
Smith, Bradford, 115
Smith, Lauren, 175, 181, 183, 209, 215, 225, 227, 237, 261, 269
Smith, Tanya Risenmay, 330
Sodeau, Michael, 146
sofas:
    before & after, 364, 369
    Norman + Quaine, 37
Sperduto, Paul, 106–7
spool table library, 250–51
staircases:
    Gorder, 5
    Heibel, 102
    Marzolf, 117
    Norris & Smith, 113
Stark, David, 94–95
Stickley, Lisa, 241
storage:
    armoires, 115, 131, 135
    Azzarito, 47
    Barb Blair's hutch, 342
    Barb's peach dresser, 345
    baskets, 150
    china cabinet, 109
    Chroma Lab's deep-sea dresser, 357
    Eric's Ikea dresser, 350
    file cabinets, 29
    flat cabinet, 97
    hidden, 147
    John's cabinet, 323
    Kara's suitcase, 359
    ladders to, 38
    Lauren's gray dresser, 353
    lockers, 70
    Lucinda's dresser, 344
    Olga's dresser, 366
    open, 11
    playroom, 165
    rolling bench, 210–11
    Shirin's trunk, 331
    underbed, 145, 161
studios:
    Ometz & Barfoot, 171
    Perna & Lee, 7
succulent brick wall, 202–3

suitcase cat bed, 216–17
Summerford, Jack, 171
sunrooms, 40, 43
sweater wreath, 206–7

T

table runners, 88
    lace doily, 200
tables:
    before & after, 324, 326, 351, 352
    coffee tables, 117
    cubby, with chair leg base, 214–15
    drafting tables, 119
    faux marble top, 354
    reconstructing, 121
    skirts for, 21
    tray, 171
table settings, inkjet transfer, 240–41
Tan, Su-Lyn, 158–59, 312
taxidermy, 68
Taylor, Rebecca, 30–31
tea towels, bleach pattern, 182–83
Teng, Eric, 350
terrarium how-to, 246–49
textiles:
    fashion, for home use, 27
    vintage, 80, 81
Thigpen, Joy & Tyler, 128–29, 315
Trienens, Sebastian, 118

U

upholstery:
    Amy's tips for, 369
    details, 288–91
    staple-gun, 281
urns, antique, 79

V

Valtierra, Pilar, 368
Varian, Michele, 168–69
vases, DIY projects, 180, 181
Voysey, Charles F. A., 61
Vu, Victoria, 358

W

Waese, Jerry, 71
wainscoting, 145
Walker, Neryl, 362
Walker, Ryan & Alissa Parker-Walker, 72–73
wallpaper:
    on ceiling, 126
    closet, 23
    creating your own, 18
    from eBay, 61
    fabric, 100
    faux-book, 53, 99
    hanging, 278
    Julia Rothman, 67
    medical posters, 103
    Neisha Crosland, 169
    Nina Campbell, 30
    Olga Kiely, 45
    Opal, 149
    ribbed, 165
    Signature pattern, 138
    Thibaut, 110
    Voysey, 61
Weinrib, Madeline, 28
Welch, Mary, 371
Wiinblad, Bjørn, 135
window films, 198–99
window treatments, DIY, 137
wine crate display case, 174–75
Wold, Thomas, 361
Wood, Britni, 134–35
wood, reclaimed, 35
wooden wax seal, 212–13
Woolley, Weston, 119

Y

Yaron, Nadia, 348

Z

Zamora, Christina, 355
Zimmerman, Lauren, 353
Zimmerman, Tassy, 247

The author and publisher wish to thank the following for permission to reproduce their photographs.

Martina Ahlbrandt: page 349
Drew Allan and Julianna Boehm: page 370
Rinne Allen: pages 156—57
Erik Anderson: page 262
Jessica Antola: pages 82—83
Jon and Heather Armstrong: pages 66—67
Graham Atkins-Hughes: pages 98—99 and 146—47
Corina Bankhead: page 367
Lincoln Barbour: pages 124—25
Belathee: page 202
Barb Blair: pages 342 and 345
Grace Bonney: pages 168—69, 180, and 184
Kimberly Brandt: page 216
Conn Brattain: page 323
William Brinson: pages 130—33
Karen Brown: page 335
Hallie Burton: pages 36—37
Ashley Campbell of Ashley Ann Photography: page 327
Emma Cassi: pages 150—51
Christine Chitnis: page 200
Tom Cinko and Jeremy Welch: page 371
Paul Clancy: pages 64—65
Patrick Cline of Brand Arts and *Lonny* magazine: pages 20—21, 23—25, 222, and 264
Beth Coleman: page 322
Alicia Cornwell: page 357
Shannon Crawford: page 186
Todd Crawford and Katrina Wittkamp: pages 102—3
Jeffery Cross: pages 355 and 365
Kathy Dalwood: pages 138—39
Juli Daoust: pages 90—91
Lori Dunbar: page 338
Elisabeth Dunker: pages 96—97
Keeley Durocher: page 351
Amanda Elmore: pages 122—23
Emersonmade: pages 86—89
Derek Fagerstrom and Lauren Smith: pages 174, 177, 179, 181, 182, 194, 196, 198, 204, 208, 214, 224, 226, 228, 230, 232, 236, 238, 240, 242, 252, 254, 256, 258, 260, and 268

Philip Ficks: pages 34—35
Eurydice Galka: page 361
K.C. Giessen: page 324
Emily Gilbert: pages 142—45
Kara Ginther: page 359
Terri Glanger: pages 54—55
Scott Goldberg: page 358
Donna Griffith: pages 68—71
John Gruen: page 363
Gustavo Campos Photography: pages 94—95
Nicole Haladyna: page 334
Michelle Hinckley: pages 326 and 329
Troy House: pages 148—49
Marvin Ilasco: pages 164—65
Ditte Isager and Tara Donne: pages 28—29
Tim James: pages 50—51
Kim Jeffery: pages 108—11 and 126—27
Laure Joliet: pages 162—63
Melissa Kaseman: pages 92—93
Dean Kaufman: pages 32—33
Olga Kaydanov: page 366
Christy Kilgore: page 352
Clara Klein: page 218
Aun Koh: pages 158—159
Sabra Krock: pages 292—93 and 297—317
Michael Lantz and Libby Gourley: page 347
Jessica Lynch: page 356
Maison 24: page 360
Jason Martin: page 339
Brett McCormack: page 354
Carmen McKee Bushong: page 328
James Merell: pages 56—59
Amy Merrick: pages 190, 192, and 244
John Meyers: pages 100—101
Joe Miller: page 336
Johnny Miller: pages 2—7, 22, 26—27, 46—49, 60—63, 78—79, 106—107, 134—35, 152—53, 210, 270, 340, 343, and 369
Johnny Miller and Grace Bonney: pages 104—105
Merry Lu Miner and Chad Kelly: page 346
Heather Moore: pages 80—81
Kimberly Munn: page 212
Lauren Nelson: page 325

Tiffany Misao Nelson: page 364
Stacy Newgent: pages 136—37
Nightwood: page 348
Halligan Norris: page 250
Cliff Norton: pages 166—67
Shay-Ashley Ometz: pages 170—71
Alissa Parker-Walker: pages 72—73
Michael Paulus: pages 120—21
Bettina Pedersen: page 188
Tec Petaja: pages 42—45
Rebecca Phillips: pages 84—85
Richard Powers: pages 18—19
Brooke Premo: page 333
Bronwyn Proctor: page 331
Kate Pruitt: pages 201, 220, 234, and 266
Jean Randazzo: pages 8—9 and 154—55
Jess Roberts: pages 112—15
Manny Rodriguez: pages 160—61
Hector M. Sanchez: pages 12—15
Kirsten D. Schueler: page 206
Jason Schulte: pages 38—41
Nick Siemaska: page 353
Shakti Space Designs: page 344
Ellen Silverman: pages 16—17
Tanya Risenmay Smith: page 330
Orlando Dumond Soria: page 337
Sprout Home: page 246
Derek Swalwell: pages 52—53
Pete Tabor: pages 74—77
Eric Teng: page 350
Joy Thigpen: pages 128—29
Lesley Unruh: pages 10—11
Pilar Valtierra: page 368
Wouter van der Tol: pages 140—41
Diana van Helvoort: page 341
Neryl Walker and Tony Owczarek: page 362
Matthew Williams: pages 30—31 and 114—19
Wondertime Photography: page 332